Palgrave Studies in Economic History

Series Editor
Kent Deng
London School of Economics
London, UK

Palgrave Studies in Economic History is designed to illuminate and enrich our understanding of economies and economic phenomena of the past. The series covers a vast range of topics including financial history, labour history, development economics, commercialisation, urbanisation, industrialisation, modernisation, globalisation, and changes in world economic orders.

More information about this series at
http://www.palgrave.com/gp/series/14632

Sabrina Joseph
Editor

Commodity Frontiers and Global Capitalist Expansion

Social, Ecological and Political Implications from the Nineteenth Century to the Present Day

palgrave
macmillan

Editor
Sabrina Joseph
American University in Dubai
Dubai, United Arab Emirates

Palgrave Studies in Economic History
ISBN 978-3-030-15321-2 ISBN 978-3-030-15322-9 (eBook)
https://doi.org/10.1007/978-3-030-15322-9

Library of Congress Control Number: 2019936155

Cover illustration: Andia/Alamy Stock Photo

This Palgrave Macmillan imprint is published by the registered company Springer Nature Switzerland AG.
The registered company address is: Gewerbestrasse 11, 6330 Cham, Switzerland

Contents

Notes on Contributors

Louise Cardoso de Mello is a Brazilian historian (Universidad de Sevilla) and anthropologist (UNED/Université de Provence), specialized in archaeology, and currently a Ph.D. candidate in Latin American History at the Universidad Pablo de Olavide, in Seville (Spain) with joint supervision at the Universidade Federal Fluminense, in Rio de Janeiro (Brazil).

Dr. Hanne Cottyn is a postdoctoral fellow at the Department of History and affiliated researcher of the Ghent Center for Global Studies of Ghent University. Her current research project traces and compares the historical trajectories of communal land rights in the Bolivian and Peruvian Highlands. Her research interests include land rights and land reform, peasant and indigenous community organization, socio-environmental conflicts, critical global studies, and Andean history.

Dr. Robrecht Declercq is postdoctoral researcher of the Research Foundation—Flanders (FWO) affiliated to the History Department at Ghent University. His main research interests include business, and global economic and ecological history. His doctoral research on the global connections of the Leipzig fur industry was nominated for the

Best Dissertation Award of the EBHA in 2016 and has been published as a book titled *World Market Transformation: Inside the German Fur Capital Leipzig 1870–1939*, Routledge, 2017.

Dr. Deborah Delgado Pugley is an Assistant Professor at the Pontificia Universidad Catolica del Peru. She is a sociologist with theoretical and applied experience in both multilateral politics and environmental issues at the community level, including extensive fieldwork in Bolivia and Peru. She holds a Ph.D. in development studies and sociology from the Université Catholique de Louvain and the Ecole des hautes études en sciences sociales of Paris.

Dr. Brigitte Howarth is an ecologist with extensive experience in desert ecology. Her first degree was in applied ecology (B.Sc. (Hons)), and her Ph.D. in ecological entomology. She is currently Associate Professor of Ecology at Zayed University in the United Arab Emirates (UAE) where she teaches courses in both ecology and biology. Having spent 20 years in the Middle East, she has a good understanding of the local species biodiversity and researches the insect biodiversity of the various terrestrial habitats found in the UAE. Dr. Howarth's research has expanded to include environmental history, specifically to investigating how and why ecosystems have altered through land use change and development, and is currently assessing how these changes are impacting species biodiversity in the United Arab Emirates. She is a lifetime member of the Al Ain Chapter of the Emirates Natural History Group which she currently chairs, with one of her roles in the ENHG being that of curator and custodian of the ENHG's entomological collection.

Dr. Sabrina Joseph is Dean of the School of Arts and Sciences and Professor of History at the American University in Dubai in the United Arab Emirates. Her research interests are in the field of Middle Eastern and Ottoman history, encompassing work on land use, environmental management, women, and inter-faith relations during the early modern and modern periods. She is the author of *Islamic Law on Peasant Usufruct in Ottoman Syria: 17th to Early 19th Century* (Brill, 2012). Her most recent research focuses on the political economy of land and water resources in the United Arab Emirates during the first half of the twentieth century. She has published her work in numerous journals including: *British Journal of Middle Eastern Studies*; *Environment and History*; *Frontiers: A Journal of Women's Studies*; *Islam and Christian–Muslim Relations*; *Journal of Muslim Minority Affairs*; and *Rural History: Economy, Society, Culture*.

Tamer Khafaga is an ecologist with more than 20 years of experience in ecology and conservation management as well as sustainable development. His M.Sc. focused on taxonomy and biodiversity with a thesis entitled "Impact of grazing on floral diversity in high altitude mountains in St. Katherine protectorate, South Sinai - Egypt". His work in the Egyptian Environmental Affairs Agency as an Environmental researcher in St. Katherine Protectorate (May 1998 till August 2006) complimented his interest and skills in the understanding of biodiversity conservation and protected area management. As team leader, his responsibilities included surveys of target species and ecosystems as well as the ecological aspects of EIAs (environmental impact assessment), culminating in the implementation of biodiversity monitoring and management interventions. Currently, he is a senior conservation manager with his role focussing on conservation and protected area research planning at the Dubai Desert Conservation Reserve. He is in the process of completing his Ph.D. (Faculty of Science, Malaga University—Spain) with his research focusing on plant functional diversity responses to grazing in an Arabian hyper-arid protected inland desert ecosystem.

Dr. James Lockhart specializes in the history of American foreign relations, global security and intelligence, and Latin American history. A member of the Cambridge, MA—based Scholars Strategy Network, he has published on the history of the CIA in the developing world, contributed to *War on the Rocks*, an online platform for analysis, commentary, debate on national security and foreign policy, and been interviewed by American and Emirati journalists. His first book, *Chile, the CIA, and the Cold War: A Transatlantic Perspective*, will be published by Edinburgh University Press. Before joining the faculty at the American University in Dubai, he lectured at the Embry-Riddle College of Security and Intelligence and at the University of Arizona, where he earned his Ph.D.

Dr. Karen R. Miller is Professor of History at LaGuardia Community College and at the Graduate Center, CUNY. She is author of *Managing Inequality: Northern Racial in Interwar Detroit* [nyupress.org] (NYU Press, 2014). Dr. Miller's articles and reviews have appeared in the Journal of American History, The Middle West Review, The International Journal of Critical Pedagogy, The Michigan Quarterly Review, Michigan Feminist Studies, and Against the Current as well as Groundwork: Local Black Freedom Struggles in America. Her article, "'Thin, Wistful, and White': James Fugate and Colonial Bureaucratic Masculinity in the Philippines, 1900-1938," is forthcoming in December 2019 in American Quarterly. Dr. Miller's current work examines internal migration in the Philippines over the course of the twentieth century.

Greg Simkins is the conservation manager for the Dubai Desert Conservation Reserve (DDCR). He is a member of the Middle East & West Asia Expert group for the green list (EAGL) and the IUCN World Commission of protected areas (WCPA) and has worked in the field of conservation and protected areas management since 2001. Simkins began his career as a Field Guide with the Emirates Group in 1999 at the newly opened Al Maha Desert Resort & Spa. In 2001, he became a Reserve Officer and was heavily involved in the planning and implementation of eco-tourism activities within the protected area of the DDCR, which was created in 2002.

In 2003, Simkins was appointed to his current position at the DDCR. He is responsible for the overall management of the Reserve and has been at the forefront of its development from conception in 2003 to its current international recognition. Simkins also manages the wildlife at the reserve looking after a number of different species including the re-introduced Arabian Oryx, Arabian Gazelles, and Houbara Bustard. He plays a major role in conducting key conservation research studies throughout the DDCR.

Dr. Indrakshi Tandon holds a Ph.D. from the Department of Anthropology at SUNY Albany. Dr. Tandon's interests include the integration of gender into development policy, participatory development, transnational and global connections, and the role of NGOs and civil society organizations in development. She currently lives and works in Dubai, where she is an instructor with Zayed University.

Dr. Sven Van Melkebeke is a Postdoctoral Fellow at Ghent University and holds a Ph.D. in history. His research focuses on the development of coffee production around Lake Kivu (former Belgian Central-Africa). He has recently published in African Economic History and is currently preparing a book chapter on the impact of colonial agronomy on labour coercion.

List of Figures

List of Tables

1

Introduction

Sabrina Joseph

The growth of the global capitalist economy has been enabled through the expansion of vast frontiers of land, labour, food, energy and raw materials, usually in areas including flatlands, valleys, mountains and forests over the past 500 years. Since the sixteenth century, extractive economies have spread across geologically and climatically distinct ecosystems, spanning most parts of the world. This transformation has been a distinguishing feature of capitalist expansion that has impacted social, political and economic structures and resulted in uneven development between core and periphery, town and countryside.[1] The cyclical nature of extractive economies and their tendency to deplete the natural resources on which they depend means that they encourage and spur further exploitation of resources, thus resulting in ever more expansion into new frontiers. The driving forces behind this process are cost reduction and increasing productivity. This process of appropriation, exploitation, dispossession and ecological fragmentation is what is identified as a 'commodity frontier', a term first introduced

S. Joseph (✉)
American University in Dubai, Dubai, United Arab Emirates
e-mail: sjoseph@aud.edu

S. Joseph (ed.), *Commodity Frontiers and Global Capitalist Expansion*,
Palgrave Studies in Economic History, https://doi.org/10.1007/978-3-030-15322-9_1

by Jason Moore.[2] Central to this concept is the idea that nature and society are 'mutually relational' and not divided.[3] As articulated by Moore, the world-ecology perspective embraces the view that 'social relations do more than produce environments…Human history, at every turn, is *co-produced*—by, with, and through extra-human natures, organic and inorganic'.[4]

This edited volume explores the dynamics of global capitalist expansion through the concept of the 'commodity frontier'. Elaborating on the concept, Moore states 'the production and distribution of specific commodities, and of primary commodities in particular, have restructured geographic space at the margins of the system in such a way as to require further expansion'.[5] The expansion of the capitalist system occurs in these frontier areas; this is 'possible so long as there remains uncommodified land'.[6] Moore highlights that socio-ecological degradation of land and labour is central to this process of expansion and extraction, leading ultimately to the exploitation of new resources and further capitalist expansion. Essentially, a commodity frontier entails a process whereby there is a shifting incorporation of new supplies of land and labour for the global marketplace. As Moore maintains, one commodity frontier can 'set into motion a vast complex of economic activities'.[7] This is not surprising given that 'the capitalist world economy is inherently expansionary…[and] based on ceaseless capital accumulation'.[8]

This book was born out of a research collaboration involving a network of scholars across the world who work extensively on topics related to global commodity production, rural societies, labour history, environmental history, political ecology and the history of capitalism. Since 2014, this network of scholars has collaborated and interacted through four separate workshops focusing on commodity frontiers:

- 'Capitalist Growth, Commodity Frontiers, and Sustainability', October 24–25, 2014, Harvard University
- 'Global Capitalism and Commodity Frontiers: A Research Agenda', December 4–5, 2015, International Institute of Social History, Amsterdam (in collaboration with Ghent University, Research Group-Communities-Comparisons-Connections, and Harvard University, The Weatherhead Initiative on Global History)

- 'Global Commodity Frontiers in Comparative Perspective', December 9–10, 2016, Institute of the Americas, University College London, and Institute of Latin American Studies, School of Advanced Study, University of London
- 'Commodity Frontiers and Global Capitalist Expansion: Social, Ecological and Resource Policy Implications', December 6–7, 2017, Zayed University (Dubai, UAE), Department of Humanities and Social Sciences (in collaboration with Ghent University, Harvard University and the International Institute of Social History).

This volume builds on the momentum generated by these workshops. It aims to provide a global, comparative and interdisciplinary perspective on the dynamics of commodity frontier development and expansion, with a particular interest in how commodity frontiers have in one way or another impacted land and nature, people's relationship to the physical environment, and social, economic and political structures. This socio-ecological transformation resulting from the rise of export-oriented agriculture and the exploitation of soil, labour and natural resources has been one of the key processes in the emergence and consolidation of global capitalism. The contributors to this volume address issues that expand upon our definition and understanding of 'commodity frontiers'. They explore the socio-ecological changes that defined capitalism and the 'market widening' and 'market deepening' processes that drove the cyclical decline and expansion of commodity frontiers.[9] They also delve deeply into the socio-economic and political dynamics at the local level that drove the emergence and expansion of frontier zones—physical and social spaces that can accommodate or facilitate economic exploitation (and thereby global economic integration) and in so doing forever alter existing social and political structures.

There is a limited body of scholarship that explores the dynamics of capitalist expansion through the lens of the commodity frontier concept. Jason Moore's research on the world-ecology paradigm as well as silver and cotton frontiers has set the stage for much of the recent research that has been done by scholars. Sven Beckert's book *Empire of Cotton* highlights the centrality of the global countryside in the expansion of global capitalism and the role of an emerging European state system in propelling this expansion through the violent control of land, labour and nature. Socio-ecological degradation fuelled the cyclical nature of cotton frontiers.[10] My own research on the United Arab Emirates in the early part of the twentieth century explores how oil frontiers generated the emergence of 'secondary commodity frontiers' centred around agricultural production. Driven by state and colonial forces, this agricultural frontier contributed to a socio-ecological reordering that served to further integrate the country and region into the global capitalist economy.[11] Building upon the paradigm of capitalism as world-ecology, Aaron Jakes examines nationalist discourses amid agro-ecological degradation in the late nineteenth and early twentieth-century Egyptian commodity frontier.[12] A related body of work explores the connection between commodities and empire building as well as the commodity chains that have driven the world economy since the sixteenth century.[13] Furthermore, there are case studies that analyse how commodity expansion and production have contributed to the evolution of working classes.[14] Finally, recent research examines an issue that is key to commodity frontiers—knowledge transfer as related to development projects and global colonialist enterprises. For instance, Joseph Morgan Hodge in his book *Triumph of the Expert* explores how the engagement between science and the state informed twentieth-century British colonial development agendas (particularly vis-a-vis land and the environment) in sub-Saharan Africa, Southeast Asia and the Caribbean. Scientific experts were, of course, key in shaping and implementing rural development projects and environmental policies, often drawing on their prior experiences in other colonial areas.[15] Finally, Toby Jones examines how the Saudi state was forged through the development of water and oil. Jones explores how the emerging Saudi state in the early twentieth century established its power by managing and controlling natural resources. Science and technology, via global networks of expertise, were key in harnessing these resources. Thus, the interplay between state institutions, multinational corporations and engineering companies proved instrumental in reshaping Saudi society and the environmental landscape.[16]

The theoretical approach of this work contributes to the existing scholarship on global capitalist expansion and provides a fresh perspective for understanding the factors that contribute to frontier creation and expansion, regardless of the commodity at hand. Specifically, the current volume brings together research on diverse frontiers across time and space with the aim of drawing out parallels and thereby broadening our understanding of 'commodity frontier' dynamics. Furthermore, it explores the role of the state and other political and economic actors in driving commodity frontier expansion and analyses how local peasants and labour shaped the evolution of frontier zones through, for example, resistance. The frontiers explored in the book include those with fossil fuels, minerals, agricultural commodities and land resources. The book approaches the issue of commodity frontiers from a bottom-up perspective, focusing on the ecological, economic, policy and/or social implications of frontier creation and perpetuation at the local level. By applying an inductive approach and not starting at the global level, the book aims to better link the local and global.

The authors address various questions aimed at further developing the 'commodity frontier' theoretical concept.

- What are the drivers of commodity frontier expansion (markets, states, science, etc.)?
- What are the key features of a commodity frontier and to what extent does this depend on the commodity at hand?
- How has commodity frontier expansion impacted local, regional and global ecologies, altered resource management/extraction/production processes and informed present-day conservation strategies and policy making?
- How have labour relations or land tenure patterns been transformed by commodity frontier expansion?
- In turn, how have local populations resisted and/or informed the trajectory of commodity frontier development?
- What is the relationship between commodity frontier expansion and state power?

The chapters in this volume are arranged according to frontier type, in a bid to facilitate the identification of common characteristics and trends within similar frontier zones and across different frontiers.

Land-Use Frontiers

The first half of the book explores land-use frontiers across different parts of the world, including South America, East Asia, South Asia and the Arabian Gulf, from the nineteenth through the twenty-first centuries. These chapters examine the dynamics of capitalist expansion through commodity frontiers that emerged out of agricultural exploitation and the demarcation of lands for pastoral purposes and as natural reserves.

In Chapter 2, Hanne Cottyn employs a world-ecological perspective to examine the dynamics shaping nineteenth-century frontier expansion into communal lands in the altiplano (Peruvian-Bolivian border region), the role of communities in renegotiating capitalist expansion through resistance, and how such contestation has been appropriated or 'externalized' by the state and elites. She explains how, with the rising global demand for wool in the nineteenth century, communal lands were commodified. Although this period witnessed the expansion of private land control and the subordination and dispossession of local peasants, community organization did not disappear but rather adapted and reinvented itself. Elite groups, supported by state land laws, led this frontier expansion and appropriation of communal land and labour through the creation of *haciendas*. Peasants, however, were not passive bystanders in this process; they actively rebelled against the emerging capitalist order in the early part of the twentieth century. Cottyn explores the motivations behind this resistance and similar forms of unrest that have taken place in the twenty-first century in response to silver mining. She ends her paper by exploring how landholding elites and the government have delegitimized and criminalized such indigenous struggles for land and political rights. Thus, community resistance itself is appropriated by and framed according to the logic of cheap nature, whereby it is reduced to ahistorical dimensions and explained in terms of its costs, risks and social impact—the assumption being that such issues can be resolved through policy interventions and technical solutions.

In Chapter 3, Karen R. Miller explores the intersection of national political interests and economic development in the creation of an agricultural commodity frontier in the Koronadal Valley in the

Philippines during the 1930s. Miller examines the role of the state in creating and developing commodity frontiers, in this case by resettling Christian Filipinos to the Koronadal Valley, an area located in a province (Cotabato) in the southwest coast of the island where Muslims and 'Pagans' were the dominant population. Although such resettlements had been taking place since the early part of the twentieth century, the government accelerated its efforts in the 1930s in preparation for realizing its vision of modernization in the country's postcolonial future. Ultimately, the Koronadal Valley project spurred the creation of an agricultural frontier zone characterized by socio-ecological degradation.

In Chapter 4, Indrakshi Tandon focuses on farmer producer companies in India and their role in shaping agricultural frontier expansion and promoting the empowerment of farmers, particularly women. Tandon begins by providing a history of agro-economic development in India since the early twentieth century. She situates the rise of cooperatives and later producer companies in the context of the emergence of neoliberal development agendas that took root from the 1990s onwards. Transnational neoliberal policies, characterized by bottom-up, participatory approaches, were a response to the failure of state-driven initiatives aimed at poverty reduction that dominated development planning during the first four decades of independent India. Tandon's research is based on an ethnographic case study of a producer company in western India (Madhya Pradesh) composed solely of women producers—the Ranapur Tribal Mahila (Women) Farmer Producer Company Limited, referred to as the FPC. Her research findings highlight the discrepancy that exists between what producer companies represent in theory and how they operate in practice. Although these companies are meant to operate with minimal government intervention, they are in fact not free from state intervention. Tandon's study explores how these companies contribute to the expansion of agricultural frontiers and calls into question their role in promoting women's empowerment and upholding community action.

Brigitte Howarth, Tamer Khafaga, Greg Simkins and I examine the ecological ramifications of the commodification of Dubai's natural habitats in lands demarcated as protected areas in Chapter 5. The authors frame the commodification of Dubai's deserts as the continuation of an earlier process of capitalist transformation in the country that resulted in the privatization of land and the spread of modern agriculture in the post-oil period. The ecological degradation that has accompanied the rise and expansion of the oil frontier (including depletion of groundwater resources and habitat fragmentation and destruction) has in part motivated the state to set aside lands for protection, as clearly articulated in laws on nature reserves. On the other hand, environmental protection is also linked to economic growth, particularly as a mechanism for stimulating tourism. Howarth et al. explore how protected lands are exploited, both for recreational purposes by tourists/visitors and for the purposes of greening the desert by the state. These activities have in turn exerted further pressure on biodiversity. The chapter ends by presenting a possible model of effective management planning of a protected area aimed at ensuring sustainable development.

Extractive Frontiers

The second half of the book explores the factors that propelled the emergence, consolidation and expansion of extractive frontiers as well as the socio-ecological and political ramifications that were born out of these transformations. The frontiers examined include those with rubber, copper, nitrate and oil, and span regions across the Americas and Africa during the nineteenth and twentieth centuries.

In Chapter 6, Louise Cardoso de Mello and Sven Van Melkebeke explore labour commodification and the social ramifications of commodity frontier expansion on native populations in Western Amazonia and the Congo Free State during the rubber boom period from the 1870s to 1910s. Their study goes beyond the existing scholarship on rubber exploitation and trade by situating the regional, social ramifications of the rubber boom in a broader global comparative perspective. Their analysis sheds light on the factors that propelled these rubber frontiers and ultimately the transformation of labour relations in both regions, engendering two forms of labour coercion distinct from pre-capitalist relations: enslavement by debt and enslavement by tax. Conversely, Mello and Melkebeke also examine the resistance and adaptation strategies employed by indigenous populations in Western Amazonia and the Congo Free State. In both regions, native populations were confronted with weak states who perpetuated colonialist and developmentalist agendas. Resistance activities ultimately informed twentieth-century human rights discourses and agendas and influenced the emergence of organized forms of institutional and political resistance carried out by local community leaders.

In Chapter 7, James Lockhart situates the expansion of mining frontiers within the broader geopolitical context of Chile during the late nineteenth and early twentieth centuries. He explores how the expansion of these frontiers propelled the formation of the modern Chilean state and its institutions. In the early part of the nineteenth century, a pro-business, pragmatic political order emerged in Chile that lasted until the end of the nineteenth century. Territorial expansion during this period was driven in large part by the push to expand Chile's mining frontiers (silver, copper, iron, nitrate and coal) in response to increasing global demand from American, European and Australian markets. This expansion contributed to industrial development and the formation of a modern Chilean navy that was instrumental in expanding Chile's borders and thus, in turn, fuelling border disputes with Peru and Bolivia. Lockhart argues that competing interests generated by commodity frontier expansion in large part triggered the War of the Pacific (1879–1883). Furthermore, he explores how foreign and Chilean investment in nitrate fields and copper mining after the War of the Pacific spurred social and political transformation in late nineteenth- and early twentieth-century Chile by contributing to political conflict, the formation of a Chilean working class and the internationalization of the Chilean labour movement. Lockhart examines these changes from the perspective of the Chilean state as an active agent in shaping its destiny rather than as a pawn of imperial powers.

In Chapter 8, Robrecht Declercq sheds light on the role of large-scale natural resource companies in driving the socio-ecological transformation and economic globalization of early twentieth-century copper frontiers, drawing on case studies from Central Africa, the USA and Central and South America. These companies, whose role has not been examined thoroughly by historians, not only played a role in exploiting resources (both land and labour), but also in organizing access to energy, labour and resources in often hostile social and natural environments. Thus, the expertise of these resource companies extended beyond geological and mining issues. Declercq's contribution provides insight into how and why developments in the copper mining business during this period were key to the development of the modern natural resource company. He also sheds light on the role of non-state agents in driving and expanding frontier zones through the appropriation, creation and application of technical and expert knowledge.

In Chapter 9, Deborah Delgado examines the social, political and ecological impact of oil exploration in the Western Amazon since the 1970s. The expansion of this oil frontier has entailed uneven development, population displacement, labour exploitation, ecological distress and economic and political transformation. Local populations as well as governments are dependent upon the cash flow from oil activities, which has in turn devastated other sources of livelihood (including fishing and agriculture) and resulted in a lack of political will to initiate legislation monitoring and regulating the industry. Delgado provides valuable insight into the actions and interactions of state actors, oil companies and indigenous populations, highlighting the complex, paradoxical and shifting nature of conflict in the frontier. She also explores the gendered dimensions of oil frontier expansion, specifically in terms of the negative impact which environmental pollution has on indigenous women. While local populations recognize the toxic health and environmental ramifications of oil exploration and have mobilized to contest such developments, they also perceive that the oil economy has contributed to the economic development of their communities. As Delgado argues, commodity frontiers are more than just sites of extraction, but also spaces where political structures are altered and new political realities are born.

Notes

1. Jason Moore, "'The Modern World System' as Environmental History? Ecology and the Rise of Capitalism," *Theory and Society* 32, no. 3 (June 2003): 325, 328, 334, 356.

2. Eric Vanhaute, "Commodity Frontiers and the Global History of Capitalism: A Discussion About Sven Beckert's *Empire of Cotton*," *Journal of World History* 28, no. 1 (2017): 104. Marta Conde and Mariana Walter, "Commodity Frontiers," in *Degrowth: A Vocabulary for a New Era*, ed. Giacomo D'Alisa, Federico Demaria, and Giorgos Kallis (New York and London: Routledge, 2015), 71.
3. Moore, "'The Modern World System' as Environmental History?" 357.
4. Moore, "Introduction World-Ecological Imaginations," *Review (Ferdinand Braudel Center)* 37, no. 3–4 (2014): 166–67.
5. Jason Moore, "Sugar and the Expansion of the Early Modern World-Economy: Commodity Frontiers, Ecological Transformation, and Industrialization," *Review* 23, no. 3 (2000): 410.
6. Ibid., 412.
7. Ibid., 427.
8. Ibid., 428.
9. Moore, "Sugar and the Expansion of the Early Modern World-Economy," 427; Moore, "Silver, Ecology, and the Origins of the Modern World," in *Rethinking Environmental History: World-System History and Global Environmental Change*, ed. Alf Hornborg, J.R. McNeill, and Joan Martinez-Alier (Lanham, MD: Rownman AltaMira Press, 2007), 129–30; Moore, "'This Lofty Mountain of Silver Could Conquer the Whole World': Potosi and the Political Ecology of Underdevelopment, 1545–1800," suppl. Special issue: Studies in World-Systems Analysis, *The Journal of Philosophical Economics* 4, no. 1 (Autumn 2010): 89–92; Moore, "'The Modern World System" as Environmental History?' 351; and Edward Barbier, "Scarcity, Frontiers and Development," *The Geographical Journal* 178, no. 2 (2012): 114.
10. Sven Beckert, *Empire of Cotton: A Global History* (New York: Alfred A. Knopf, 2014); Sven Beckert, *Empire of Cotton: A New History of Global Capitalism* (London: Alan Lane and Penguin, 2014).
11. Sabrina Joseph, "Farming the Desert: Agriculture in the Oil Frontier, the Case of the United Arab Emirates, 1940s–1990s," *British Journal of Middle Eastern Studies* 45, no. 5 (2018): 678–694, https://doi.org/10.1080/13530194.2017.1320977.
12. Aaron Jakes, "Boom, Bugs, Bust: Egypt's Ecology of Interest, 1882–1914," *Antipode* 49, no. 4 (2017): 1035–59.
13. Ulbe Bosme, *The Sugar Plantation in India and Indonesia: Industrial Production, 1770–2010* (Cambridge: Cambridge University Press, 2013); Steven Topik, Zephyr Frank, and Carlos Marichal, eds.,

From Silver to Cocaine: Latin American Commodity Chains and the Building of the World Economy, 1500–2000 (American Encounters and Global Interactions) (Durham and London: Duke University Press, 2006); and Matthew Evenden, "Aluminum, Commodity Chains, and the Environmental History of the Second World War," *Environmental History* 16, no. 1 (January 2011): 69–93.

14. Jean Stubbs, *Tobacco on the Periphery: A Case Study in Cuban Labour History, 1860–1958* (Cambridge: Cambridge University Press, 1985); Joshua Howard, "The Politicization of Women Workers at War: Labour in Chongqing's Cotton Mills During the Anti-Japanese War," *Modern Asian Studies* 47, no. 6 (November 2013): 1888–1940; and Jan Rus, "Coffee and the Recolonization Highland Chiapas, Mexico: Indian Communities and Plantation Labor, 1892–1910," in *The Global Coffee Economy in Africa, Asia and Latin America, 1500–1989*, ed. William Gervase Clarence-Smith and Steven Topik (Cambridge: Cambridge University Press, 2003), 257–85.
15. Joseph Morgan Hodge, *Triumph of the Expert: Agrarian Doctrines of Development and the Legacies of British Colonialism* (Athens: Ohio University Press, 2007).
16. Toby Jones, *Desert Kingdom: How Oil and Water Forged Modern Saudi Arabia* (Cambridge: Harvard University Press, 2010).

Bibliography

Barbier, Edward. "Scarcity, Frontiers and Development." *The Geographical Journal* 178, no. 2 (2012): 110–22.

Beckert, Sven. *Empire of Cotton: A Global History*. New York: Alfred A. Knopf, 2014.

Bosme, Ulbe. *The Sugar Plantation in India and Indonesia: Industrial Production, 1770–2010*. Cambridge: Cambridge University Press, 2013.

Conde, Marta, and Mariana Walter. "Commodity Frontiers." In *Degrowth: A Vocabulary for a New Era*, edited by Giacomo D'Alisa, Federico Demaria, and Giorgos Kallis, 71–74. New York and London: Routledge, 2015.

Evenden, Matthew. "Aluminum, Commodity Chains, and the Environmental History of the Second World War." *Environmental History* 16, no. 1 (January 2011): 69–93.

Hodge, Joseph Morgan. *Triumph of the Expert: Agrarian Doctrines of Development and the Legacies of British Colonialism*. Athens: Ohio University Press, 2007.

Howard, Joshua. "The Politicization of Women Workers at War: Labour in Chongqing's Cotton Mills During the Anti-Japanese War." *Modern Asian Studies* 47, no. 6 (November 2013): 1888–1940.

Jakes, Aaron. "Boom, Bugs, Bust: Egypt's Ecology of Interest, 1882–1914." *Antipode* 49, no. 4 (2017): 1035–59.

Jones, Toby. *Desert Kingdom: How Oil and Water Forged Modern Saudi Arabia*. Cambridge: Harvard University Press, 2010.

Joseph, Sabrina. "Farming the Desert: Agriculture in the Oil Frontier, the Case of the United Arab Emirates, 1940s–1990s." *British Journal of Middle Eastern Studies* 45, no. 5 (2018): 678–694. https://doi.org/10.1080/13530194.2017.1320977.

Moore, Jason. "Introduction World-Ecological Imaginations." *Review* (*Ferdinand Braudel Center*) 37, no. 3–4 (2014): 165–72.

———. "'The Modern World System' as Environmental History? Ecology and the Rise of Capitalism," *Theory and Society* 32, no. 3 (June 2003): 307–77.

———. "Silver, Ecology, and the Origins of the Modern World." In *Rethinking Environmental History: World-System History and Global Environmental Change*, edited by Alf Hornborg, J.R. McNeill, and Joan Martinez-Alier, 123–42. Lanham, MD: Rownman AltaMira Press, 2007.

———. "Sugar and the Expansion of the Early Modern World-Economy: Commodity Frontiers, Ecological Transformation, and Industrialization." *Review* 23, no. 3 (2000): 409–33.

———. "'This Lofty Mountain of Silver Could Conquer the Whole World': Potosi and the Political Ecology of Underdevelopment, 1545–1800." suppl. Special issue: Studies in World-Systems Analysis, *The Journal of Philosophical Economics* 4, no. 1 (Autumn 2010): 58–103.

Rus, Jan. "Coffee and the Recolonization Highland Chiapas, Mexico: Indian Communities and Plantation Labor, 1892–1910." In *The Global Coffee Economy in Africa, Asia and Latin America, 1500–1989*, edited by William Gervase Clarence-Smith and Steven Topik, 257–85. Cambridge: Cambridge University Press, 2003.

Topik, Steven, Zephyr Frank, and Carlos Marichal, eds. *From Silver to Cocaine: Latin American Commodity Chains and the Building of the World Economy, 1500–2000*. American Encounters/Global Interactions. Durham and London: Duke University Press, 2006.

Vanhaute, Eric. "Commodity Frontiers and the Global History of Capitalism: A Discussion About Sven Beckert's *Empire of Cotton*." *Journal of World History* 28, no. 1 (2017): 101–5.

2

Making Cheap Nature on High Altitude: A World-Ecological Perspective on Commodification, Communities and Conflict in the Andes

Hanne Cottyn

Introduction: The Dialectics of Capitalist Expansion and Rural Community (Trans)Formation on the Altiplano

Over the last years, the Ombudsman of Peru observes and monitors a stark rise in conflicts in the rural Andes. In 2017, the *Defensoría del Pueblo* in Peru registered 256 social conflicts, of which 66.4% were identified as 'socio-environmental' conflicts and mostly concentrated in the (South-)Andean region.[1] The label of 'socio-environmental' refers to conflicts caused by a real or perceived incompatibility between different systems of control, use, management, access or exploitation of territories and their natural resources. The recent creation of this distinctive category is an indicator of the rise in this kind of conflict, pointing to the growing awareness of how unequal social power relations correlate with nature, and denoting a fundamental critique to injustice

H. Cottyn (✉)
Ghent University, Ghent, Belgium
e-mail: hanne.cottyn@ugent.be

S. Joseph (ed.), *Commodity Frontiers and Global Capitalist Expansion*,
Palgrave Studies in Economic History, https://doi.org/10.1007/978-3-030-15322-9_2

reproduced by specific economic models.[2] These conflicts have been explained as 'ecological distribution conflicts' and relate directly to a process of expanded commodity production.[3] Latin American rural communities are in the eye of a storm brewed by high commodity prices and expanding extractive operations. Maristella Svampa has framed this storm as the product of a paradigmatic and strategic shift to a 'Commodities Consensus'.[4] This shift is marked by the large-scale exportation of raw materials that thrives on the identification of previously considered 'unproductive' assets as new (the last?) reserves of exploitable resources. It is a race to the bottom that sparks numerous social struggles in the region, with Peru undoubtedly as one of its most emblematic hot spots. Different from the more paradoxical discourse of its 'progressive extractivist' neighbours, Peru legitimizes this violent extractivist turn by deliberately matching a neoliberal development model with a neo-developmentalist discourse.

If Peru would have had an Ombudsman in 1917, he (very unlikely a she) would have observed a similar increase in social conflicts. In the late nineteenth century, liberal policies targeting communal landholdings as obstacles to modernity and progress unleashed a new, violent cycle of land dispossession and rural protest, particularly in the Andean highlands.[5] But would the Ombudsman also define what he observed as 'socio-ecological' conflicts? The way in which the neoliberal extractivist turn 'discovers' communal territories as vacant terrain, which comes with the design of appropriate narratives and legal frameworks that enable and justify interventions, starkly resembles Latin America's liberal extractivist turn around 1900. Equally, the explosion of social conflicts that accompanies the current Consensus seems all too familiar. Literature on contemporary environmental justice struggles is booming,[6] and the parallels with the transitions of a century earlier are clear to all, yet comprehensive analyses of this historical interconnectedness are lacking.

In order to juxtapose these parallel historical moments of community transformation, this chapter urges for a deeper historical, systemic and dialectical understanding of current commodity booms and their effect on communal territories. This chapter questions the 'survival' of community-based systems, unveiling this survival as a central paradox of historical capitalism. The premise is that the global countryside forms the prime terrain of action of historical capitalism. The interaction between rural societies and capitalist expansion is embedded in a long, uneven historical trajectory. The strategies through which communal worlds are opened up as providers of land, labour and nature to nurture new waves of capitalist expansion, as well as the communal strategies to counter this appropriation, rest on accumulated historical experiences of community-based participation in an evolving capitalist world system. Hence, communal territories must be understood as the product of social change. As new actors and industries seek to reorganize rural spaces and heighten the pressures on communal lands, community demands, organization and memories are reactivated. This context of community threats and revitalization has pushed peasant communities—once a prominent domain of sociological research and social policies but since the 1980s progressively marginalized—back on the academic and political agenda.[7] In response to this renewed, often idealized interest in communal forms of organization and resistance, this chapter underscores the need to understand communities in a relational and processual way. As Diez states, these institutional formations are in constant change through adaptation, resistance and self-reinvention—they 'are transformed while they remain'.[8]

Focusing on the contestation over land and power in communal territories, and the attempts on the part of central governments and elite groups to neutralize this conflict, this chapter attempts to demonstrate the eco-'logic'-al continuities between the ruptures of Andean rural uprisings of the liberal and the neoliberal era. It argues that these moments were part of the same sort of world-ecological transformation. The method of 'incorporated comparison' is adopted to interconnect these moments in relation to a systemic process—the commodification of nature, and particularly of relations (access, control and property) to land. This systemic process is approached from the perspective of world-ecology, 'a perspective that joins the accumulation of capital and the production of nature in dialectical unity'.[9] It is a perspective that unveils the contradictions of capitalist development. The concept of 'commodity frontier' serves as an analytical tool to disentangle the dialectics of commodity production and community reproduction in a non-dichotomist way. This notion, coined by Jason W. Moore, refers to the world-systemic processes of land, labour and nature incorporation and appropriation, pushed forward by capitalism's inherent ecological contradictions.[10] By historically specifying episodes of expanding commodification in a particular time/space context, and by developing the analysis from the frontier (not from the core), this chapter problematizes the idea of capitalism's systemic development as a uniform and linear historical project.

This chapter centres on the contentious nature of these frontier dynamics in peripheral places, in order to understand the role of 'peripheral agency' in the commodification of nature and its contestation. The repercussions and limits of advancing commodity frontiers will be explored through the history of Aymara communities of the Andean high plateau, or 'altiplano'. Through its early incorporation as a vital, silver-providing periphery, the altiplano was restructured into a world-ecological frontier zone, both functional and disruptive to the smooth expansion of a capitalist world order. Based on an extensive literature study in combination with insights from field and archival research in Puno,[11] Peru, this chapter interconnects formative episodes, situated, respectively, at the turn of the twentieth and twenty-first centuries, in the commodification of land rights and Andean rural transformation.

In what follows, I first elaborate on the notions of world-ecology, 'cheap nature' and commodity frontiers as analytical concepts to understand the transformation of communal land systems in a dialectical way. In the third section of this chapter, I provide a historical assessment of commodity frontier dynamics in relation to pastoralist communities on the altiplano. Then, I zoom in on the dramatic moment of the simultaneous breakthrough of commodity booms and a liberal discursive apparatus in the nineteenth century. With the case studies on peasant revolts in the province of Chucuito, I assess not only the methods but also the limits of pastoralists' deepening incorporation within a world-ecological order. In the fifth section, I focus not only on how this incorporation was contested by Andean communities, but also on how the proliferation of rural conflicts was being appropriated by state and corporate leaders. Here, I provide a comparative analysis with the way socio-environmental conflicts are portrayed and 'managed' in the current neoliberal age. I finish with a metaphorical allusion to *soroche*, Andean altitude sickness, that seems to impede commodity frontiers' full-fledged development on the altiplano.

Land Rights and the Paradoxes of Commodity Frontier Expansion

How to forge the link between contemporary socio-environmental conflicts in the Peruvian Andean highlands and rural unrest of a century ago as specific expressions of rural communities' incorporation in a world-ecological order? In order to explain distinct moments as 'relational parts of a singular (historically forming) phenomenon', McMichael proposes a method of 'incorporated comparison'.[12] Unlike conventional comparison, it is a method that does not abstract cases from their temporal and spatial context, but on the contrary allows to historically specify particular time/space instances in relation to a systemic process.[13] Examples are Arrighi's comparison of accumulation cycles as instances of the historical project of capitalist expansion[14] or McMichael's juxtaposition of contemporary free trade with nineteenth-century British imperial market rule.[15] Separate instances of a formative global phenomenon become conceptually interconnected, and the mutual shaping of the overall process and particular instances can be explained. In this case, we take two distinct (liberal and neoliberal) moments of heightened vulnerability of community lands as specific episodes in the globalization of a modern land regime, understood as a formative world-ecological process. This section forms the conceptual foundations of this endeavour; it introduces the concepts of world-ecology and commodity frontier to grasp the commodification of nature, identifies the mechanisms behind this process and points to its paradoxical development.

World-ecology offers a framework to understand capitalism not as acting upon nature, but as product and producer of nature, capitalism as a multi-species world-ecological order.[16] Hence capitalism cannot be understood only as world-economy, but also as a way of organizing nature; it 'does not have an ecological regime; it is an ecological regime'.[17] Cheap nature, that is how to get 'nature—human nature too!—to work for free or very low-cost', is its main strategy.[18] A world-ecology perspective unveils the creation of cheap natures (the appropriation of labour, food, energy and raw materials) as capitalism's simultaneous strength and weakness, the driver of its expansion and the roots of its inherent contradictions.[19] The contemporary 'environmentalization' of social struggles in Latin America[20] demonstrates a growing awareness of this contradictory character.

As McMicheal explains, the recurrence (rather than the modification or 'progression') of earlier phases of systemic expansion and consolidation can be explained by identifying the mechanisms and rhetoric through which this expansion is operationalized.[21] I understand the mechanism through which nature is 'made' cheap as commensuration, which has been theorized as a specific form of standardization or calculation that 'reduces quality to quantity' and 'culminates with a common metric'.[22] It is through commensuration that the Cartesian dichotomy is imposed, enabling a separation between society and nature. It means nature, including human life, food, energy and raw materials, being stripped from its non-economic value, and spiritual bonds to land, rivers or mountains being replaced by commodity value. The reduction of part of human life to a cheap labour supply is a highly racialized and gendered process. Separating humans versus the rest of nature enforces the domination of the former over the latter as 'the web of life could be reduced to a series of external objects—mapped, explored, surveyed, calculated for what Nature could do for the accumulation of capital'.[23] The outcome is abstract social nature. As an effect, commensuration opens the 'possibility of appropriation'[24] of an increasingly larger arena of the 'web of life' as economic 'input' for the sake of the endless accumulation of capital.

Inherently contradictory and hence exhaustive, the cheap nature strategy thrives on crisis. Consequently, production processes are constantly moved into new terrain. This movement and its spatial constellation is what Jason W. Moore has labelled a 'commodity frontier'.[25] As Hall explains, a 'specific frontier often follows a complex path, a trajectory, of incorporation with successive strengthening and weakening phases'.[26] The trajectory of a frontier of incorporation describes a 'dialectical historical process'.[27] I adopt 'commodity frontier' as an analytical tool to capture commodity-community dialectics, that is, to describe and explain how capitalist power extends into new, uncommodified spaces and the localized dynamics that give shape to this process. Rasmussen and Lund emphasize the mutually constitutive disintegration of social order and restructuring of space as 'frontier moments' and 'territorialisations'.[28] Through commodity frontiers, we trace how pre-existing social and territorial logics are materially broken up and reshuffled, and rhetorically reimagined and 're-socialized'. Commodity frontiers develop through conflict and struggle, shaping a dynamic development of commodity production (the creation of cheap nature) and community reproduction (the paradoxes of cheap nature). They materialize in frontier zones—the spatial expression of commodity frontiers—where the incorporation of new places and peoples is under negotiation.

World-ecological paradoxes refer to the unintended encounters that drive capitalism. That is, how capitalist expansion fuels itself 'by attempting to divert or attach itself to other kinds of energy or logic'[29] and is 'continuously interrupted by other logics'.[30] Instances of 'friction',[31] of conflicting social interactions, hint at capitalism's instability and reveal how it develops by responding to its own contradictions. These encounters give rise to new imaginaries that undermine the pretended imposition of a Cartesian divide, and materialize in co-existing alternative spaces of social reproduction and imagination. With respect to Latin America, Svampa has referred to an 'ecoterritorial turn', a new vocabulary at the intersection of indigenous-communitarian and environmental discourses that emerges in response to the extractivist moment and the concomitant proliferation of conflict.[32] But the paradoxical character of commodity frontier expansion appears also when and where a frontier seems static, where things seem to remain in place, as in resistant 'untouched' indigenous territories. The frontier's apparent immobility relates to dynamic counterforces that temporally balance or frustrate the incorporation process. Here, a 'countercyclical' fuelling link can be identified between the pulsatile (contraction and expansion) development of capitalist space and the cycles of (often indigenous) community-based resistance movements.[33] The notion of frontier thus reveals the imagined *surviving* margins of capitalism as the messy or paradoxical product of the social and territorial reorganizations that come with commodity frontier expansion. To understand these dialectical reconfigurations, more empirical insight into the formation of commodity frontiers in concrete places is necessary.

This chapter delves into a concrete and constitutive frontier process, the commodification of land rights. The expansion of global capitalism is the expression of a fundamental transformation of land rights.[34] The struggle over rights to access, withdraw, manage, exclude or alienate land shapes an uneven trajectory of land rights commodification, materializing in a modern land regime centred that linked land to capital.[35] The globalization of a private property regime intensified from the nineteenth century on, through colonial, developmentalist and neoliberal state projects. The world contained by this regime intersects and coexists—not dichotomously, but dialectically yet asymmetrically—with silenced but resilient communal worlds. Today, the control over a surprisingly large share—over 50%—of the world's land area is in communal hands.[36] The rural Andes appear as one of these 'surviving' margins of this globalizing land system, though thoroughly shaped by the forces of that regime.

Strategies and practices of the commons appear as enclosure's 'other', pointing again to the dialectical relation that binds 'commodification' and 'community'.[37] These dialectics, fuelled by the partial incorporation of customary tenure systems, undercut the logic and outlines of a neatly commodified land regime. Peluso and Lund capture this in the notion of constantly (re)created 'new frontiers of land control'. These frontiers 'are not sites where 'development' and 'progress' meet 'wilderness' or 'traditional lands and peoples'', but 'where authorities, sovereignties, and hegemonies are … challenged by new enclosures, territorializations, and property regimes'.[38] In other words, territories that 'survive' under communal control are not overlooked by frontier-driven reorganizations, nor did they become fully fledged integrated into the newly envisioned order. These communal territorial formations, reflected in land being kept under community control, can be read through a *longue durée* history of commodity frontiers moving into, reordering or circumventing, exhausting or retreating from a specific environment. They resonate both the effect and the rejection of the cheap nature strategy.

The Altiplano as a World-Ecological Frontier Zone

The altiplano serves as an excellent illustration of the dialectical way in which commodity spaces and community spaces co-evolve. This vast arid plain is situated entirely above 3500 metres above sea level across the Peruvian-Bolivian border. Over the centuries, mining and urbanization have dramatically altered the landscape, yet without displacing livestock herding and communal organization as key features that structure rural life. The altiplano countryside is dominated by the semi-desert ecosystem of the 'puna', where llamas, sheep and vicuña thrive, and microclimates—especially around Lake Titicaca—where rural communities grow potatoes and quinoa. Ethnically, these communities predominantly self-identify as Aymara or quechua, and only a tiny, vulnerable minority still presents itself as the region's original inhabitants, the Uru. Economically, these peasants are oriented towards subsistence agro-pastoralist activities and (cross-border) trade, organized within a social agro-pastoralist system.[39] Due to the scarcity of resources in this harsh environment and the highly developed transport competences of llama-herding households, pastoralists developed a remarkable expertise in long-distance exchange relations with complementary production zones. Because of the need for vast open pasture land to support their main means of transport—the llama, collective land management is extremely important in these societies. Land control, production and exchange explain why pastoralist communities develop a specific relation to the market sphere and to the state apparatus.[40] These factors are to a large extent structured by communal access regulations, highly reliant on supra-local exchange relations through inter-ecological barter and markets, and negotiated through tributary relations with the state.

The outcome of this trajectory is the continuing weight of these communal structures, which becomes particularly clear in terms of land control. In Peru, around 35% of the total land surface is either designated for the communities or held collectively by communities.[41] In Peru's southern highlands, most of these lands are in hands of *comunidades campesinas* (peasant communities).[42] In the Aymara zone of the Puno department, on which this research centres, most rural land is controlled under the legal figure of these 'peasant communities', but also of the *parcialidad*.[43] The latter is an older institution of territorial control consisting of parcels of land under family tenure, where a certain degree of individual autonomy is matched by a communal form of political-administrative organization.[44] Although locals attribute different meanings to the *parcialidad*,[45] it is commonly understood as the antecedent of the 'peasant communities', which were formed as regroupings of individual peasant, communal and hacienda lands in the 1970s after Peru's Agrarian Reform. In Puno, only 0.2% of the plots of rural lands is accessed and transferred through customary land rights, but these terrains comprise almost half of the department's surface.[46] In what follows, the focus will be placed on the province of Chucuito, situated south from Lake Titicaca and entirely Aymara territory (Fig. 2.1).

This particular relationship between pastoralist communities, centralized state power and market dynamics developed through a centuries-long process of world-ecological incorporation. Stubbornly peripheral, the altiplano took shape as a vital commodity frontier zone of the emerging and expanding capitalist world system more than five centuries ago. The commodity frontier history of altiplano communities developed through the cyclical intensification and slowdown in the production of particular commodities (time), communal territorial reconfigurations within a commodity frontier zone (space) and the transformation of particular pastoralist logics to relate to nature (ecology). Over the centuries, the altiplano has been discovered and reorganized as a frontier of peasant labour for mines and haciendas, of animal labour for transport, of animal resources for the wool market, of mineral wealth for the monetary and industrial economy. This process started during the sixteenth-century 'commodity revolution' that linked the Potosí silver mines

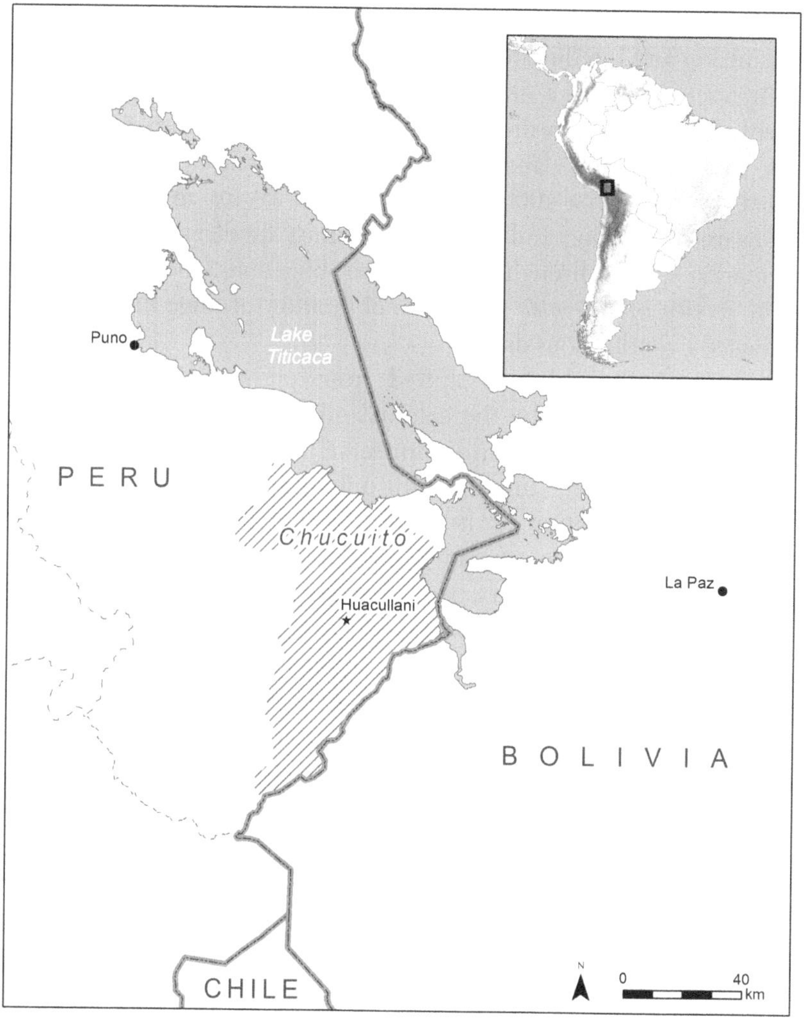

Fig. 2.1 The highland community of Huacullani is located at the heart of the province of Chucuito in the department of Puno, Peru (Map designed by Hans Blomme)

to European capital and empire.[47] The extraction of silver in Potosí was the epicentre of one of the most powerful 'open vein' of the Americas[48]; 'the principal motor force of structural change that affected all facets of economic life and social relations throughout the Andes'.[49] The silver economy acted as the pumping heart of a new regional labour division, reorganizing and interlinking communal livelihoods, economic flows and labour reserves within a unified socio-economic space that spread from current Ecuador to North-Chile.[50] It activated numerous provisioning lines, supplying food, labour, mercury and practically everything else needed to survive in a 4000-metre-high and arid city, and redrawing silver towards the Pacific. Indigenous community dwellers were drawn into this market sphere through two-year tax obligations, the forced mining labour service of the *mit'a* and the mobilization of huge llama caravans conducted by indigenous drivers.

Over time, the altiplano shifted from perhaps capitalism's most critical vein, embodied by the colonial mines of Potosí, to one of the many peripheral veins which do not serve but to postpone capitalism's imminent exhaustion. This dramatic incorporation process implied a profound transformation of the countryside. After the *encomienda* system allocated native population groups to the conquistadores decayed in the late sixteenth century, the *reducciones* reform—imposed under the Spanish viceroy de Toledo—resettled hamlets in centralized communities within a (for the Spanish) 'legible' and segregated administrative structure.[51] The Andean 'community', which is usually referred to as *ayllu* and is today being defended as a space of autonomy against advancing commodification, was first created as a Spanish colonial institution for tax and labour extraction. Ever since, the *ayllu* has been exposed to cheap nature strategies but also been re-appropriated as a communal negotiation lever. Hence, contrary to the dominant thesis that the community is a colonial product, it makes much more sense to understand this institution as a much younger creation, an adaptation to more recent challenges to rural livelihoods, a product of the nineteenth-century hacienda (and of the struggles against it), as has been suggested by Alejandro Diez.[52] Indeed, the nineteenth century constitutes a crucial moment in the trajectory of Andean community lands.

By the late eighteenth century, the decay of Potosí disrupted the South-Andean socio-economic space. Moreover, the independence wars divided the altiplano politically between Peru and Bolivia, condemning Puno to a somewhat awkward dependence to Lima. Mining lost its articulating power and the Peruvian–Bolivian border deteriorated the fragmenting effect on the colonial economic space. The transition period to independence was marked by a lower pressure by landowners on rural society, enabling altiplano communities to enlarge their herds and strengthen their control over territory in the Peruvian[53] and Bolivian[54] altiplano. Despite the proclamation of liberal decrees that sought to replace communal land systems by private property titles, the policy makers of the new republics had to adapt their anti-corporate legislative designs to that reality.[55] Gradually, however, a new phase in the cheap nature strategy took off. In Puno, this phase was driven in the first place by rising wool prices on the world market. Because of initially comfortable position of indigenous herding communities, the take-off of the wool boom relied on these communities as the largest wool producers.[56] However, old and new landlords redressed that reality into the old colonial feudal image as opposed to a modern, but lacking, land market. This brings to mind what Grosfoguel has called 'feudalmania', the discursive mechanism to establish a distance between an inferior and superior moment that legitimates a 'catch-up'.[57] First, communities were to be un-thought as an enabling basis for indigenous peasant market participation and imagined as immobilized and marginalized from expanding commercial networks.[58] This enabled a neo-colonial reframing of community lands as a frontier of cheap nature, a still illegible reserve, and hence in need of abstraction and commensuration.

Pastoralists and Liberal Land Grabbing at the Turn of the Twentieth Century

In the nineteenth century, the community lands in the highlands of Puno were converted into commodities. Before, the value of land was secondary to, or simply included in, that of the livestock—the real capital—that grazed on it.[59] The specific commensuration scheme that 'mobilized' the community was private property, as a vehicle that would absorb not only land, but also labour—the indigenous body—within the circulation of commodities. The discursive framework for this transition was the 'triumph of liberalism', which came with the implementation of a legal-technical apparatus. A new state-capital-science nexus was forged, enabling the identification and seizure of new reserves of cheap nature through mapping, codification, surveying and other categorization techniques.[60] In Puno, the liberal land laws of the 1820s that sought to distribute individual lands among indigenous families provided the legal basis to the later assault on community lands. Still, until the post-1850s boost in the land market, these laws paradoxically helped to keep the balance between peasant and hacienda land control in place.[61] Land scarcity, state incapacity and peasant responses impeded the full reign of liberal principles.[62] This section zooms in on the advance of private landholdings in an altiplano province, explores why and how this advance constituted a frustrated process, and reflects briefly on the recurrence of this conflictive episode in recent times.

The economic effect of neo-colonial commodity booms—first guano, and later wool and minerals—on national treasuries, and the concomitant emergence of a new rural elite was decisive for the breakthrough of this shift. Increasing revenues from commodity production and exportation freed the treasury from its 'colonial' dependency upon indigenous fiscal contributions (which require the protection of communities), until this cycle started to lose power by 1920. Politically, this shift is framed in a process of national reconstruction that started in the wake of the War of the Pacific (1879–1884). Around 1900, the Peruvian Andean countryside was marked by political reconfigurations. National elites opted for railroads, white 'modern' migration and schooling as the tools to integrate the Andean countryside, thereby forging a link between the 'indigenous question' and the 'national question'. In practice, this facilitated the subordination of local peasantries through the monopolization of land control, mercantile capital and public offices in the hands of new rural power groups, the so-called *gamonales*[63] or *mistis* (white and mestizo rural elites). This did not simply materialize in colonial-like extractive pressures upon Andean communities—which continued to spark revolts—but in new legal measures and attitudes that scaled the ambitions up to the total elimination of the communities.[64] This trend resembles the recent and ongoing series of neoliberal *paquetazos* or reform packets pushed through in Peru, prioritizing large-scale investments of 'national interest' over achieved but precarious community rights.[65]

Nineteenth-century liberalism pretended to provide the conditions for a capitalist transition of the country by converting indigenous collectives into a class of individual entrepreneurial smallholders. On the ground, liberalism's grand ambitions took a very different course, dictated by economic realities rather than ideological directives. The key drive behind dispossession on the Peruvian altiplano was the rising demand for sheep and camelid wool, particularly by English capital, and was facilitated by the introduction and expansion of railways. By the 1850s, the export of wool to Europe had come to constitute the altiplano's most important source of income.[66] This went together with the building out of a hierarchical complex for wool appropriation through trade houses connected to the southern city of Arequipa and intermediaries that covered up to the smallest corners of the altiplano countryside.[67] Highland communities in the provinces of Chucuito, Lampa and Huancané were particularly important in the supply of alpaca wool.[68] The wool demand and the legal veneer of private property rights incentivized the massive absorption of communal land and labour within a semi-feudal hacienda complex of large-scale landholdings. The liberal discourse on the elimination of the 'dead hands' justified not only land's commercialization, but also its usurpation, either through fraudulent practices or plain grabbing. The consolidation of a hacienda complex involved fraud and speculation, such as by wool *rescatistas* paying ahead wool production as a mechanism to appropriate peasant plots, but also legal tricks, plain lies and violence.[69]

Between 1870 and the 1930s, the altiplano witnessed an expansion of private land control on a scale unprecedented since the sixteenth century. In the case of Puno, the number of haciendas rose between 1876 and 1915 from 702 to 3699, although this doesn't take into account the size and concentration of those haciendas.[70] This number contains multiple rather small and mainly livestock-oriented units, and they continued to co-exist with indigenous territorial units.[71] However, *hacendados*, while appropriating the most valuable lands, pushed autonomous community peasants into ever higher and more marginal territories. Haciendas started to expand also into the highest areas dedicated to pastoralism, such as the provinces of Chucuito and Huancané (Puno), where communal usufruct had remained strongest in place in contrast to the quasi-individual properties at the shores of the Titicaca lake.[72] In the Chucuito province, the number of haciendas rose five times from 49 to 242 between 1876 and 1915, with a particular increase after 1895.[73]

Inaccessible vs. *Inaki* Land: Making Cheap Nature and Pastoralist Resistance

Post-colonial wool and mining commodity booms restructured power and property relations in altiplano communities profoundly, albeit without eliminating Aymara socio-territorial logics. From roughly 1870 to 1930, the high demand for Peruvian wool and a general demographic boom between 1876 and 1940, including a population increase of community peasants of possibly 50–60%,[74] heightened the pressures on land and resources. The wool commodity boom and indigenous community organization constituted two competing spheres over land, resources, labour, in short, nature. The level of mutual incompatibility erupted in the 'Great Peasant Revolts' of the early twentieth century.[75] What is still known as the 'altiplano storm'[76] can be examined in terms of socio-environmental conflicts, as was explained earlier in this chapter, and hence in world-ecological terms.

Puno's 'great' indigenous peasant rebellions consisted of a series of multiple simultaneous protests, with major eruptions in the 1910s and the 1920s, and (partly) linked to *indigenista* (pro-indigenous) organizations.[77] The highest regions, where pastoralist communities roamed and community organization was most solid, were strongly involved in these cycles. Yet, there is discussion about the drivers behind these rebellions. Usually, these struggles are understood as primarily driven by economic factors, mainly over land. Other investigations, focusing on the highest zones of the Aymara region, frame these pastoralist struggles in the first place as directed against labour appropriation and the widespread climate of abuses. Flores and Palacios, in a case study on pastoralist protest in 1901 in Chichillapi (today part of the recently created El Collao province), hold that there were no struggles over land nor attempts to usurp land in the highest region, which they attribute to the lack of large haciendas and the strength and extension of the communities.[78]

Calisto also criticizes the dominant assumption that Aymara peasant protest was about land, and insists on the role of political claims.[79] Indeed, the struggle for social justice and political rights was key and involved sending out *mensajeros* (messengers) who brought indigenous complaints to the capital. Yet, land was definitively a factor of social protest in pastoralist territories, as several cases indicate (see for instance in the following section on colonial legacies). According to Rodrigo Montoya, it was the pastoralists of communal (non-hacienda) lands—the *comuneros parcelarios* (community members of *parcialidades*)—who formed the vanguard of Peru's early twentieth-century land struggles.[80] Moreover, while indigenous peasant revolts were indeed often sparked by the conditions of labour exploitation, they were understood as inherently linked to a longer history of land usurpation.

Rather than choosing one side in the debate over the genuine drivers of the peasant revolts, I hold that land, labour, political rights and cosmovision all entangled in the way pastoralist communities sensed the increased vulnerability to which they were exposed. 'The late nineteenth-century liberal assaults on indigenous forms of subsistence and community threatened, as perhaps only the European conquest had done, the intricate webs that bound most Andean peasantries to their mountainous world and all that it had to symbolize'.[81] I argue that this cycle of resistance was not just about land conflicts or political power, but that there was a much more profound, systemic, indeed, 'world-ecological' dimension to it. This was clearly a moment of deepening world-ecological incorporation with a very violent character.

In terms of a world-ecological phase, the response to this appropriation of communal land must be understood from an Aymara socio-territorial logic rooted in a non-Cartesian notion of the interrelation between kinship, land and territory. The following testimony of a peasant woman, Manuela Ari, about communal dispossession in the Chucuito province (Puno) in the early twentieth century, recorded in the late 1990s, demonstrates how this non-Cartesian reasoning and the cheap nature strategy clashed.[82] When landowner Tovar told the comunarios that '[t]hese houses and these land will be mine.... If you don't sell them voluntarily, I'll know how to kick you out', Ari's father-in-law responded that the land was 'mine since [the time of] the ancestors of my ancestors. I cannot sell it to you'. These lands pertained integrally to a sphere that was inaccessible for cheap nature. So Tovar ordered to burn the house down and to take away the animals. 'Tovar grabbed the lands without having given any money', Manuela recounts, '*inaki, chama paru athini sisna*'; 'For free, he won by force'. *Inaki* is Aymara for free. Nature is not cheapened, but taken freely, both the land and the labour. Manuela's husband became *pongo* (domestic worker) of the hacienda. Manuela adds, 'Before, the mestizo did not do this, because he was the *patrón*', hinting at a prior moral economy that guided landlord and community interrelations. The dissolution of this moral economy pushed several comunarios to eventually sell their land.

Colonial Legacies and the Limits of Cheap Nature

Empirical research on the wool boom in Puno (Peru) has demonstrated that the end of communal land control did not equal its replacement by capitalist property relations.[83] This adds to Congost's argument for a realistic and relational analysis of property, and equally other 'institutional' bonds, in order to overcome legalist interpretations which only capture the lettered world of the decision-makers.[84] Hacienda expansion, while aggressive, resulted in a rather weak control over land and labour. Jacobsen claims that the 'legacy of colonialism' was determinant in halting capitalism on the altiplano, by which he does not refer to the lasting impact of Hispanic cultural and political traits, but to 'the tendency of most social groups in the altiplano (…) to use polarized visions of society'.[85] Access to resources was secured through colonial binaries of colonized/colonizer, Spaniard/indian, or civilized/barbaric, which liberal administrative, fiscal, legal, and other categorizations–essential for the cheap nature strategy—struggled to replace. Even critics of indigenous exploitation such as government inspector Maguiña remained faithful to that framework. In his influential stringent report of 1902 on the situation in the province Chucuito, he formulated the assumption that the *indios* wanted to stick to slavery.[86]

Colonial dichotomist notions continued to regulate power relations, resulting in the incomplete materialization of reforms based on new concepts of property into secure and complete rights.[87] Rural property was invisible and unavailable to people from outside with no personal ties or commercial contacts in the area. Even though private property was incorporated in the local vocabulary, this was not reflected in corresponding property practices. Simultaneously, an 'internal appropriation' of lands materialized within non-absorbed communities, through which new rural elites consolidated their local power base. Control over labour remained equally very fragile. To an important degree, *hacendados* had to extract complementary input for their residential labour from outlying communities, which partly explains the simultaneous subordination and autonomy of hacienda *colonos* (peons).[88] The limited reach and impact of the cheap nature strategy in the post-colonial altiplano demonstrates how commodity frontiers move through the interplay between Aymara communities caught up in advancing commodity frontiers, Andean states pretending to regulate frontier movements, and new (local to transnational) elite groups leading frontier expansion, and how that interplay is embedded within a historically charged environment. In the process, pre-existing practices and imaginaries were also appropriated by indigenous peasants to vindicate and reinvent the community as an alternative and resistant space, in that way deviating the projected transition.

The weight of colonial procedures and memories in the unwinding of counter-commensuration revolts on the altiplano is illustrated by the following case in the district of Huacullani. When hacienda expansion came to a 'closure' and consolidated during the first phase of wool export expansion, around 1910,[89] a first large-scale rebellious moment started to mount. This included highland communities in the Chucuito province, where both non-hacienda and hacienda peasants mobilized against the ongoing land usurpation. In 1912, in the district of Huacullani, both 'free' peasants and hacienda *colonos* sought to physically and symbolically counter the appropriation of communal land through the execution of a land demarcation in the *fincas* of hacienda 'Pichupichuni'.[90] The hacienda, equipped with a mill, had become property of the Eduardo family, who had usurped these lands in former decades.[91] The action was led by the indigenous ex-messenger Santiago Mallca. Interestingly, he adopted a Spanish introduced, albeit communally internalized, instrument for fixing and standardizing access to land; the *deslinde* or land demarcation. Moreover, he presented himself with the authority of a judge, declaring that he was entrusted by the Supreme Government to install new landmarks and take judicial possession of the usurped *fincas*. Those lands were declared as 'not private property but of the community'. The ultimate proof of its communal status was in the communities' possession of authentic colonial property deeds. A letter announcing the action and signed by the *comunarios* of *parcialidad* Sales declared that 'as the properties of the community cannot be sold without the strict consent of the comunarios, it is established that not any sale will be recognized'.[92] Here, the colonial legal-discursive apparatus was vital in condemning and fighting the abuses and appropriation on the part of new provincial elites.

In this context of widespread upheaval, the communities that remained out of the scope of hacienda seizure did not just persist as a 'reserve buffer' or refuge, but were (re)created as such, as communal formations, in intimate interaction with the succeeding enclosure movement. Throughout successive phases of intensified commodity production, the altiplano countryside transformed profoundly yet incompletely due to both the strength of colonial dichotomist notions and of indigenous socio-territorial logics. Through this imperfect process, Andean peasant communities have become more intimately connected to the rhythms and scales of the market and the state, albeit in different and often ambiguous ways. The resulting different modes and degrees of capitalist incorporation and resistance influenced the possibilities for communities and their leaders to renegotiate the margin for communal land control.

From the Great Peasant Revolts to the *Aymarazo*

The recurrence of the patterns explored above through early twentieth-century rural unrest becomes clear when assessing recent violent transitions in the Andean countryside. This section draws a link with a region-wide protest that has been labelled as the *Aymarazo*.[93] In 2011, the Aymara (and some quechua) communities of Puno rose in response to the large-scale silver mining project 'Santa Ana', to be implemented in the district of Huacullani by the Canadian Bear Creek Mining Company. While there is debate (and lacking research) on the regionalist political dimension of the mobilization, which shifted as the conflict developed, the conflict had an explicit environmental and even eco-ethno driver.[94] A detailed assessment of the conflict is beyond the scope of this chapter, but what is of interest here, is the remarkable recurrence in commodification mechanisms and rhetoric.

According to Pinto Herrera, the principal causes of the conflict were the land concession politics, company-community clientelism and political state-company-community alliances, and the project's environmental implications.[95] The way in which the company had acquired land concessions—even on terrain that was legally inaccessible to mining enterprises for being situated within fifty kilometres from the international border[96]—reflects how Peru's deliberate modification of its legal frameworks opened the door for a new land-grabbing episode. Under the rhetoric disguise of 'the national need for private, national and foreign, investment in productive activities (...) in the border zones' and by linking this need to the mining project's 'important influence on the community's wellbeing',[97] the government constructed a justification similar to the liberal 'dead hands' argument. The clientelism and alliances allude to efforts, on the part of the business sector and the government, to remould principles of a local moral economy that guided communities' external relations into 'corporate social responsibility'. Moreover, no true consultation, through which the affected communities could have expressed their concerns and demands, was executed.[98] While Peru has ratified the ILO Convention 169 which guarantees the right to free, prior and informed consent to indigenous people, Peru's strategy is to canalize protest through negotiation roundtables which in fact serve to impose a pre-established outcome. With respect to the communities' relation to land, territory and nature, this conflict evidences the role of additional (negative) qualitative properties attached to land in defining twenty-first communal territories. That is, through centuries-long accumulated contamination, mainly in relation to mining activities, altiplano communities do not just struggle against 'classic' land usurpation by private and public agents, but against 'dispossession by accumulation' as extreme levels of pollution risks to leave them with unproductive lands.[99]

At the time of writing, the legal unwinding of the *Aymarazo* is still developing. A reactivation of the mining project seems unlikely, but the company is still active in the region, while the affected communities now need to mobilize on two fronts—to defend their territorial rights and to combat the criminalization of their collective actions. Further research will teach us more about how the involved communities relied on (or reinvented) pre-existing resistance strategies to enhance their negotiation power, and how their accumulated historical experiences constellated into alternative spaces. Understanding this episode within a longer dialectical trajectory and exploring the diachronic interconnections between historical moments helps to break the walls constructed around the 'modern Andean present' that convert indigenous communities deliberately into 'simply the result of the inertias of history' ready to be opened to new commodity frontiers.[100]

Managing the Costs of Cheap Nature: Conflict as Externality

Throughout the sketched history of commodity production and community reorganization, rural conflict acts as a shaping force in capitalist expansion. Jacobsen has stressed how social power on the altiplano is structured by the continuities in agrarian societal organization, and above all, by hacienda-community struggles.[101] As Charles Walker indicates, serious historical research on these 'stormy' years of peasant revolts has been abandoned in the last decades, despite the important guidance provided by the work of Ramos, Manuel Burga and Alberto Flores Galindo,[102] ànd in spite of the striking parallels with present-day dynamics. This section delves deeper into the tactics deployed to neutralize community resistance and assesses the way in which socio-environmental conflicts, then and now, are subjected to commensuration mechanisms.

Through their actions and alliances, pastoralist communities in Puno managed to secure a small but important degree of independence. This sparked panic on the part of the local landholding elites. Collective claims for territorial justice were delegitimized and dehumanized by depicting them as irrational but major threats: 'Great Revolts'. Moreover, the 'Great Peasant Revolts' that marked this neo-colonial, liberal extractivist turn were reduced to either 'land wars' or 'race wars'. An exaggerated and essentialist portrayal helped, in the first place, to justify the criminalization of communities and their leaders, and even the further dispossession of their properties. In Puno, rural elites labelled the unrest as a *guerra de castas* or caste war, which served as an excuse to organize themselves into *Ligas de Hacendados* which they denominated as 'Proprietors Associations'.[103] Similarly, *La Sociedad Ganadera del Departamento de Puno* was created, presided by Alejandro Cano, publisher of *El Pueblo*, a lobby-magazine to push the government to protect their properties against the imminent rebellion.[104] Across the altiplano, terror for the rise of a general movement that would take the cities and reinstall the *Tawantinsuyu* (the Inca empire), implying total extermination of the white population, took shape. Hacendados even invented indigenous rebellions, as a new tactic to justify land grabbing and provoke indigenous reactions, after which the very same hacendados could then present themselves as victims, request judicial and police protection.[105] In this context of heightened tensions, an important and ambiguous intermediary role was played by mestizo individuals and pro-indigenous associations which deserves further research.

Here, the question of who was behind those revolts becomes a very loaded one. The depiction of 'free' *comuneros* in a leading role might be the version which the *gamonales* wanted people to believe, as this could generate a divide between 'savage' non-hacienda peasants and 'obeying' hacienda peasants. In addition, the threatened landlords critizied the role of non-indigenous intermediaries, denouncing the damage caused by 'marionettes' of revolutionary, anarchist or socialist political movements, pro-indigenous committees, evangelist missionaries, scrupulous merchants and lawyers. They equally criticized the central state, its laws, institutions (such as obligatory military service) and lower authorities.[106] Thus, in a second step, indigenous agency was not just criminalized, but erased.

Yet, while indigenous agency was of course key, we cannot understand the altiplano rebellions without scrutinizing the ambiguous alliance with mestizo and white intermediaries. Ramos has explored this issue for Puno,[107] and I examined the intermediation of local elites in Aymara rebellions in Bolivia,[108] but much more research is needed regarding the nature and consequences of these alliances. A particularly interesting aspect of mediation in these resistance movements is the role of the *mensajeros*, who travelled to the national capitals in search for justice. In any case, the opposition between indigenous and mestizo rural dwellers was never as absolute as usually assumed. This is also demonstrated in the 1912 revolt in Huacullani (cf. supra), where Santiago Mallca, the leader of the action, was entitled as ex-messenger, was identified as 'extortionist' by his opponents, and reportedly 'advised' by a *misti*. In the course of this rebellious episode, overlapping class and ethnic tensions were redrawn through this kind of collaboration, which often materialized out of pragmatism (increased social power) and at other times (partly) out of idealism (for instance by the white *indigenistas*).

In a third step, the portrayed danger and passivity on the part of indigenous insurgents justified the simplification of these clashes to quantifiable externalities. This made conflicts predictable, hence rational solutions and adaptation schemes could be designed. Making complex social relations calculable is commensuration, the cheap nature strategy, in action. It was a way of appropriating social conflicts for political purposes, essentially the disciplining of the rural masses. Several politicians would seize the conflicts to lobby for pro-indigenous legislation and education, yet with the aim of overcoming illiteracy and political abuses without addressing the protagonists and strategies of land grabbing.[109] Initially, education was clearly promoted as a way to neutralize rather than to empower communities. Encinas, an allegedly 'pro-indigenous' *puneño* deputy to the Peruvian Parliament, stated for instance that the *indios* needed pedagogy and not laws; as the latter would be as 'ridiculous' as 'giving a new chronometer to someone who does not know how to tell the hour or has no concept of time'.[110] Over the longer term, 'disciplining' intervention schemes such as military conscription and schooling, would match bottom-up demands from the communities themselves.[111]

The delegitimation and criminalization of rural struggles for land, social and political rights, and their 'appropriation', knew a similar upsurge in the wake of the Aymarazo. As in the above-described steps, first the conflict in itself was represented as an irrational, dangerous outbreak of ethnic violence, reifying the existing urban fears for the 'rebellious aymaras'.[112] This exaggeration and essentialization, further facilitated by the lack of an anthropological investigation during the trial, justified the following criminalization of legitimate social protest and its alleged leaders.[113] About one hundred indigenous community authorities were accused of extortion, insinuating they formed a criminal organization intended to extort the state.[114] Second, the identification of a single main leader and the accusation of this individual acting as 'immediate author' is one of the ways in which the agency of the Aymara community peasants is erased, reducing their expressed will and organizational capacities to manipulation on the part of this leader.[115] While more elements can be added and complicated regarding the Aymarazo, this development hints at the deployment of the next step—the design of rational intervention techniques. As will be reflected upon in the following, in order to guarantee the further appropriation of nature, socio-environmental conflicts need to be reconfigured as externality.

As Svampa comments on twenty-first-century Latin American socio-environmental conflicts, '[t]he aim is to limit collective resistance and close off the possibility for considering other notions of development and to install a comprehensive-historical threshold in regard to alternatives'.[116] To explain the logic of 'conflict as externality', I compare this with the scientific symptomization and remediation of Andean altitude sickness, known as *soroche*. When industrial mining started to conquer the Peruvian Andes, the lack of oxygen at high altitudes presented itself as a 'natural' barrier to mining expansion. In order to prevent the slowdown of the mining frontier, this obstacle had to be controlled and overcome. Identified as *soroche*, its medical analysis attracted great interest, portrayed as a matter of national economic progress.[117] The mining sector and the state were in pressing need of establishing the 'cost' of, and hence the professional remedy for the pathology. Without assuming conflicts to be an 'organic' phenomenon, the *soroche* history helps us understand the logic and efforts on the part of the mining sector and the state in the context of 'neoliberal' commodity boom to control socio-environmental conflicts and mitigate its brake on mining expansion. These are externalized as a disturbing side-effect for which a scientific 'cure' can be designed. Just as *soroche*—the 'Peruvian disease'—was associated with national development, current social leaders are being portrayed as 'anti-development' obstacles and their movements as pathologies from which the country should and can be 'cured'—in the same vein as their labelling as 'infantile ecologism' or 'colonial environmentalism' elsewhere.[118] Current President Pedro Pablo Kuczynski, for instance, a former investment banker seeking to revive investments in the wake of the global commodities bust, promised during his presidential campaign in 2016 to ease opposition to mining projects by delivering 'the benefits of development' to local people early on. Social leaders, however, are already warning for the divide-and-rule effect of implementing social programs as a palliative measure.[119]

Today, the shift towards a Commodities Consensus, seeking efficient ways of opening up communal resources, as well as the concomitant explosion of socio-environmental conflicts and exacerbating vulnerability of communities foster an interest in conflict prevention and remediation. This triggers the pursuit for deeper insight into the community's internal resource management, its external resilience and dynamics of communal resistance. In the process, community conflicts tend to be reduced to technicity expressed in terms of 'costs', 'inefficiency', 'negative social impact' and 'risks' that can be calculated even in monetary terms.[120] The assumption then is that these can and should be overcome through a technical solution, 'good governance' or corporate 'responsibility', as a recent study on company-community conflicts in extractive industries expresses: 'The good news is that, as my UN business and human rights mandate demonstrated, the kinds of policies and processes that extractive companies (and others) need to put in place to prevent and address negative social impacts and their associated costs are clear and increasingly well-understood. The study highlights the connections between key systems – for identifying social impacts, responding to grievances, and tracking performance – that responsible companies in the extractive sector are putting into place and refining in order to better manage their social impacts'.[121]

Complex, territorialized and historically rooted conflicts are reassembled into legible abstractions, enabling policy interventions. This is basically the 'cheap nature strategy' at work. It allows for the reproduction of ahistorical interpretations reflected in the attempts to neutralize socio-environmental conflicts, whether these attempts have the intention to guarantee the smooth commodification of communal territories or to secure their protection and resilience. These efforts tend to reduce those territories to passively 'surviving' objects; thereby overlooking the *longue durée* dialectical relation between these territories and capitalist expansion. Yet the cheap nature strategy is not a watertight strategy; frictions can be ironed out, but not eliminated. Interpretations that miss this messy dimension lead to policy responses that exacerbate rather than 'resolve' the conflictive drive of the current rush for communal resources, as the aforementioned strategy of Peruvian President Kuczynski indicates. Around 1900, as around 2000, commodity frontier expansion in both countries reopened the debate over the role of these communities in relation to national development—as defenders of sovereign interests, to-be-consulted stakeholders, or as hindrances to the road to progress.

Concluding Thoughts: The *Soroche* Effect

This chapter argues for a world-ecological approach to conflicts linked to processes of expanded commodity production. By scrutinizing the interconnections between two conflictive moments of advancing commodity frontiers in the post-colonial altiplano, this chapter gives insight into how communal territories have been divested and (re)constructed as 'cheap' reserves for accumulation. Unthinking the Cartesian divide requires making the constant and violent (re)creation of a separation of nature from humans visible. In the search for new reserves of cheap labour and land, communities, their families, lands and resources are imagined and legally classified as non-humans, banned from society, and communal land control depicted as 'vacant' hence free to take and 'improve'. Just as the appropriation of human and animal labour as cheap nature for the extraction and transportation that shaped the colonial mining frontier was far from a complete transition, the absorption of community land, animal resources (wool) and cheap human labour (*colonos*) in the liberal wool and mining frontier was not free from paradoxes. In the neoliberal mining frontier, pastoralists and their llamas seem to have been exhausted as cheap nature, in an advancing mining landscape that hardly needs cheap labour.

Since the 'triumph of Liberalism', a modern Andean present has been constructed and walled off, expelling Andean rural communities to the fate of the 'inertia of history'. This becomes visible in the way community-based conflicts are dealt with and discursively framed. Through the lens of cheap nature, communal resistance becomes a matter of conflict management and calculating 'costs'. Communal spaces and agency seem to endure, stripped to mere (externalized) obstacles. However, far from 'empty' reservoirs, they also appear as 'counter-spaces',[122] (em)powered by the struggles and achieved or (re)appropriated political (including property) rights throughout a long commodity frontier history and a constant reminder/instance of capitalism's flexibility. The conflictive character of the cheap nature strategy is thus understood beyond a black-white opposition between a commodification that erases everything, and a resistant de-commodification that knows no dialogue. It exposes a dialectical, messy trajectory that results in a 'dizzy' commodity frontier expansion, constituting a frontier zone suffering from a kind of *soroche*, gasping for oxygen.

Notes

1. Defensoría del Pueblo, *Vigésimo primer informe anual 2017* (Lima: Defensoría del Pueblo, 2017), 146–48.
2. Anthony Bebbington and Denise Humphreys Bebbington, "Actores y Ambientalismos: Conflictos Socio-Ambientales en Perú," *Iconos. Revista de Ciencias Sociales* 35 (2009): 117–28.
3. Mario Pérez-Rincón, Julieth Vargas-Morales, and Zulma Crespo-Marín. "Trends in Social Metabolism and Environmental Conflicts in Four Andean Countries from 1970 to 2013," *Sustainability Science* 13, no. 3 (2018): 635–48.

4. Maristella Svampa, "Commodities Consensus: Neoextractivism and Enclosure of the Commons in Latin America," *South Atlantic Quarterly* 114, no. 1 (2015): 65–82.
5. Brooke Larson, *Trials of Nation Making: Liberalism, Race, and Ethnicity in the Andes, 1810–1910* (Cambridge: Cambridge University Press, 2004), 7.
6. Joan Martinez-Alier, Leah Temper, Daniela Del Bene, and Arnim Scheidel, "Is There a Global Environmental Justice Movement?" *The Journal of Peasant Studies* 43, no. 3 (2016): 731–55.
7. Alejandro Diez Hurtado, "Nuevos Retos y Nuevos Recursos Para Las Comunidades Campesinas," in *Tensiones y Transformaciones en Comunidades Campesinas*, ed. Alejandro Diez Hurtado (Lima: CISEPA, 2012), 7.
8. Diez, "Nuevos Retos," 10.
9. Jason W. Moore, "Transcending the Metabolic Rift: A Theory of Crises in the Capitalist World-Ecology," *The Journal of Peasant Studies* 38, no. 1 (2011): 1–46.
10. Moore, "Transcending"; Jason W. Moore, "'This Lofty Mountain of Silver Could Conquer the Whole World': Potosí and the Political Ecology of Underdevelopment, 1545–1800," *The Journal of Philosophical Economics* 4, no. 1 (2010): 58–103.
11. I am very grateful for the support I received at the CISEPA research center (Pontificia Universidad Católica del Perú) in Lima, the Regional Archive of Puno, and the NGO IDECA in Puno. This research was made possible thanks to funding through travel grants for a long-term research stay of the Faculty of Arts and Philosophy (Ghent University) and by the Research Foundation—Flanders (FWO).
12. Philip McMichael, "Incorporating Comparison within a World-Historical Perspective: An Alternative Comparative Method," *American Sociological Review* 55, no. 3 (1990): 385–97; "World-Systems Analysis, Globalization, and Incorporated Comparison," *Journal of World-Systems Research* V, no. 3 (2000 [1990]): 672.
13. McMichael, "World-Systems Analysis," 672.
14. Giovanni Arrighi, *The Long Twentieth Century: Money, Power, and the Origins of Our Times* (London: Verso Books, 1994).
15. McMichael, "World-Systems Analysis."
16. Jason W. Moore, *Capitalism in the Web of Life: Ecology and the Accumulation of Capital* (London and New York: Verso, 2015).

17. Moore, "Transcending," 1.
18. Jason W. Moore, "Introduction," in *Anthropocene or Capitalocene?* ed. Jason W. Moore (Oakland: PM Press, 2016), 11.
19. Moore, *Capitalism in the Web of Life.*
20. The term 'environmentalization' in relation to social protest was formulated by Enrique Leff. See Svampa (2015, 68).
21. McMichael "World-Systems Analysis," 672.
22. Wendy Nelson Espeland, *The Struggle for Water Politics, Rationality, and Identity in the American Southwest* (Chicago: University of Chicago Press, 1998), 24.
23. Moore, "The Rise of Cheap Nature," 87.
24. Lawrence Grossberg, "Modernity and Commensuration," *Cultural Studies* 24, no. 3 (2010), 322.
25. Jason W. Moore, "Sugar and the Expansion of the Early Modern World-Economy: Commodity Frontiers, Ecological Transformation, and Industrialization," *Review: A Journal of the Fernand Braudel Center* 23, no. 3 (2000), 412.
26. Thomas D. Hall, "Frontiers, Ethnogenesis and World-Systems: Rethinking the Theories," in *A World-Systems Reader: New Perspectives on Gender, Urbanism, Cultures, Indigenous Peoples, and Ecology*, ed. Thomas D. Hall (Oxford: Rowman & Littlefield Publishers, 2000), 244.
27. Wilma A. Dunaway, *The First American Frontier: Transition to Capitalism in Southern Appalachia, 1700–1860* (Chapel Hill: University of North Carolina Press, 1996), 467.
28. Mattias Borg Rasmussen, and Christian Lund, "Reconfiguring Frontier Spaces: The Territorialization of Resource Control," *World Development* 101, Supplement C (2018): 388–99.
29. Vinay K. Gidwani, *Capital, Interrupted: Agrarian Development and the Politics of Work in India* (Minneapolis: University of Minnesota Press, 2008), xix.
30. Gidwani, *Capital, Interrupted*, xxiv.
31. Anna L. Tsing, "Natural Resources and Capitalist Frontiers," *Economic and Political Weekly* 38, no. 48 (2003): 5100–6.
32. Svampa, "Commodities Consensus," 69.
33. Thomas D. Hall and James V. Fenelon, *Indigenous Peoples and Globalization: Resistance and Revitalization* (Boulder: Paradigm Publishers, 2009), 120.
34. Farshad Araghi, and Marina Karides, "Land Dispossession and Global Crisis: Introduction to the Special Section on Land Rights in the

World-System," *Journal of World-Systems Research* XVIII, no. 1 (2012): 1–5.

35. Hanne Cottyn, "A World-Systems Frontier Perspective to Land: Exploring the Uneven Trajectory of Land Rights Standardization in the Andes," *Journal of World-Systems Research* 23, no. 2 (2017): 515–39.
36. Oxfam, International Land Coalition, and Rights and Resources Initiative, *Common Ground: Securing Land Rights and Safeguarding the Earth* (Oxford: Oxfam, 2016); "Global Platform of Indigenous and Community Lands," LandMark, accessed November 15, 2017, www.landmarkmap.org.
37. Alex Jeffrey, Colin McFarlane, and Alex Vasudevan, "Rethinking Enclosure: Space, Subjectivity and the Commons," *Antipode* 44, no. 4 (2012): 1247–67.
38. Nancy Lee Peluso, and Christian Lund, "New frontiers of land control: Introduction," *The Journal of Peasant Studies* 38, no. 4 (2011): 668.
39. Erik Thoen, "'Social Agrosystems' as an Economic Concept to Explain Regional Differences. An Essay Taking the Former County of Flanders as an Example (Middle Ages-19th Century)," in *Landholding and Land Transfer in the North Sea Area (Late Middle Ages—19th Century)*, ed. Peter Hoppenbrouwers and Bas Van Bavel (Turnhout: Brepols Publishers, 2004), 47–66.
40. Jorge Flores Ochoa, "Enqa, Enqaychu Illa y Khuya Rumi: Aspectos Mágico-Religiosos entre Pastores," *Journal de la Société des Américanistes* 63 (1974): 245–62.
41. Rights and Resources Initiative, *Who Owns the Worlds Land? A Global Baseline of Formally Recognized Indigenous & Community Land Rights* (Washington, DC: RRI, 2015), 7.
42. According to the national census of 2012, the Puno department contains 22.7% of Peru's 6115 recognized *comunidades campesinas*, making it the region with the largest concentration of peasant communities (INEI 2014). These peasant communities occupy 41.9% of the departments' land area. Edgardo Rodríguez, *Balance de la campaña de titulación de tierras en el departamento de Puno* (Lima: CEPES, 2000).
43. Ministerio de Cultura, *Aimaras. Comunidades rurales en Puno* (Lima: Ministerio de Cultura, 2014).
44. Antonio Peña Jumpa, *Justicia comunal en los Andes del Perú: el caso de Calahuyo* (Lima: Pontificia Universidad Católica del Perú, Fondo Editorial, 1998), 75.

45. Ministerio de Cultura, *Aimaras*, 50.
46. Rodriguez, *Balance de la campaña*.
47. Moore, "This Lofty Mountain of Silver."
48. Eduardo Galeano, *Las venas abiertas de América Latina*, 26th ed. (México D.F.: Siglo Veintinuno Editores, 2013 [1971]).
49. Brooke Larson, and Olivia Harris, *Ethnicity, Markets, and Migration in the Andes: At the Crossroads of History and Anthropology* (Durham: Duke University Press, 1995), 15–16.
50. Carlos Sempat Assadourian, *Minería y espacio económico en los Andes: siglos XVI–XX* (Lima: Instituto de Estudios Peruanos, 1975).
51. Jeremy Ravi Mumford, *Vertical Empire: The General Resettlement of Indians in the Colonial Andes* (Durham: Duke University Press, 2012); Tamar Herzog, "Indigenous Reducciones and Spanish Resettlement: Placing Colonial and European History in Dialogue," *Ler História*, no. 72 (2018): 9–30.
52. Alejandro Diez Hurtado, "Tres hipótesis sobre el origen de la comunidad indígena campesina en el Perú: una exploración a partir de las comunidades de Carumas en Moquegua." Presentation at the *IV Encuentro Latinoamericano de Estudios Agrarios* (Lima, 19 April 2018).
53. José Luis Rénique, *La Batalla por Puno: Conflictos Agrarios y Nación en los Andes Peruanos, 1866–1995* (Lima: Editoriales IEP/CEPES/SUR, 2004), 29; Nils Jacobsen, "Campesinos y Tenencia de La Tierra en el Altiplano Peruano en la Transición de la Colonia a la República," *Allpanchis* 23, no. 37 (1991): 25–92.
54. Erick D. Langer and Robert H. Jackson, "El Liberalismo y el Problema de la Tierra en Bolivia (1825–1920)," *Revista de Historia* 5 (1990): 9–32.
55. Nils Jacobsen, "Libre Comercio, Élites Regionales y Mercado Interno en el Sur del Perú, 1895–1932," *Revista Andina* 7, no. 2 (1989): 409–49.
56. Rénique, *La Batalla por Puno*, 29.
57. Ramón Grosfoguel, "Developmentalism, Modernity, and Dependency Theory in Latin America," *Nepantla: Views from South* 1, no. 2 (2000): 350.
58. Nils Jacobsen, *Mirages of Transition: The Peruvian Altiplano, 1780–1930* (Berkeley: University of California Press, 1993), 5.
59. Jacobsen, "Campesinos y Tenencia de La Tierra," 25.

60. Jason W. Moore, "The Capitalocene Part II: Accumulation by Appropriation and the Centrality of Unpaid Work/Energy," *The Journal of Peasant Studies* 45, no. 2 (2017): 1–43.
61. Jacobsen, "Campesinos y Tenencia de La Tierra," 69–70.
62. Ibid., 65.
63. In its broadest sense, *gamonalismo* is the phenomenon of local 'privatized' politics that is mutually defined by *latifundismo* (large scale private estates), both referring to a feudal property control over land sustained by the exploitation of the peasants, in or outside the hacienda. Yet, not all *hacendados* are *gamonales*, as the latter have superior political and economic influence. Thus, *gamonalismo* must be understood beyond landownership, also including the exploitation by (indigenous) intermediaries. Manuel Burga, and Alberto Flores Galindo, *Apogeo y Crisis de la República Aristocrática* (Lima: Ediciones Rikcha y Perú, 1981), 104; José Carlos Mariátegui, *7 Ensayos de Interpretación de La Realidad Peruana* (Lima: Empresa Editora Amauta, 1974); and Marcela Calisto, "Peasant Resistance in the Aymara Districts of the Highlands of Peru, 1900–1930: An Attempt at Self-Governance" (PhD diss., University of California at San Diego, 1993), 11.
64. Larson, *Trials of Nation Making*.
65. Lynda Sullivan, "Peru Passes a Packet of Neoliberal Reforms, Erodes Environmental Protections and Labor Rights," *Upside Down World*, July 25, 2014.
66. Jacobsen, *Mirages of Transition*, 152.
67. Alberto Flores Galindo, *Arequipa y el Sur Andino: Ensayo de Historia Regional, Siglos XVIII–XX* (Lima: Editorial Horizonte, 1977).
68. Burga and Flores Galindo, *Apogeo y Crisis*, 89.
69. Jorge Mariano Cáceres-Olazo Monroy, "La Gran Sublevación Campesina en Puno, 1920–1924," *X-storia*, no. 1 (2000): 50–51.
70. Flores Galindo, *Arequipa y el Sur Andino*.
71. These units were known as *ayllus*, *parcialidades* and *comunidades*, yet the exact characteristics and functioning of each of these denominations and how they transformed during the twentieth century remains understudied. Ministerio de Cultura, *Aimaras*, 48.
72. Cáceres-Olazo, "La Gran Sublevación," 52.
73. Emilio Romero, *Monografía del Departamento de Puno*, 3rd ed. (Puno: Universidad Nacional del Altiplano, 2013 [1928]), 425.
74. Jacobsen, *Mirages of Transition*, 270.

75. Alberto Flores Galindo, *Movimientos Campesinos en el Perú: Balance y Esquema*. Cuaderno Rural (Lima: Pontificia Universidad Católica del Perú, 1976).
76. Augusto Ramos Zambrano, *Tormenta altiplánica rebeliones indígenas de la provincia de Lampa-Puno, 1920–1924* (Lima: Gráfica Espinal, 1990).
77. Jorge Mariano Cáceres-Olazo Monroy, "La Gran Sublevación Campesina En La Provincia de Chucuito: Puno 1920–1924," *X-Storia*, no. 2 (2002): 65–84.
78. Jorge Flores Ochoa, and Felix Palacios Rios, "La Protesta de 1901. Un Movimiento de Pastores de La Puna Alta a Comienzos Del Siglo XX," in *III Congreso Peruano el Hombre y la Cultura Andina (31 de Enero-5 de Febrero de 1977). Volume 2. Actas y Trabajos*, ed. José Matos Mar (Lima: Secretaría General del Congreso, 1980).
79. Calisto, *Peasant Resistance*, 2–4.
80. Rodrigo Montoya, *Lucha por la tierra, reformas agrarias y capitalismo en el Peru del siglo XX* (Lima: Mosca Azul, 1989), 137.
81. Larson, *Trials of Nation Making*, 21.
82. Cáceres-Olazo, "La Gran Sublevación," 55.
83. Jacobsen, *Mirages of Transition*.
84. Rosa Congost, Jorge Gelman, and Rui Santos, *Property Rights in Land: Issues in Social, Economic and Global History: Perspectives in Economic and Social History* (London and New York: Routledge, 2016).
85. Jacobsen, *Mirages of Transition*, 3–4.
86. Alejandrino Maguiña, "Memoria que el Ministro de Gobierno y Policia Sr. Leonidas Cardenas presenta al Congreso Ordinario de 1902," in *Rebelión india*, ed. Pablo Macera, Alejandrino Maguiña, and Antonio Rengifo (Lima: Ediciones Rikchay Perú, 1988), 21–55.
87. Jacobsen, *Mirages of Transition*, 5–6.
88. Jacobsen, *Mirages of Transition*.
89. Bertram, cited in Grimaldo Antonio Renfigo Balarezo, *Lanas y movimientos indígenas de Puno 1890–1930* (Puno: Universidad Nacional del Altiplano, 2013), 58.
90. File *Denunciante don Juan de la Cruz Eduardo por delito de usurpación contra Santiago Mallca, Provincia Chucuito, Huacullani, 1912*. Series 'Usurpaciones', Criminales, 15 H. Archivo Regional de Puno, Puno.
91. Two years before, the 'indigenous' children of Pablo Quiñones claimed to be the rightful owners and denounced the dispossession of the land by other families. Notarial proceedings, provincia de July, File 014, No. 19, distrito de Zepita, 1897; Lawsuit 21 October 1899, Series 'Escrituras

públicas', distrito de Huacullani, File 25, Book 6. Archivo Regional de Puno, Puno.

92. Letter 14/10/1911. File *Denunciante don Juan de la Cruz Eduardo por delito de usurpación contra Santiago Mallca, Provincia Chucuito, Huacullani, 1912*. Series Usurpaciones, Criminales, 15 H. Archivo Regional de Puno, Puno.
93. Ideca Perú, "Juicio del 'aimarazo' es un caso de criminalización de la protesta," *Los Andes*, May 17, 2017.
94. Emma McDonell, "The Co-constitution of Neoliberalism, Extractive Industries, and Indigeneity: Anti-mining Protests in Puno, Peru," *The Extractive Industries and Society* 2, no. 1 (2015): 112–23.
95. Honorio Pinto Herrera, "Conflicto minero en Santa Ana (Puno)," *Investigaciones Sociales* 17, no. 31 (2013): 207–20.
96. Julio Mejía, *Aymaraso* (Puno: Derechos Humanos y Medio Ambiente Puno, 2014), 1.
97. Mejía, *Aymaraso*, 1.
98. Pablo Ricardo Abdo, "El 'aymarazo', un caso de criminalización de la protesta," *Servindi*, October 8, 2016.
99. Thomas Perreault, "Dispossession by Accumulation? Mining, Water and the Nature of Enclosure on the Bolivian Altiplano," *Antipode* 45, no. 5 (2013): 1050–69.
100. Fernando Eguren, "Prólogo a Dos Manos," in *Los Nietos de La Reforma Agraria. Tierra y Comunidad en el Altiplano de Bolivia*, ed. Miguel Urioste, Rossana Barragán, and Gonzalo Colque (La Paz: Fundación TIERRA, 2007), xviii.
101. Jacobsen, *Mirages of Transition*.
102. "Prólogo a 'Ezequiel Urviola y el indigenismo puneño'," Charles Walker, accessed August 3, 2017, http://charlesfwalker.com/prolo-go-a-ezequiel-urviola-y-el-indigenismo-puneno-2016/; Ramos, *Tormenta altiplánica*; Burga and Flores Galindo, *Apogeo y Crisis*; and Flores Galindo, *Movimientos Campesinos*.
103. Cáceres-Olazo, "La Gran Sublevación," 67.
104. Ibid.
105. Calisto, *Peasant Resistance*, 35.
106. Ibid., 41.
107. Ramos, *Tormenta altiplánica*.
108. Hanne Cottyn, "Renegotiating communal autonomy: communal land rights and liberal land reform on the Bolivian altiplano: Carangas, 1860–1930" (PhD thesis, Ghent University, 2014).

109. Calisto, *Peasant Resistance*, 23.
110. Ibid., 39.
111. Dan Chapin Hazen, *The Awakening of Puno: Government Policy and the Indian Problem in Southern Peru, 1900–1955* (PhD diss., Yale University, 1985).
112. See also Ramón Pajuelo Teves, *'No hay ley para nosotros…' Gobierno local, sociedad y conflicto en el altiplano: el caso Ilave* (Lima: Asociación Servicios Educativos Rurales, Instituto de Estudios Peruanos, 2009), 44.
113. Abdo, "El 'aymarazo'."
114. Thomas McDonagh, and Aldo Orellana López, "Protesta social en Perú: criminalización extrema de comunidades indígenas Aymaras," *openDemocracy*, July 11, 2018.
115. McDonah and Orellana, "Protesta social."
116. Svampa, "Commodities Consensus," 67.
117. Jorge Luis Lossio Chávez, "Nación, Ciencia y Salud: Investigación Médica en los Andes y la Construcción de una 'patología de las alturas'," *Historica* 33, no. 1 (2009): 65–86.
118. Svampa, "Commodities Consensus," 67.
119. Teresa Céspedes, "Empresarios mineros de Perú, preocupados porque protestas se agudicen en próximo Gobierno," *Reuters*, May 20, 2016.
120. Rachel Davis, and Daniel Franks, *Costs of Company-Community Conflict in the Extractive Sector*. Corporate Social Responsibility Initiative Report No. 66 (Cambridge: Harvard Kennedy School, 2014), 7.
121. Ruggie in Davis and Franks, *Costs of Company-Community Conflict*, 6.
122. Henri Lefebvre, "Contradictory space," in *The Production of Space*, ed. Henri Lefebvre (Oxford and Cambridge: Blackwell, 1991), 292–351.

References

Primary Sources

Archivo Regional de Puno, Puno.
Series 'Usurpaciones'.
Notarial proceedings, province of July.
Series 'Escrituras públicas'.

Literature and Published Sources

Abdo, Pablo Ricardo. "El 'aymarazo', un caso de criminalización de la protesta." *Servindi*, 8 October 2016.

Araghi, Farshad, and Marina Karides. "Land Dispossession and Global Crisis: Introduction to the Special Section on Land Rights in the World-System." *Journal of World-Systems Research* XVIII, no. 1 (2012): 1–5.

Arrighi, Giovanni. *The Long Twentieth Century: Money, Power, and the Origins of Our Times*. London: Verso Books, 1994.

Assadourian, Carlos Sempat. *Minería y espacio económico en los Andes: siglos XVI-XX*. Lima: Instituto de Estudios Peruanos, 1975.

Bebbington, Anthony, and Denise Humphreys Bebbington. "Actores y Ambientalismos: Conflictos Socio-Ambientales en Perú." *Iconos. Revista de Ciencias Sociales* 35 (2009): 117–28.

Burga, Manuel, and Alberto Flores Galindo. *Apogeo y Crisis de la Répública Aristocrática*. Lima: Ediciones Rikcha y Perú, 1981

Cáceres-Olazo Monroy, Jorge Mariano. "La Gran Sublevación Campesina en Puno, 1920–1924." *X-storia* 1 (2000): 45–73.

———. "La Gran Sublevación Campesina En La Provincia de Chucuito: Puno 1920–1924." *X-Storia* 2 (2002): 65–84.

Calisto, Marcela. "Peasant Resistance in the Aymara Districts of the Highlands of Peru, 1900–1930: An Attempt at Self-Governance." Unpublished PhD diss., University of California at San Diego, San Diego, 1993.

Céspedes, Teresa. "Empresarios mineros de Perú, preocupados porque protestas se agudicen en próximo Gobierno." *Reuters*, May 20, 2016. https://mx.reuters.com/article/businessNews/idMXL2N18F0TP.

Congost, Rosa, Jorge Gelman, and Rui Santos. *Property Rights in Land: Issues in Social, Economic and Global History: Perspectives in Economic and Social History*. London and New York: Routledge, 2016.

Cottyn, Hanne. "Renegotiating Communal Autonomy: Communal Land Rights and Liberal Land Reform on the Bolivian Altiplano: Carangas, 1860–1930." PhD thesis, Ghent University, 2014.

———. "A World-Systems Frontier Perspective to Land: Exploring the Uneven Trajectory of Land Rights Standardization in the Andes." *Journal of World-Systems Research* 23, no. 2 (2017): 515–39.

Davis, Rachel, and Daniel Franks. *Costs of Company-Community Conflict in the Extractive Sector*. Corporate Social Responsibility Initiative Report No. 66. Cambridge: Harvard Kennedy School, 2014.

Defensoría del Pueblo. *Vigésimo primer informe anual 2017*. Lima: Defensoría del Pueblo, 2017.

Diez Hurtado, Alejandro. "Nuevos Retos y Nuevos Recursos Para Las Comunidades Campesinas." In *Tensiones y Transformaciones en Comunidades Campesinas*, edited by Alejandro Diez Hurtado, 21–35. Lima: CISEPA, 2012.

———. "Tres hipótesis sobre el origen de la comunidad indígena campesina en el Perú: una exploración a partir de las comunidades de Carumas en Moquegua." Presentation at the *IV Encuentro Latinoamericano de Estudios Agrarios*. Lima, 19 April 2018.

Dunaway, Wilma A. *The First American Frontier: Transition to Capitalism in Southern Appalachia, 1700–1860*. Chapel Hill: University of North Carolina Press, 1996.

Eguren Fernando. "Prólogo a Dos Manos." In *Los Nietos de La Reforma Agraria. Tierra y Comunidad en el Altiplano de Bolivia*, edited by Miguel Urioste, Rossana Barragán, and Gonzalo Colque, xvii–xxii. La Paz: Fundación TIERRA, 2007.

Espeland, Wendy Nelson. *The Struggle for Water Politics, Rationality, and Identity in the American Southwest*. Chicago: University of Chicago Press, 1998.

Flores Galindo, Alberto. *Movimientos Campesinos en el Perú: Balance y Esquema*. Cuaderno Rural. Lima: Pontificia Universidad Católica del Perú, 1976.

———. *Arequipa y el Sur Andino: Ensayo de Historia Regional, Siglos XVIII-XX*. Lima: Editorial Horizonte, 1977.

Flores Ochoa, Jorge. "Enqa, Enqaychu Illa y Khuya Rumi: Aspectos Mágico-Religiosos entre Pastores." *Journal de la Société des Américanistes* 63 (1974): 245–62.

Flores Ochoa, Jorge, and Felix Palacios Rios. "La Protesta de 1901. Un Movimiento de Pastores de La Puna Alta a Comienzos Del Siglo XX." In *III Congreso Peruano el Hombre y la Cultura Andina (31 de Enero-5 de Febrero de 1977). Volume 2. Actas y Trabajos*, edited by José Matos Mar. Lima: Secretaría General del Congreso, 1980.

Galeano, Eduardo. *Las venas abiertas de América Latina*. 26th ed. México D.F.: Siglo Veintinuno Editores, 2013 [1971].

Gidwani, Vinay K. *Capital, Interrupted: Agrarian Development and the Politics of Work in India*. Minneapolis: University of Minnesota Press, 2008.

Grosfoguel, Ramón. "Developmentalism, Modernity, and Dependency Theory in Latin America." *Nepantla: Views from South* 1, no. 2 (2000): 347–74.

Grossberg, Lawrence. "Modernity and Commensuration." *Cultural Studies* 24, no. 3 (2010): 295–332.

Hall, Thomas D. "Frontiers, Ethnogenesis and World-Systems: Rethinking the Theories." In *A World-Systems Reader: New Perspectives on Gender, Urbanism, Cultures, Indigenous Peoples, and Ecology*, edited by Thomas D. Hall, 237–70. Oxford: Rowman & Littlefield Publishers, 2000.

Hall, Thomas D., and James V. Fenelon. *Indigenous Peoples and Globalization: Resistance and Revitalization*. Boulder: Paradigm Publishers, 2009.

Hazen, Dan Chapin. "The Awakening of Puno: Government Policy and the Indian Problem in Southern Peru, 1900–1955." PhD diss., Yale University, New Haven, 1985.

Herzog, Tamar. "Indigenous Reducciones and Spanish Resettlement: Placing Colonial and European History in Dialogue." *Ler História* 72 (2018): 9–30.

Ideca Perú. "Juicio del 'aimarazo' es un caso de criminalización de la protesta." *Los Andes*, May 17, 2017. http://www.losandes.com.pe/Regional/20170517/106158.html.

Instituto Nacional de Estadística e Informática. "Las comunidades campesinas y nativas como persona jurídica del sector agropecuario." In *Características Socioeconómicas Del Productor Agropecuario En El Perú, IV Censo Nacional Agropecuario 2012*, edited by Instituto Nacional de Estadística e Informática. Lima: INEI, 2014.

Jacobsen, Nils. "Libre Comercio, Élites Regionales y Mercado Interno en el Sur del Perú, 1895–1932." *Revista Andina* 7, no. 2 (1989): 409–49.

———. "Campesinos y Tenencia de La Tierra en el Altiplano Peruano en la Transición de la Colonia a la República." *Allpanchis* 23, no. 37 (1991): 25–92.

———. *Mirages of Transition: The Peruvian Altiplano, 1780–1930*. Berkeley: University of California Press, 1993.

Jeffrey, Alex, Colin McFarlane, and Alex Vasudevan. "Rethinking Enclosure: Space, Subjectivity and the Commons." *Antipode* 44, no. 4 (2012): 1247–67.

LandMark, "Global Platform of Indigenous and Community Lands." World Resources Institute, 2017. Accessed November 13, 2017. www.landmarkmap.org.

Langer, Erick D., and Robert H. Jackson. "El Liberalismo y el Problema de la Tierra en Bolivia (1825–1920)." *Revista de Historia* 5 (1990): 9–32.

Larson, Brooke. *Trials of Nation Making: Liberalism, Race, and Ethnicity in the Andes, 1810–1910*. Cambridge: Cambridge University Press, 2004.

Larson, Brooke, and Olivia Harris. *Ethnicity, Markets, and Migration in the Andes: At the Crossroads of History and Anthropology*. Durham: Duke University Press, 1995.

Lefebvre, Henri. "Contradictory Space." In *The Production of Space*, edited by Henri Lefebvre. Oxford and Cambridge: Blackwell, 1991.
Lossio Chávez, Jorge Luis. "Nación, Ciencia y Salud: Investigación Médica en los Andes y la Construcción de una 'patología de las alturas'." *Historica* 33, no. 1 (2009): 65–86.
Maguiña, Alejandrino. "Memoria que el Ministro de Gobierno y Policia Sr. Leonidas Cardenas presenta al Congreso Ordinario de 1902." In *Rebelión india*, edited by Pablo Macera, Alejandrino Maguiña, and Antonio Rengifo, 21–55. Lima: Ediciones Rikchay Perú, 1988.
Mariátegui, José Carlos. *7 Ensayos de Interpretación de La Realidad Peruana*. Lima: Empresa Editora Amauta, 1974.
Martinez-Alier, Joan, Leah Temper, Daniela Del Bene, and Arnim Scheidel. "Is There a Global Environmental Justice Movement?" *The Journal of Peasant Studies* 43, no. 3 (2016): 731–55.
McDonagh, Thomas, and Aldo Orellana López. "Protesta social en Perú: criminalización extrema de comunidades indígenas Aymaras." openDemocracy, 11 July 2018.
McDonell, Emma. "The Co-constitution of Neoliberalism, Extractive Industries, and Indigeneity: Anti-mining Protests in Puno, Peru." *The Extractive Industries and Society* 2, no. 1 (2015): 112–23.
McMichael, Philip. "Incorporating Comparison Within a World-Historical Perspective: An Alternative Comparative Method." *American Sociological Review* 55, no. 3 (1990): 385–97.
———. "World-Systems Analysis, Globalization, and Incorporated Comparison." *Journal of World-Systems Research* VI, no. 3 (2000): 68–99.
Mejía, Julio. *Aymaraso*. Puno: Derechos Humanos y Medio Ambiente Puno, 2014.
Ministerio de Cultura. *Aimaras. Comunidades rurales en Puno*. Lima: Ministerio de Cultura, 2014.
Montoya, Rodrigo. *Lucha por la tierra, reformas agrarias y capitalismo en el Peru del siglo XX*. Lima: Mosca Azul, 1989.
Moore, Jason W. "Sugar and the Expansion of the Early Modern World-Economy: Commodity Frontiers, Ecological Transformation, and Industrialization." *Review: A Journal of the Fernand Braudel Center* 23, no. 3 (2000): 409–33.
———. "'This Lofty Mountain of Silver Could Conquer the Whole World': Potosí and the Political Ecology of Underdevelopment, 1545–1800." *The Journal of Philosophical Economics* 4, no. 1 (2010): 58–103.

———. "Transcending the Metabolic Rift: A Theory of Crises in the Capitalist World-Ecology." *The Journal of Peasant Studies* 38, no. 1 (2011): 1–46.

———. *Capitalism in the Web of Life: Ecology and the Accumulation of Capital.* London and New York: Verso, 2015.

———. "The Rise of Cheap Nature." In *Anthropocene or Capitalocene?* edited by Jason W. Moore, 78–115. Oakland: PM Press, 2016.

———. "The Capitalocene Part II: Accumulation by Appropriation and the Centrality of Unpaid Work/Energy." *The Journal of Peasant Studies* 45, no. 2 (2017): 1–43.

Mumford, Jeremy Ravi. *Vertical Empire: The General Resettlement of Indians in the Colonial Andes.* Durham: Duke University Press, 2012.

Oxfam, International Land Coalition, and Rights and Resources Initiative. *Common Ground: Securing Land Rights and Safeguarding the Earth.* Oxford: Oxfam, 2016.

Pajuelo Teves, Ramón. *'No hay ley para nosotros…' Gobierno local, sociedad y conflicto en el altiplano: el caso Ilave.* Lima: Asociación Servicios Educativos Rurales, Instituto de Estudios Peruanos, 2009.

Peluso, Nancy Lee, and Christian Lund. "New Frontiers of Land Control: Introduction." *The Journal of Peasant Studies* 38, no. 4 (2011): 667–81.

Peña Jumpa, Antonio. *Justicia comunal en los Andes del Perú: el caso de Calahuyo.* Lima: Pontificia Universidad Católica del Perú, Fondo Editorial, 1998.

Pérez-Rincón, Mario, Julieth Vargas-Morales, and Zulma Crespo-Marín. "Trends in Social Metabolism and Environmental Conflicts in Four Andean Countries from 1970 to 2013." *Sustainability Science* 13, no. 3 (2018): 635–48.

Perreault, Tom. "Dispossession by Accumulation? Mining, Water and the Nature of Enclosure on the Bolivian Altiplano." *Antipode* 45, no. 5 (2013): 1050–69.

Pinto Herrera, Honorio. "Conflicto minero en Santa Ana (Puno)." *Investigaciones Sociales* 17, no. 31 (2013): 207–20.

Ramos Zambrano, Augusto. *Tormenta altiplánica rebeliones indígenas de la provincia de Lampa-Puno, 1920–1924.* Lima: Gráfica Espinal, 1990.

Rasmussen, Mattias Borg, and Christian Lund. "Reconfiguring Frontier Spaces: The Territorialization of Resource Control." *World Development* 101, Supplement C (2018): 388–99.

Rengifo Balarezo, Grimaldo Antonio. *Lanas y movimientos indígenas de Puno 1890–1930.* Puno: Universidad Nacional del Altiplano, 2013.

Rénique, José Luis. *La Batalla por Puno: Conflictos Agrarios y Nación en los Andes Peruanos, 1866–1995*. Lima: Editoriales IEP/CEPES/SUR, 2004.

Rights and Resources Initiative. *Who Owns the Worlds Land? A Global Baseline of Formally Recognized Indigenous & Community Land Rights*. Washington, DC: RRI, 2015.

Rodríguez, Edgardo. *Balance de la campaña de titulación de tierras en el departamento de Puno*. Lima: CEPES, 2000.

Romero, Emilio. *Monografía del Departamento de Puno*. 3rd ed. Puno: Universidad Nacional del Altiplano, 2013 [1928].

Sullivan, Lynda. "Peru Passes a Packet of Neoliberal Reforms, Erodes Environmental Protections and Labor Rights." *Upside Down World*, 25 July 2014.

Svampa, Maristella. "Commodities Consensus: Neoextractivism and Enclosure of the Commons in Latin America." *South Atlantic Quarterly* 114, no. 1 (2015): 65–82.

Thoen, Erik. "'Social Agrosystems' as an Economic Concept to Explain Regional Differences. An Essay Taking the Former County of Flanders as an Example (Middle Ages-19th Century)." In *Landholding and Land Transfer in the North Sea Area (Late Middle Ages—19th Century)*, edited by Peter Hoppenbrouwers and Bas Van Bavel, 47–66. Comparative Rural History of the North Sea Area 5. Turnhout: Brepols Publishers, 2004.

Tsing, Anna Lowenhaupt. "Natural Resources and Capitalist Frontiers." *Economic and Political Weekly* 38, no. 48 (2003): 5100–6.

Walker, Charles. Prólogo a "Ezequiel Urviola y el indigenismo puneño". 2016. Accessed August 3, 2017. http://charlesfwalker.com/prologo-a-ezequiel-urviola-y-el-indigenismo-puneno-2016/.

3

Agricultural Commodities on the Philippine Frontier: State-Sponsored Resettlement and Ecological Distress in the 1930s

Karen R. Miller

In November 1938, a delegation of Filipino government officials and "technical advisors" traveled from Manila down to Zamboanga City by boat on their way to the Koronadal Valley in southern Mindanao. Zamboanga was the seat of the regional government for Mindanao, the Philippines' second largest island. Unlike the rest of the island, which was either majority Muslim or populated by groups of people who practiced native religions, Zamboanga was majority Christian. It made sense as a starting point for the delegation, whose Manila members were representatives of the almost exclusively Christian Filipino central state. A few days later, the original group of twelve stopped in Cotabato City and picked up 11 more members. While Cotabato City was majority Muslim, these men, all of whom held high positions in the local and regional government, were also Christian Filipino and linked, politically, to the central state.[1]

K. R. Miller (✉)
LaGuardia Community College, City University of New York,
New York City, NY, USA
e-mail: kamiller@lagcc.cuny.edu

S. Joseph (ed.), *Commodity Frontiers and Global Capitalist Expansion*,
Palgrave Studies in Economic History, https://doi.org/10.1007/978-3-030-15322-9_3

Koronadal Valley, a tract of land spanning almost 97,000 hectares, was about 80 kilometers long and ranged from 10 to 12 kilometers wide.[2] It was in Cotabato, a province on the southwest corner of the island, where Muslims and "Pagans"—a state designation meaning neither Christian nor Muslim—outnumbered Christian Filipinos by 8 to 1. Muslims were 62% of a population of 220,000, "Pagans" were 24%, and Christian Filipinos were 13%. Just under 500 "Foreigners" lived in the province, representing less than one half of 1% of the total population.[3] The party was traveling south to conduct a "reconnaissance survey." It was assessing whether the Koronadal Valley would be a good site for the state-sponsored settlement of Christian migrants from northern islands onto an "agricultural colony" of unprecedented proportions.

The reinvention of space in Koronadal Valley was an environmental project on a grand scale. It was linked to governing elites' idea that a sovereign Philippine economy would be based on the exploitation of nature on the archipelago's periphery, a periphery that they characterized as practically untouched, certainly underutilized, and ripe for agricultural commodity production. State leaders cast the area as extremely lush, drawing on ideas about "tropical nature" that animated elite fantasies about the limitless potential of peripheral Philippine space.[4] In a 1935 report outlining his vision for frontier development, General Paulino Santos, head of the reconnaissance team, translated these ideas into technocratic language. He imagined that southwest Mindanao had a "most favorable" landscape in the archipelago, with "soil conditions of great promise to diversified agriculture."[5]

The Philippine colonial state had been promoting Christian Filipino migration from provinces it designated as "densely populated" onto tracts of "unoccupied" public land in non-Christian areas for decades. These programs promised migrants access to land they could farm as owners, rather than tenants or sharecroppers, and thus access to a level of stability previously unknown to them. The state also promoted this project in an effort to develop commodity production on the frontier. Finally, state leaders hoped that these programs would turn the land, itself, into a commodity. By moving land out of public and into private hands, state leaders hoped that would eventually have a monetary exchange value.

Between 1913 and 1930, the state established ten large-scale "agricultural colonies" in Cotabato, seven of which remained by 1930.

These colonies had a combined population of about 12,000 people who lived on 16,000 hectares of land. Four of the seven colonies had a "mixed" Christian and "Mohammedan" population, but the vast majority of families were Christian and had migrated from Cebu. Most held plots that were 16 hectares, far larger than the plots they would have farmed in the Visayas. The agricultural colonies in Cotabato represented about one half of one percent of the total land mass of the province, and their residents were about five percent of the total population. However, the Christian population of these "colonies" was between 30 and 35% of the total Christian population of the province.[6] Mindanao was also the site of smaller-scale colonies as well as individual migration supported by the state. Approximately 18,000 additional Christian migrants moved mostly from the Visayas, but also from regions in Luzon by the early 1930s.

In the mid-1930s, the Philippine government passed a law designed to accelerate this process as part of its preparation for the country's postcolonial future. This law was partly a response to the Tydings–McDuffie Act of 1934, US legislation that put the Philippines on a path toward independence. The Act called on Filipino lawmakers to draw up a new constitution and put it up for a national referendum. Once the constitution was passed, the Philippines would remain a US colony for ten years, although it would be "self-ruled." Subsequently, the archipelago would attain full sovereignty. The shift to official self-rule under the new constitution was politically significant, but it was not particularly dramatic on the ground, since Philippine elites and members of the middle class had dominated the ranks of the colonial government at all levels for over twenty years. Indeed, by 1934, they held 21,492 of these jobs, while Americans retained only 327.[7]

Most Philippine elites embraced the idea that the Philippines must modernize and unite before its population was prepared for independence; most accepted the model that sovereignty would follow from the forms of capitalist development favored by the colonial state. This development was oriented toward the expansion of agricultural commodity production, the consolidation of wealth and power in the hands of elites, and the uncompromising management and repression of dissent among the poor and disenfranchised. Internal migration, they believed, could help deliver these building blocks for sovereignty.

Philippine lawmakers were also working to expand internal migration as a response to changing international trade relations: to both remake the Philippine economy and reimagine what the nation should do with its land. State leaders' concerns about building a new national economy were amplified by the plan for independence, which would, over ten years, end the Philippines' free trade arrangement with the United States.[8] Resettlement was one part of a set of proposals designed to move national production away from cash crops like sugar, which depended on access to American markets for its viability, and toward agricultural goods that would continue to be profitable in the face of tariffs, including crops they believed would do well domestically and regionally.[9] Santos' report from the reconnaissance mission reflected these priorities. He self-consciously used his report to "justify the raising of such crops needed in the Philippines and to discourage the further raising of hemp and copra, because of their very uncertain market." This was not a turn away from agricultural commodity production, however. Rubber and cotton, he argued, "should be the principal money crops for Koronadal."[10]

The 1935 Act, to "Facilitate and Promote the Occupation and Cultivation of Public Land at Present Unoccupied by the Establishment of Settlement Districts," produced guidelines for what settlement would look like and committed one million pesos to this endeavor. Rather than plantation-style development, legislators lay the groundwork for owner-occupiers to move into ostensibly "unoccupied" spaces, but they attempted to limit migrants' control of the landscape. For example, "each applicant," the Act declared, would "bind himself" to plant sixty percent of their land in crops chosen by a local superintendent in consultation with the Department of Plant Industry. While migrants would be allowed to use some of their land as they liked, more than half of it would be committed to commodity crop production dictated by the state. In addition, while settlers were deemed owners, their land was not exchangeable until they paid off their considerable debts to the government. In other words, they could not sell the land until they owned it outright, which could take as few as five years, but was likely to take many more. Furthermore, if the settler was "declared incompetent" before their debt was paid in full, the state could cancel their application, repossessing the land and any improvements they had made.[11] Finally, while the bill promised a vast reshuffling of the national population and massive new agricultural development, it was modestly funded. Legislators contributed limited capital, but imagined that migrants' sweat equity could close the gap between their vision and the state's investment.

Resettlement was a developmentalist solution to poverty that was informed by the notion that populations deemed surplus in one region could build new political economies in another. Homesteading supporters thus blamed population distribution, rather than exploitation or inequality, for poverty. The Philippines, according to this logic, faced a mismatch: Ostensibly overpopulated islands had too few opportunities and rich, tropical Mindanao had too few workers. On one hand, authors of the Act called on governmental bureaus dedicated to managing land, health, and public works to administer the environmental aspects of the program. On the other, they invited the Department of Labor to support and oversee settlers and ultimately reintegrate migrants back into the political terrain as owners of property. The act's authors thus imagined that the frontier agricultural economy was being built with two distinct resources. These were land, which they characterized as naturally fertile but underutilized, and labor, which they characterized as maldistributed. The technocratic state would prepare the terrain for farming. No longer exclusively American, its expertise would be dispensed by a Christian Filipino professional-managerial class with deep transnational ties to scientific communities pursuing similar aims. A different arm of the state would organize the human terrain: The Department of Labor was responsible for overseeing both production and reproduction. It would build houses for settlers, as well as reproductive institutions like schools and infrastructure like roads and warehouses to support commerce. The Act cast laborers as able to perform the physical work of farming, but unable to organize or manage production on a large enough scale to satisfy either their own interests or the ambitions of the program. Ultimately, it called on the scientific state to produce land ready for cultivation and the administrative state to turn settlers into producers and ultimately owners.

Indeed, the homesteading program relied on workers from afar to build agricultural frontier terrains oriented toward commodity production because of the perceived deficits of indigenous populations—in both their size and capacities. Administrators were vocal about their belief that people native to Mindanao were unable to farm appropriately. In their minds, peasants' use of *kaingin*, or swidden cultivation, was particularly backward, and non-Christian Filipinos were the worst culprits. Filipino legislators would have been familiar with the findings of countless studies that characterized *kaingin* as primitive, damaging to the land and unconnected to the marketplace.[12] Indigenous people were also extremely unlikely to hold government recognized titles to the land they lived on and worked and were often reluctant to apply for this kind of official recognition of ownership from the state. They were also a problem for the homesteading program because of the local resources they could muster to escape the program's harsh discipline. Furthermore, their local knowledge, while consistently dismissed as damaging, could challenge the expertise of scientists and technocrats. Authors of the 1935 legislation embraced a broad sensibility about both indigenous and migrant labor that was also connected to ideas about the environment, where indigenous people damaged the land, but migrants, managed by a state that curated their choice of seeds, agricultural tools, and approaches to farming, would be more amenable to following the priorities of the government.

Authors of the 1935 legislation embraced this broad sensibility about both indigenous and migrant labor and applied its logic to internal migration.[13] Settlers from majority-Christian areas signed up to migrate as a strategy for seeking relief from the poverty and coerced labor they faced on their home islands. The allure of the program was its promise of individual ownership and the freedom that would hopefully deliver. However, when they arrived on newly cleared land, settlers confronted a system of harsh control and debt, not unlike peasants' experiences as tenants and sharecroppers on their islands of origin, where landlords would have extended credit in the form of draft animals, farm implements, and small amounts of cash, just as the state promised it would for homesteaders on public land. While Christian migrants would certainly bring farming knowledge from their own localities, their lack of familiarity with the terrain in Cotabato amplified their reliance on "expert" advice and innovations. Furthermore, without social or political networks in the area, they would have more difficulty protecting themselves from the demands of the state. They could not call on local supporters for solidarity or take shelter with relatives, strategies they may have used on their home islands, to extract themselves or their labor from the demands of the program.

The 1935 Act called on state agents to build an agricultural terrain oriented toward the regional marketplace. Indeed, the program was developed with these aims in mind and was an effort to push against peasants' notoriety (among modernizing elites) for preferring subsistence farming over market-oriented agriculture. For example, settlers were required to agree to continuous cultivation, a provision that meant they could not let land lay fallow and thus could not practice *kaingin*. In addition, homesteaders had to claim 16-hectare plots (about 40 acres), a piece of land that was far larger than most smallhold farms in the archipelago. Land that size required "modern" inputs like irrigation, fertilizer, draft animals, and agricultural machinery, inviting settlers' dependence on the program.

Few small landholders had the resources to use these techniques. In order to support this scale of agriculture, the Bureau of Labor and its superintendents would establish organizations in each settlement designed to foster "a cooperative spirit" among settlers, "through which Government aid [could] be efficiently extended to them." These organizations would buy "tractors, agricultural implements, draft animals and other equipment" for work individual settlers could not accomplish alone. They would also build district warehouses for storing produce, sell goods in bulk, and negotiate favorable prices for members. Described as supportive of settlers' pursuits in the 1935 Act, these organizations would help bind homesteaders to the land through uncompensated labor and an extra layer of debt.

During their fifth year of occupancy, settlers would have to begin paying the state back for any investment it had made in the land they occupied. These investments included *all* expenses associated with settlement: surveying, clearing, and breaking the land, as well as the houses, farm implements, carabao, and seeds that they received. Settlers would also be asked to pay 4% interest per year on that debt. In addition, they would be responsible for investing in the local cooperative institution set up by the district supervisor, and as a group be responsible for paying back loans, also with 4% annual interest. Homesteaders had ten years to pay back the state, and if they missed more than two months payments along the way, they were subject to losing their farms. Although they could stay on as tenants, this meant that they would lose any equity they had been trying to build in the property. Migrants could not sell the land or otherwise enter into "any contract relative to it" before all debts were paid. As a group, they attained a compromised form of "ownership"—one that was difficult, precarious, and almost always elusive. These harsh terms mirrored the compromised sovereignty that the Philippines had negotiated with the USA.

Like colonists' ability to control their land, their ownership of their labor was compromised under the terms that brought them to Mindanao. The 1935 Act required settlers to work on communal projects for the colony at "wages as are generally paid by agricultural concerns in the locality." These wages were extremely low, and colonists would only receive "the portion of their wages considered necessary for… subsistence," with the balance credited to their "indebtedness to the settlement."[14] In other words, settlers had to prioritize repayment and could not make decisions about this income based on their own priorities. The Department of Labor set up corporations designed to collectivize some of the risks of farming among members of a single settlement, something that could be beneficial for individual migrants. However, it offered no program for the development of political structures in the area and essentially had migrants move into spaces run by local superintendents with no input from settlers themselves.

In January and February, 1935, Attorney Lamberto Siguion Reyna, who was serving as special investigator for the Department of Interior, traveled to Mindanao and Sulu for 49 days to survey the southern islands. Reyna took his trip before the new law had gone into effect, so his observations about resettlement were less about the effects of the newly passed legislation than they were about the existing program. Rather than painting a portrait of possibility and success, Reyna found that many of the agricultural colonies were "failures," since scores of colonists were indebted to the state and few had been able to pay back "their obligations." One family, for example, owed 3000 pesos to the government. In other words, migrants' independence, the promise that attracted them to the program, was elusive at best, and perhaps even unattainable with the program in its current state. While Reyna' findings were less than positive, his diagnosis of the problems aligned him with legislators who had passed the new law. Like them, he believed that a better managed program could succeed. The project, he argued, had been hampered by the selection of the "wrong… sites" and the "wrong kind of workers." The flaws, in other words, were not with the original vision, but with the particular spaces and people that had been selected. The problem with the land, he explained, was that it was "not suited" for the crops that settlers were growing. Different land, he argued, needed to be selected for a project that would continue with its original goals in mind. Like the legislators who crafted the new law, he blamed migrants for their lack of expertise and their ostensible unwillingness to work hard enough. Ultimately, while Reyna criticized resettlement, his assessment stood in line with legislators' perception that the resettlement model was sound. If technocrats, he believed, made better decisions, including choosing the people best suited for the program, then migrants would be able to prosper.[15]

At the same time that poor migrants faced often insurmountable challenges in their efforts to become independent land owners in Mindanao, native people confronted exclusion of from homesteading and settlement projects. In 1935, Gouverneur Frank Mosher, Bishop of the Philippine Islands, complained that several Tiruray families whom he had encouraged to attain and farm homesteads were having trouble acquiring titles to the lands they were cultivating. Tiruray people were indigenous to Mindanao and at the time were considered "pagan" by the state. Mosher appealed to the director of the Bureau of Forestry to reverse its decision rejecting their applications for titles. Mosher suggested that the government should favor Tiruray settlement, since it would help reduce swidden or shifting cultivation and support settled farming. "May we hope that you will take personal interest in helping us in our effort to get these people to stop [swidden farming], to abandon their nomad existence and to settle down in homesteads?" While lack of attention to this group of Tirurays certainly reflected administrative ineptitude—the Bureau of Forestry had failed to classify the lands, even though the homesteaders had been cultivating it for "four or five years"—the consistency with which non-Christians faced bureaucratic barriers suggests that their challenges were systematic.[16]

Indeed, Muslim Filipinos' claims to public lands in Mindanao were often summarily rejected by colonial and Commonwealth administrators, who characterized them as a nuisance and saw their claims as an obstruction to the modernizing project of settlement. In January 1935, a few days after President Roosevelt signed the Philippine Agricultural Colonization Act into law, Salipada Pendatun, a Muslim Filipino law student from a prominent family in Cotabato Province, appealed to Acting Governor-General Joseph Hayden to help Mindanao's native residents acquire homesteads. Pendatun was concerned that the new law would displace Muslim Filipinos from land they had occupied for generations and that Muslims would lose "the race with their Christian brothers" to acquire property. While Christian Filipinos from areas deemed "overpopulated" were being assisted by agents from the Bureau of Lands, Pendatun observed, non-Christian natives were provided with no such help. Furthermore, he pronounced, their "ignorance [would] undoubtedly handicap them." Pendatun was interested in the modernization project that homesteading represented, and while he was Muslim, he shared condescending ideas about Moros, as a population, with Christian Filipino elites. He suggested that the state should set aside land designated for Muslim settlement "like the way that American Fathers did for the Indians," to "help solve the problem."[17] Other Muslims in Mindanao, conversely, rejected the notion that non-Christians would benefit from either homesteading or its implicit goal of integrating the island into the Philippine nation. Dimakaling, celebrated by non-elite Muslims as the "defender of Islam in Mindanao," fought against homesteading by attacking and killing settlers and representatives of the Bureau of Lands between the mid- and late-1930s, when he was killed by Philippine authorities. While resettlement projects failed to deliver on their promises to lift rural migrants out of poverty, this remained the model favored by the state. This suggests that there were ways that this model served the needs of state leaders, even as it failed those people who moved far from their homes.

Koronadal Valley

The most ambitious project to come out of this legislation was the settlement in the Koronadal Valley which opened to its first migrants in 1939. In this section, I will consider the work of the reconnaissance party, which assessed whether the area was appropriate for a settlement of this scale. I will show that the development aims and visions of the reconnaissance party were shaped by a tension between concerns about the sustainability of the proposed agricultural project and the sometimes explicitly dishonest optimism of its boosters. Team members' impressions of the space and conclusions about how the state and migrants should handle the land emerged in dialogue with contemporary debates about environmental questions. But, they were also shaped by governing elites' broader interest in building political economies that would sustain the Philippines as a sovereign nation without significantly disrupting existing relations of power or sinking too much cash into the program. The technocratic practice of the land survey was a performance of scientifically informed due diligence, but the political economic priorities of governing elites contributed as much to shape of the landscape as ostensibly neutral ecological considerations.

General Santos, chief of staff of the Philippine Army, traveled from Manila to Mindanao to lead the survey team. Santos knew he would be appointed head of the National Land Settlement Administration (NLSA), the government agency that would oversee the project, and believed that his leadership of the reconnaissance party would set the project off on the right path. Santos had been an enthusiastic promoter of resettlement for the last decade. As head of the Bureau of Prisons in the early 1930s, he spearheaded the Davao Penal Colony, a giant agricultural settlement and prison that aimed to use convict labor to feed the national prison population as a tool for the reformation and uplift of incarcerated men. In addition to their agricultural labor for the Bureau, incarcerated men were given individual plots of land to tend. They were required to use these plots for personal sustenance. Santos believed that these small farms would help reform incarcerated men by instilling in them a sense of ownership, an understanding of the necessity of hard work, and the agricultural skills that would allow them to establish small farms upon their release. Like he would as head of the NLSA, Santos understood himself as a social engineer and saw the autocratic control he was able to assert over incarcerated men's lives as a positive model for a national resettlement program. For him, agricultural resettlement projects produced opportunities for the reinvention of Filipinos as much as the reinvention of Philippine space in Mindanao. Santos believed that previous settlements had failed because they were poorly sited. It was "imperative," he declared in his 1935 "Tentative Plan for the Development of Agricultural Colonies under the New Colonization Law," that the man charged with the "final responsibility" for an agricultural colony "lead the selection party."[18]

Before he joined his team, Santos spent eight days with Charles Burnett, head of the Bureau of Insular Affairs (BIA), the division of the US War Department that oversaw the United States' island colonies. Burnett was responsible for "unincorporated territories" that were, like the Philippines, *not* on a path to statehood. Indeed, the Philippines was headed in the opposite direction: It was scheduled to attain its sovereignty seven years later, and would become an independent nation in 1946. Together, Santos and Burnett flew over Mindanao on an "inspection tour" of the Western provinces of Lanao and Cotabato and the southeastern province of Davao. When Burnett left the Philippines at the end of November, according to one reporter, he exclaimed that he [was] favorably impressed with the government plans for the settlement and development of Mindanao."[19] Burnett did not join the reconnaissance team, but he embraced and promoted its mission. Like them, he saw Christian migration into non-Christian spaces in Mindanao as the lynchpin for Philippine progress.[20] Like them, he believed that the production of agriculture commodities for export was and should remain the engine of the Philippine national economy. US leaders were working on industrial recovery at home, but promoting agricultural expansion in the Philippines, extending the uneven development that had characterized colonial rule.

Burnett, who was also a general, had served in Mindanao between 1901 and 1903, during the brutal US war against Philippine independence. This meant that in his first encounters with Mindanaoans, he participated in a violent military campaign to secure US dominance over the islands. Burnett's 1938 trip to the Philippines as head of the BIA had important parallels with his 1901 tour of duty. In both cases, he traveled to the islands to help secure an international system favorable to the interests of the United States: one based on deep global and local inequalities. By the late 1930s, US leaders and their elite Philippine allies no longer used the language of "benevolent assimilation" to justify their dominance, but their enthusiasm about market-oriented "development" operated in much the same way: as the ideological lynchpin for promoting global capitalist relations of power and elite Filipino rule. Governing Filipino elites saw their interests as congruent with the aims of global capital, including its developmentalist vision and its environmental sensibility.[21]

About twenty-five men joined General Santos on the 1938 survey team. Many of them held high ranks in their agencies, including the Commissioner of Mindanao and Sulu, the chief of the animal husbandry division of the Bureau of Animal Industry, and the Assistant Director of Prisons for the Commonwealth. This suggests that participation in the reconnaissance mission was based less on the scientific role a participant could play than it was related to political considerations. In other words, it is likely that officials went on the trip in order to secure a place either for themselves or their agencies in the newly expanding settlement program.

These men were joined by a handful of officials from Cotabato City, including the District Engineer, the Chief of Police, and a "ranger." Every member of the team, including those from Cotabato, a Muslim-majority region, was Christian Filipino. While some Muslims worked in local governments in Mindanao and Sulu, none participated in the reconnaissance mission, reflecting their exclusion from leadership in development projects based on interisland resettlement, an exclusion that actually amplified in the 1930s. Muslims and non-Christians had been integrated into previous Mindanaoan settlement districts alongside Christian migrants from other provinces during the 1910s. But, they would not be allowed to participate in these new programs, pointing to a hardening, rather than a softening, of inequalities rooted in state-recognized social difference.

When the group arrived in Dadiangas, a bayside town near Koronadal Valley which became the site of modern-day General Santos City, it was met by three members of the Philippine Constabulary and by Francisco Natividad, who Santos described as "one of the pioneers in the development of Southern Cotabato." Together, these men had "prepared the way" for the reconnaissance survey and would coordinate the trip. Natividad was well established in the area and held considerable power and wealth. In 1920, he chose to settle in the Koronadal Valley after touring the entire island of Mindanao with a group of business-people from Luzon. He moved south with 35 other families from Nueva Ecija, a province on Luzon, approximately eighty miles north of Manila. Together, they brought "modern farm machinery" and 70 carabaos (Philippine water buffalo), an indication of their prosperity.[22] Natividad likely saw the siting of a state-subsidized settlement project as a boon for him and the region. In fact, he had been involved in an effort to persuade Santos to locate the Davao Penal Colony in Koronadal. While Santos chose not to site the prison there, he had stayed in touch with Natividad, who accompanied the 1939 mission on its tour. Among other favors, Natividad hosted the team for a meal and a meeting at a *tienda*, a restaurant and store that he owned in one town, Sitio Tupi, and had them stay overnight in his home in another town, Polomulok.

Natividad also shuttled the reconnaissance team around the Valley in his "new International truck," which, General Santos explained, allowed them to move far more quickly than they otherwise would have. The group covered about 50 kilometers on their first day, a pace made possible by the truck, and facilitated by Natividad's practice of "blazing new trails." As the party traveled, Natividad cut through barbed wire fences to facilitate movement across the Valley. This practice was motivated by the team's haste, but perhaps more importantly, it illustrates that both Natividad and the reconnaissance party did not see themselves as beholden to existing enclosures, whether those enclosures represented the borders of state-recognized property or they pointed to conventions and practices vis-a-vis local landholding. Even though members of the reconnaissance team were simply surveying the land, they clearly came to the area with the belief that the development that they were promoting gave them the right to reshape the terrain without respecting existing boundaries. This was also reflected in their propensity to assign new names to mountains and hills. For example, they renamed the mountain ranges that framed the Valley "Quezon" and "Roxas," after prominent Filipino politicians, and renamed a hill "Carpenter Hill" after an American governor, who, Santos claimed, "did so much for the development of Mindanao and Sulu."[23]

This sense that the reconnaissance team saw the Koronadal Valley as essentially theirs to manipulate shaped their relationship to the land and their ideas about how development would work. As they traveled, the group stopped to collect soil samples and climbed up hills to get a "bird's eye-view" of the landscape. They also held meetings to assess the "possibilities of the areas covered" and to discuss how they would handle the terrain if it became the site for the agricultural colony. At their meeting on the first day, for example, they considered whether "cotton and cattle-raising" would work well in the area and concluded that they should take initial steps to clear the way for these practices. They agreed that Mr. San Buenaventura, a "Special Delegate" from the Department of Agriculture and Commerce, should ask the Bureau of Forestry to discontinue the pasture leases held in the area. He was also tasked with urging the Bureau of Lands to suspend "pending applications for sale of public lands" and to "carefully check" existing holdings in order "to facilitate the adjustment of landholdings later."[24] In other words, he was taking the first steps toward dissolving ownership of property in the area that might get it the way of its reinvention as the site for the colonization project.

On the second day of their trip, at a meeting in Natividad's store, the team outlined some of its initial suggestions. First, 70,000 pesos should be made available to build a road that would allow easier travel from the settlement site, Paidu Pulangi, to Makar, the nearest port (now a port in General Santos City). Second, they suggested, Mount Matutum should "be reserved as a National Park to conserve its forests and protect sources of future water supply." Finally, the Bureau of Forestry should reserve "communal forests" that would "benefit the greatest possible number of settlers." These conservation impulses were rooted in experience. The team agreed that "sufficient timber land along creeks [should] be left intact to serve as water shade and thus prevent soil erosion" in order to correct for mistakes made "in opening land in Davao Penal Colony."[25]

While some suggestions made by the reconnaissance team were informed by environmental lessons that members had learned from previous projects, General Santos and his political allies resisted the idea that their vision should be constrained by the limits of the terrain. For example, when Professor Mariano Raymundo, Chief of the Propagation Division at the Bureau of Plant Industry, suggested that the proposed settlement plans would not work because settlers would certainly need to use commercial fertilizer "due to the apparent low fertility of the soil," his concerns were dismissed. Dr. Alicante, head of the Soil Survey at the Bureau of Science dispensed advise that Santos embraced. Alicante claimed that the Koronadal Valley was "fertile enough" so that settlers would not need "fertilizer for at least the next ten years." Santos told Dr. Raymundo to delete his reservations about the soil from his report. The settlement program depended on very low state investments, and its ambitions could not be sustained with these kinds of inputs.

Santos maintained an autocratic approach toward migrants that extended to their farming practices and thus to the management of the land. Some of his controlling impulses were economic and social. For example, while migrants were required to work for the NLSA their compensation for that work would be used for their "subsistence and clothing" first, and then to pay off their debts to the state. Cash, he explained, would only be advanced "in very exceptionally meritorious cases." Furthermore, Santos declared, "community spirit would be encouraged, if not enforced."[26] Other top-down aspects of the program were directly related to land management. For example, settlers were required to plant either rubber or cotton on five hectares of their twelve-hectare plots and use seed they received from the Bureau of Plant Industry. All of these requirements meant that settlers could neither learn from locals, developing farming strategies that had evolved in that area over generations, nor could they develop their own approaches that emerged in dialogue with the terrain. Indeed, promoters of the settlement project came out of a long tradition of imagining that independent farming, especially swidden cultivation, was environmentally destructive, and ironically saw their top-down program as an elixir against environmental degradation.

Ultimately, foresters, botanists, and managers of agricultural land, as well as farm workers, peasants, and *kaiganeros*—men and women who practiced swidden agriculture—produced a range of discourses, some written and others enacted, about these questions. As Brendan Luyt and others have shown, since its inception, the Philippines' Bureau of Forestry attempted to limit swidden cultivation, or what was called *kaingin* locally. The Bureau criminalized the unauthorized use of *kaingin* and promoted the notion, widely accepted among foresters in colonial South and Southeast Asia, that peasants destroyed forests.[27] In the early twentieth century, this concern focused more on the loss of value from timber extraction. By the 1930s, there was more concern about the conservation of the forest as a strategy for producing a climate amenable to sustainability and agriculture.

In the end, the Koronadal Valley project, a product of an effort to develop commodity agriculture on the frontier, transformed the cultural and physical terrains of southwestern Mindanao. In its first two years, over ten thousand migrants claimed plots of land in the settlement district, both those who received support from the state to migrate and those who came on their own. New forms of intensive agricultural production did not pull the vast majority of migrants out of the poverty they faced on their home islands, although it did radically transform the landscape, undercutting the political power of indigenous locals and producing and agroecological terrain that was constantly in crisis. As Hiromitsu Umehara explains, by the 1980s, Cotabato has "extensive stretches of bald mountains and grasslands where once stood lush old-growth forests... ecological destruction has turned Mindanao into the land of the unfulfilled promise."[28]

Notes

1. Paulino Santos, "Appendix No. I, Itinerary, Activities and Notes of Conferences, Mindanao Reconnaissance Survey Party," 1939, General Paulino Santos Museum, Notre Dame of Dadiangas University, General Santos City, Philippines.

2. Karl J. Pelzer, *Pioneer Settlement in the Asiatic Tropics* (New York: American Geographical Society, 1945), 143.
3. Dionesio Gutierrez, "Miscellaneous Information Regarding Cotabato Province and Its Needs," April 20, 1931, Joseph Ralston Hayden Papers (hereafter HP), Box 27, Folder 28, Bentley Library, University of Michigan, Ann Arbor (hereafter Bentley).
4. For an expanded discussion of this sensibility about natural resources and American colonial logic, see Theresa Ventura, "American Empire, Agrarian Reform and the Problem of Tropical Nature in the Philippines, 1898–1916," PhD diss., Columbia University, 2009.
5. Paulino Santos and Inocencio Elayda, "Tentative Plan for the Development of Agricultural Colonies Under the New Colonization Law," n.d., HP, Box 29, Folder 6.
6. "Annual Report of the Director of Non-Christian Tribes for the Fiscal Year 1934," n.d., HP, Box 28, Folder 22; Provincial Governor, "Miscellaneous Information Regarding Cotabato Province and Its Needs," April 20, 1931, HP, Box 27, Folder 29.
7. Carlos Quirino, "America's Colonial Blunders," *Commonwealth Advocate* 1, no. 8 (August 1935): 13–16.
8. US Congress, "The Philippine Independence Act," *Approved*, March 24, 1934.
9. The American Agricultural Commissioner stationed in Shanghai, Owen Dawson, argued that the Philippines should vastly reduce its production of sugar, increase its production of rice, and make other adjustments to its organization of agricultural production in light of the changing terms of trade it would face with the USA over the course of the Commonwealth. Owen L. Dawson, U.S. Agricultural Commissioner at Shanghai, "Preliminary Report on Agricultural Tendencies in the Philippines," September 13, 1936, US Department of Agriculture Records, National Archives and Records Administration, College Park, Maryland.
10. Santos, "Appendix No. I."
11. "An Act to Facilitate and Promote the Occupation and Cultivation of Public Land at Present Unoccupied by the Establishment of Settlement Districts…" Approved, February 12, 1935, HP, Box 29, Folder 6.
12. For a discussion of *kaingin* and its political meanings during this period, see Brendan Luyt "Narratives, Shifting Cultivation, and Knowledge Projects in the Philippines, 1901–1941: A Cautionary Tale," *Library &*

Information History 33, no. 1 (2017): 35–54; Owen Lynch, Jr., "The Philippine Indigenous Law Collection: An Introduction and Preliminary Bibliography," *Philippine Law Journal* 58 (1983): 457–534.

13. As Julie Greene demonstrates, labor migration was an essential element of American empire partly because imperialists believed that migrants were uniquely dominable. She demonstrates that colonial officials believed that they would be easier to manage than indigenous workers because they were "alienated from their home environments." Colonial officials, Greene explains, believed that indigenous workers "would not work hard enough, would leave labor sites to return home, or would cause trouble." Julie Greene, "Movable Empire: Labor, Migration, and U.S. Global Power During the Gilded Age and Progressive Era," *The Journal of the Gilded Age and Progressive Era* 15 (2016): 6.
14. "An Act to Facilitate and Promote the Occupation and Cultivation of Public Land at Present Unoccupied by the Establishment of Settlement Districts," p. 4.
15. "Prober Back from South with Report," *Manila Daily Herald*, February 27, 1935.
16. Gouverneur Frank Mosher to The Hon. Arthur F. Fischer, October 28, 1935, HP, Box 27, Folder 29; Gouverneur Frank Mosher, "A Memorandum concerning Tiruray Applications for land grants in the Awang District, Cotabato," October 12, 1935, HP, Box 27, Folder 29.
17. Salipada Pendatun, "Memorandum for His Excellency, The Honorable Acting Governor-General J.R. Hayden, Malacanang," January 15, 1935, HP, Box 29, Folder 6.
18. Paulino Santos and Inocencio Elayda, "Tentative Plan for the Development of Agricultural Colonies under the New Colonization Law," HP, Box 29, Folder 6. Santos described the Davao Penal Colony as the "most recent development in internal colonization," and suggested that his experiences had prompted him "to make some suggestions."
19. "News Summary: October 13–November 11, 1938," *Philippine Magazine*, December 1, 1938, http://www.gov.ph/1938/12/01/news-summary-philippine-magazine-october-13-november-11-1938/.
20. "Brigadier General Charles Burnett, Chief of the U.S. Bureau Arrived Last Monday on a Visit in the Philippines," October 30, 1938, *The Sunday Tribune Magazine*.
21. General Burnett's 1938 trip to Mindanao just happened to coincide with the beginning of the reconnaissance mission, but it makes sense

that Burnett would have met with Santos, since the development of agricultural commodities stood at the heart of Philippine modernization programs.

22. Andrea Villano-Campado, "The Tuna Country at the Southern Edge of Mindanao: General Santos City, 1939–2000," accessed January 4, 2012, http://www.notredamegensan.org/gscbk; Hon. Shirlyn L. Bañas-Nograles SPPR NO. 2017: "Resolution Conferring Posthumous Recognition and Honor to Don Francisco Natividad for His Cultural and Historical Contributions toward the Growth and Development of General Santos City."
23. Santos, "Appendix No. I, Itinerary, Activities and Notes of Conferences, Mindanao Reconnaissance Survey Party," p. 8.
24. For a discussion of swidden agriculture and how it was understood in the first half of the twentieth century, see Luyt, "Narratives, Shifting Cultivation, and Knowledge Projects in the Philippines."
25. Ibid., p. 3-4.
26. Santos, "Appendix No. I, Itinerary, Activities and Notes of Conferences, Mindanao Reconnaissance Survey Party," p. 29.
27. "An Act to Facilitate and Promote the Occupation and Cultivation of Public Land at Present Unoccupied by the Establishment of Settlement Districts," p. 4.
28. Hiromitsu Umehara, "Agricultural Colonization and Environmental Change in Koronadal Valley, South Cotabato," in *Communities at the Margins: Reflections on Social, Economic, and Environmental Change in the Philippines*, ed. Hiromitsu Umehara and Germelino M. Bautista (Manila: Ateneo de Manila University Press, 2004), 58.

Bibliography

Manuscript Collections

General Paulino Santos Museum, Notre Dame of Dadiangas University, General Santos City, Philippines.

Joseph Ralston Hayden Papers, Bentley Library, University of Michigan, Ann Arbor.

U.S. Department of Agriculture Records, The National Archives at College Park.

Newspapers

Manila Daily Herald.
Philippine Magazine.
The Sunday Tribune Magazine.

Printed Primary and Secondary Sources

Bañas-Nograles, Hon. Shirlyn L. SPPR NO. 2017. "Resolution Conferring Posthumous Recognition and Honor to Don Francisco Natividad for His Cultural and Historical Contributions toward the Growth and Development of General Santos City."

Greene, Julie. "Movable Empire: Labor, Migration, and U.S. Global Power During the Gilded Age and Progressive Era." *The Journal of the Gilded Age and Progressive Era* 15 (2016): 4–20.

Luyt, Brendan. "Narratives, Shifting Cultivation, and Knowledge Projects in the Philippines, 1901–1941: A Cautionary Tale." *Library & Information History* 33, no. 1 (2017): 35–54.

Lynch, Owen, Jr. "The Philippine Indigenous Law Collection: An Introduction and Preliminary Bibliography." *Philippine Law Journal* 58 (1983): 457–534.

Pelzer, Karl J. *Pioneer Settlement in the Asiatic Tropics.* New York: American Geographical Society, 1945.

Quirino, Carlos. "America's Colonial Blunders." *Commonwealth Advocate* 1, no. 8 (August 1935): 13–16.

U.S. Congress, "The Philippine Independence Act," *Approved*, March 24, 1934.

Umehara, Hiromitsu. "Agricultural Colonization and Environmental Change in Koronadal Valley, South Cotabato." In *Communities at the Margins: Reflections on Social, Economic, and Environmental Change in the Philippines*, edited by Hiromitsu Umehara and Germelino M. Bautista, 57–83. Manila: Ateneo de Manila University Press, 2004.

Ventura, Theresa. "American Empire, Agrarian Reform and the Problem of Tropical Nature in the Philippines, 1898–1916." PhD diss., Columbia University, 2009.

Villano-Campado, Andrea. "The Tuna Country at the Southern Edge of Mindanao: General Santos City, 1939–2000." Accessed January 4, 2012. http://www.notredamegensan.org/gscbk.

4

Gendering Farmer Producer Companies at the Agricultural Frontier of India: Empowerment or Burden?

Indrakshi Tandon

Introduction

The concept of commodity frontiers permits a holistic, broad view of the socio- and agro-ecological impacts of capitalist expansion, laying bare the very real ways in which local agricultural economies are incorporated into global markets. Jason Moore describes a frontier as "a specific kind of space defined by the forward movement of the (capitalist) system".[1] It is a zone of surplus production of particular commodities, where resources are extracted but not utilized, instead being directed to urban centers. Frontiers are spaces which tend toward further expansion, as long as the physical geography and capitalist system they are located within allow it. Thus, they are "profoundly transformative of land and labor".[2] Against this background, this chapter seeks to draw transnational connections between local agro-ecological transformations in India and global market

I. Tandon (✉)
Department of Anthropology, University at Albany SUNY,
Albany, NY, USA

Zayed University, Dubai, UAE

S. Joseph (ed.), *Commodity Frontiers and Global Capitalist Expansion*,
Palgrave Studies in Economic History, https://doi.org/10.1007/978-3-030-15322-9_4

economies through the concept of Farmer Producer Companies, contextualized amidst the state's national development goals of farmer (women's) empowerment, changing labor patterns, and ecological degradation.

The ideology behind cooperatives is significant in that it forges transnational connections between global consumption and grassroots production; between the world economy and local ecosystems. Shifting global needs and retail structures in the food sector have specific impacts on rural farmer producers, their labor patterns, and ecosystems. Anika Trebbin recognizes the spread of supermarkets and modern retail from Western economies to developing countries as a leading cause for the attempt to "modernize" traditional farming economies.[3] She notes, "The emergence of modern retailers in a country's food retail market also affects agricultural production and farmers, as supermarkets build new supply chains or modernize existing ones to facilitate the enforcement of stringent quality standards".[4] In the Indian context, modern retail structures in the food sector became popular around the early 2000s, re-organizing traditional supply chains with increased input of private funds. It is not uncommon for stringent quality standards and high demand for specific products to be accompanied by an influx of private capital. However, as a result small-scale farmers end up occupying the bottom of supply chains with poor bargaining positions, and the inability to deliver high-quality produce can at times eliminate them from supply chains altogether.

To combat farmer immiseration and exploitation, the organization of primary producers (farmers) into collectivities or cooperatives is argued to be the one of the more notable means of protection available to small farmers in modern, neoliberal, competitive markets. Their main objectives are to mobilize small-scale farmers to collectivize and organize in order to gain collective bargaining power, in the process empowering farmers and eliminating the need for middlemen. Trebbin astutely notes that despite vast scholarly attention given to the rise of modern retail in India over the past few decades, surprisingly little has been said of how farmer collectivities can more beneficially link small-scale farmers to the emerging modern food retail sector.[5] It is this chapter's assertion that even less attention has been paid to the failure of collectivities to effectively empower farmers and to a certain extent address the ecological ramifications that accompany frontier expansion.

This chapter will first introduce the Indian state and its changing policies toward agricultural development and poverty alleviation. Given the vast literature on more than two centuries[6] of South Asia's integration into the global economy, a comprehensive historical account of the region's capitalist development is beyond the scope of the current study. Instead, I will present a brief account of the state's economic development spanning the twentieth century in order to contextualize its current position on agricultural expansion, rural development, and farmer empowerment. The notion of empowering farmers takes on added significance in the Indian case as contemporary narratives on farmer empowerment have become increasingly gender focused, calling for mandatory inclusion of women in most development projects. Subsequently, a number of women-only producer companies have been established with inadvertent consequences. Through an examination of ethnographic data collected in the tribal regions of Western India, I shall demonstrate how mandatory inclusion as a participation tool often serves to disempower and further burden women. While such inclusion can prove crucial to enhancing women's decision-making roles and does have certain benefits, I ask whether this approach to farmer (women's) empowerment remains meaningful in realizing the goals of producer companies in a context where external support for women to succeed is not provided.

Lastly, I will address the issue of ecological degradation as one of the primary byproducts of agricultural frontier expansion. As an arid, drought-prone region, agriculture in Western India is greatly groundwater-dependent. Intensive exploitation of groundwater reserves over the past 50 years have resulted in severe depletion of these reserves. For instance, the Green Revolution pushed the use of water-intensive high-yield and hybrid variety seed cultivation. Additionally, increased cultivation of cash crops such as soybean, of which the state of Madhya Pradesh in Western India is the largest producer, continues to further deplete soil productivity.[7] Literature on producer companies, specifically on companies composed of women,[8] suggests that with their new-found bargaining power local actors such as farmers would, in theory, be more willing to undertake conservation activities and tackle ecological degradation. It is worthwhile to analyze this assumption that romanticizes grassroots communities as selfless caretakers of the environment in a rapidly changing capitalist economy by asking why farmers, particularly women, should have to bear the immense burden of combating ecological degradation?

Agro-Economic Development in India

In the early twentieth century, the belief that colonizers were beneficent and colonized subjects needed help reaching certain levels of progress and modernity made the notion of planned change explicit within the colonial administration. Thus, responsibility for economic development in colonized nations was complemented by incorporating welfare objectives including health, education, and nutrition programs for the colonized populations. In post-World War Europe and North America, economic growth and modernity were seen as the foundations of development "and it was generally believed that economic growth would 'trickle down' to the poor, while transfer of new technology would bring material benefits".[9] This was classic modernization theory which argued that in order for traditional, low-income societies to "develop," a philosophy of modern, capitalistic economic change was required, which would be based on "financial investment, improved governance and modern technologies."[10] This would in turn enable these societies to grow and progress, ultimately setting them "on a course of self-sustaining growth".[11] By the middle of the century, newly independent India followed suit with similar reasoning.

While still under colonial rule, in 1938 the Indian National Congress set up a National Planning Committee responsible for drawing up rudimentary plans focused on India's economic and social restructuring. The committee was a response by India's nationalist movement to critiques of exploitative British policy and inaction regarding the colony's economic underdevelopment. Leaders of the freedom movement had long blamed high land revenues and colonial tendencies to divert raw material out of India as key reasons for poverty and malnutrition. Most focused their critiques on flawed fiscal policies that prevented industrialism from bringing benefits to the poor, while others like Gandhi saw industrialism as a modern evil.[12] Regardless of differences, Indian nationalism and calls for independence had become inextricably tied to desires for economic progress and social change. As David Ludden has pointed out, the creation of India was synonymous with the creation of "a development regime," what he calls an industrial complex "created by colonial capitalism and bourgeois nationalism."[13]

During this time a prominent Indian scientist, Meghnad Saha, posed a pertinent question to the President of the Indian National Congress, Subhas Chandra Bose. He asked: "May I enquire whether the India of the future is going to revive the philosophy of village life, of the bullock-cart – thereby perpetuating servitude, or is she going to be a modern industrialized nation which, having developed all her natural resources, will solve the problems of poverty, ignorance and defence and will take an honoured place in the comity of nations and begin a new cycle of civilization?" This question encapsulates the unique struggle faced in India's development experience. Bose responded that, while not all members of the Indian National Congress agreed, "the rising generation are in favour of industrialization."[14] However, as postcolonial Indian theorists have shown, under the guise of democracy and inclusive development rhetoric, the Indian state continued operating much like the colonial government, exploiting its agrarian-based economy in order to prop up a more modern, industrial one. A passive reformist agenda had replaced the active agrarian revolution that previously defined India's freedom struggle. Bourgeois industrialization displaced peasant revolutions and became normalized in the imaginations of Indian communities.[15]

In 1950, the independent Government of India set up the Planning Commission under its first prime minister, Pandit Jawaharlal Nehru, which was tasked with solving the "problem" of India's underdevelopment through "rational and scientifically" conceptualized five-year development plans. Antithetical to the Gandhian view of developing self-sustaining village communities, the initial five-year plans pursued an aggressive industrialization agenda starting with the release of the first plan in 1951. Wary of unthinkingly mimicking First World development models, yet impatient to catch up, Nehru's administration sought a different path to development. Enamored by the rapid progress of socialist nations and Second World industrialization, Stalin's Soviet model, Meiji Japan, and China served as benchmarks for Indian development. State-run enterprises took over management of heavy industries such as mining, energy, hydroelectricity, steel, and cement at the expense of the environment and public land. However, unlike socialist models, private businesses were allowed to function within state regulations.[16] All the while Nehru reiterated commitment to reinvigorating the agricultural sector, calling it "the key-stone of our planning."[17] Achieving industrialization would be near-impossible without support from surplus generated by the agrarian economy. Thus, agricultural intensification through *scientific* practices—large-scale irrigation, industrial inputs, such as fertilizer, seed, pesticide, and heavy machinery—was also included in the initial five-year plans.[18]

However, by the 1960s it became increasingly evident that agricultural outputs were not matching up to expectations. Amid two wars with Pakistan and two consecutive years of rainfall failure, India began importing food grains. Over the next two decades, the nation-state faced inflationary pressures and a worsening balance of payments. Severe drought conditions in 1972–1973, followed by shortages of various essential consumer goods and critical raw materials and inputs contributed to a deteriorating economic situation. By the late 1980s, the Planning Commission echoed a widely held opinion when it declared that the strategy of "focusing on industrial development through import substitution which was encouraged through a tight control over imports and maintenance of high tariffs" had failed.[19] The government was criticized as being "over-active in industry" and "under-active" in areas relating to social development. Moreover, the public sector was seen as being "too involved" and complicit in "exercising strict control over private investment… and all important industries." However, it was not until the 1990s that wide-ranging economic reforms aimed at "decontrolling and debureaucratising the economy was initiated."[20] These reforms radically shifted the paradigm of development from industrial "trickle-down" to neoliberalist, decentralized, and participatory, which have since endured.

In 1991, the then finance minister of India, Manmohan Singh,[21] announced a program for the liberalization of the Indian economy to counter foreign exchange deficit. According to Akhil Gupta, the middle class in India widely held that the foreign exchange crisis was exacerbated by former prime minister Rajiv Gandhi's decision to allow imported consumer goods, such as television sets, to be purchased using foreign currency.[22] The deregulation of foreign currency, compounded by increasing oil prices due to the Gulf War, led India dangerously close to defaulting on foreign debt. Eventually, an economic crisis was abated by a bailout from the International Monetary Fund, which was conditional to the implementation of structural adjustment reforms. Succeeding decades have seen dramatic transformations in the Indian state driven by globalization and the opening up of markets. From large-scale availability of consumer goods and introduction of call centers to serve global outsourcing, new opportunities have arisen including in information technology, medicine, and finance, to name a few. However, these benefits are mainly received by India's urban populace and a privileged few in rural areas.

While centralized and socialist planning dominated development discourse in the first four decades of independent India, current or post-liberalization development planning has been shaped by transnational neoliberal policies.[23] By opening up the Indian economy, the nation-state became open to global discourses of development, and neoliberalism and market forces were seen as crucial to helping India's rural poor receive the benefits of a booming economy. IMF guidelines strictly channeled India's government expenditure, impacting certain subsidy and welfare programs. While some programs were defunded, others were simply remade in the image of neoliberalism. As Gupta[24] asserts, "[N]eoliberalism was accompanied by a new set of antipoverty initiatives that stressed self-help and emphasized that the poor could take the initiative and use the market to help themselves rather than rely on government assistance and handouts."[25] Development jargon began increasingly employing terms such as community, self-help, market forces, microfinance, and empowerment. These were "technolog[ies] of neoliberal self-government… linked with a wide variety of ideas and practices, including radical politics, persistent action and reflection, just and liberatory social change, development, participatory and decentralized governance, self-regulation, self-esteem, and self-actualization."[26]

It bears mentioning that such discourse harks back to Gandhi's call for grassroots empowerment, self-ruling village systems, and bottom-up, decentralized governance.

The rationale for why "bottom-up" and participatory approaches would work to better the situation of farmers and the poor in India can be found within this neoliberal logic of development. The belief was that where centralized, top-down approaches had failed, increased community involvement would succeed by promoting self-regulation and self-actualization by the target population. In fact, the logic of decentralization takes as its point of departure the failure of initial attempts at poverty reduction by largely state-controlled and implemented programs. These programs were "devised by bureaucrats and engineers, usually in collaboration with big business and large farmers' lobbies, and with very little popular participation,"[27] resulting in frequently exacerbated and multiplied social inequalities. The solution to this developmental problem was seen to be programs designed by the communities for themselves, with "external" help from development practitioners and the state. It is within this neoliberal logic that the ideology behind cooperatives, and eventually producer companies, can be located. However, as the ethnographic example in this chapter shows, producer companies still have a long way to go before being able to adequately empower farmers and solve India's poverty issues.

The Logic of Farmer Producer Companies

Despite being seen as the primary path to reduction in poverty and increased well-being of rural populations, studies show that cooperatives across the developing world have been more of a failure than success due to exclusion of the really poor, issues of elite capture, promotion of differentiation over equity in rural communities, government interference, and corruption. In India specifically, cooperatives have had an unpleasant history, as they have been largely state promoted, with a focus on welfare rather than along business lines. They have been characterized as inward-oriented, informally organized, with relative independence to function according to local customs and traditions of the farming community.[28] Apart from the large dairy,[29] sugar, and fertilizer cooperatives set up in the 1970s and 1980s, new cooperatives have not established any demonstrable success in achieving these goals.[30]

In 2003, as an amendment to the Indian Companies Act, the Government of India enacted producer companies as legal entities that would enable existing and new cooperatives to operate as companies, while ensuring that the unique elements of cooperatives remained intact within regulatory frameworks similar to those of private companies. Some of the organizing principles of the producer companies were based on the same principles as cooperatives: "[V]oluntary and open membership; equal voting right independent of shareholding; elected board from amongst members; limited return on share capital; and distribution of surplus on patronage basis."[31]

The central activities of producer companies are to form backward linkages, such as inputs for seeds, fertilizer, credit, insurance, knowledge, and extension services; and forward linkages, such as collective marketing, processing, market-led agriculture production, and so on. Producer companies are differentiated from traditional cooperatives as being outward-oriented, performing a "bridging function… as interface structures between their members and the external world. They are more formal… organized on economic principles but rooted in local customs… [and] run in a more professional way."[32] At its core, the objective is to empower farmers, build capacity, and eliminate the middleman.

In India's fast transforming food retail sector, large retailers are able to dominate small-scale farmers and the means of production through a process of "vertical coordination." This term describes "the explicit coordination of agricultural production processes by lead firms, such as retail chains... [and] describes the most explicit types of agrofood chain governance where buyers have strong control over the means of production."[33] Such market processes effectively disempower marginal farmers who not only face structural constraints such as small land holdings and the lack of bargaining power,[34] but also run the risk of "becoming simple pieceworkers on their land, while corporate enterprises control the means of production and the output."[35] However, in theory, producer companies have the ability to mobilize farmer collectivities and empower them via collective bargaining power over the terms of production. According to Trebbin and Hassler,[36]

> Producer companies are an example of changes towards more profit-oriented forms of organization arising among farming communities. In India these changes can be seen as reactions to a new market and regulatory environment. Unlike top-down models of smallholder market integration, such as contract farming or outgrowing, producer companies create and nurse an entrepreneurial spirit at the community level. By leaving production decisions and major assets in the hands of farmers, they contribute to their reempowerment. At the same time, producer companies try to enable access to new markets by establishing flexible linkages to highly specialized demand.

A producer company can be formed with equity contribution by members and is limited to them. Members buy shares of the producer company, in some cases, they are distributed equally among all, and in others, it is variable. In each producer company, a management team of two to three professionals with agribusiness backgrounds are hired from the market. Day-to-day operations are managed by these professionals under the direction of the Board of Directors, which can range from including five to 15 persons. These directors are elected or selected by the General Body of the producer company for a specific tenure from within the participating farmers with the belief that leadership chosen from within the community will ensure its acceptance.[37] The senior most individual of the management team performs the duty of a CEO (legally required) while others look after the production, marketing and accounting jobs. The Chairman (or Chairperson) of the board also works as a full-time member in the management team and is a co-signatory of the bank account of the producer company. All members of the company are primary producers or farmers who contribute directly to it. Theoretically, a cluster of 12–15 villages is the ideal size for constituting a company, and farmers must fill out an application form to join, membership being approved by the General Body. Typically, a functioning producer company should have 800–1000 members, which changes depending on the product which is being developed through that company (crop, seed, fertilizer, artisanal product, and so on).[38]

Ethnographic Case Study[39]

As of mid-2011, there were just over 156 producer companies throughout the country,[40] and by 2015, over 2000 had been formed.[41] Some of the most researched producer companies in India, and the longest running ones, are located in Western India, in the state of Madhya Pradesh. The state government of Madhya Pradesh under the District Poverty Initiative Project (DPIP), along with a World Bank poverty reduction project, have jointly financed producer companies since 2005. A mid-size NGO located in Bhopal, Madhya Pradesh, with significant state-wide recognition, was chosen to facilitate the formation and activation of 14 producer companies. The data for this paper were collected in 2013 in the district of Jhabua, Madhya Pradesh, among the Bhil tribal community where the NGO was promoting the establishment of more producer companies. The company that is the focus of this ethnographic case study—from here on referred to as FPC—was established in 2011 with financial support from the Mahila Kisan Sashaktikaran Yojana (MKSY or MKSP),[42] a government program aimed at empowering women farmers. The FPC is composed solely of women producers, and as per producer company rules, ten women from within the FPC have been appointed to the Board of Directors. A management team which provides support has been externally hired, and at the time of fieldwork, the FPC's activities were limited to producing incense sticks for sale in nearby markets and selling vegetables.

Observation of the FPC's annual general meeting for shareholders revealed certain realities about how capacity building and empowerment strategies are implemented, and how the state "performs" support for empowerment programs. A general meeting is required to be held as per the rules of the producer company to discuss profits and other specific issues related to its management. This particular meeting had been organized in a hurry in one of the MKSP program villages in the district. Before heading to the meeting, I visited one of my key informants, a young Bhil mother, who had been waiting with other women from the village for transportation to the meeting which the NGO had organized. On reaching the village where the meeting was to take place, I saw similar tractors arriving with Bhil women from other program villages. A stage had been built at one end of a school courtyard, set up with chairs, and decorated with banners and flowers. The women were asked to sit in rows facing the stage on a carpeted floor. There were many village men and boys (young adults) in attendance as well. Despite an already late start, the chief guest of the event, a government official in the Jhabua District Council, had not yet arrived. When he eventually did, accompanied by other state representatives, a small prayer ceremony was performed on stage to mark the beginning of the meeting and some Bhil women were invited from the audience to light candles, a Hindu custom performed before important events in India. The all-female Board of Directors of the FPC were then invited to the front of the audience and given flower garlands. The male guests were given chairs to sit on stage while the women directors sat facing the stage. Each of the male guests then took turns giving speeches on the advantages of producer companies and the benefits of signing up for them. They also talked about various other government programs being implemented in the region. In a few hours, after all the speeches were concluded, some time was devoted to taking questions from the women in the audience.

While on paper, the state's involvement in the FPC extends to providing financial support via the MKSP program, in reality that is not the case. The meeting was a performance pandering to government officials in the district, with a number of lengthy speeches made to showcase how the government was supporting farmer- and women-oriented agricultural schemes. Participation in annual general meetings is supposed to be restricted to shareholders; however, as a matter of "visibility of women" in the eyes of the state, a large number of women from different villages were asked to gather at certain locations from where they were brought to the event site. How many of these women, apart from those on the Board of Directors, were actual shareholders was unclear. Subsequent interviews revealed that while some women were interested in attending the event and hearing what the organizers had to say, more often than not they were going because they had been told to. This is consistent within the context of a region heavily dependent on development interventions, as attending an event such as this could lead to future benefits. Moreover, as a member of the NGO staff later told me, this particular meeting had been organized only for women farmers and producers, but many village men attended uninvited just "to hear the program, to see what happens." This in itself implies a deep unease with women-focused development programs on the part of rural men, despite superficial acceptance of them.

Such meetings are representative of how many development initiatives play out in the region. Despite promoting "bottom-up" participatory approaches, community-led interventions, and women-oriented programs, popular development practices in India can be said to operate at a superficial level. The ineffectiveness of events such as the annual general meeting was aptly summarized in a passing comment made by a well-meaning NGO staff member. Frustrated, he lamented that main issues, such as voting for a new Chairman of the Board (the previous one having quit) and informing the shareholders about profits received from the FPC, were not even discussed during the day-long meeting. He added: "These people [the government official and other guests] should not have been called today. The important work that was to be completed with the women [shareholders] was not even done." Later I heard that the tractors meant to transport the women back to their villages had refused to drop them off close to their homes. Many women had to walk back to their homes caught in an afternoon downpour, and I was left wondering what empowerment, if any, the women had received that day.

Empowerment or Burden?

While the creation of women-only producer companies could arguably prove crucial to enhancing empowerment and women's decision-making roles, it is also necessary to understand how using mandatory inclusion as a participation tool can serve to disempower and enhance inequality between women themselves, as well as between men and women. Mandatory inclusion in the FPC was not an intentional objective of the NGO; rather, it was a by-product of mainstreaming gender narratives currently popular with development initiatives and supported by state policies, as well as a result of extant beneficiary-organizing methods.

According to some studies,[43] the creation of producer companies on the basis of common interest groups rather than individual membership is more effective for integration into larger markets. Similarly, others[44] maintain that up-scaling already-formed common interest groups such as Self Help Groups (SHGs) as per the principles of producer companies can help quicken their spread. With this approach, the FPC has been built on the basis of previous membership to women-only SHGs and to a lesser extent Water Users' Groups, which were created as part of other participatory development programs. In theory, these groups are already strengthened; therefore, their participation in the FPC will be more effective. In reality, the criteria for participation in these groups were flawed to begin with, which resulted in the exclusion of certain categories of women who are more in need of agricultural intervention and access to social, human, and physical capital. For instance, only women who have the means to consistently contribute money toward SHGs in their primary function as savings groups are guaranteed membership to the SHG and as a result the FPC, thus capitalizing on their already present social capital (membership in groups and social networks) and financial capital. This practice reveals how inclusion on the basis of previous membership to a group can work adversely to the spirit of empowerment, by excluding marginal and very poor women who are not already members in SHGs.

Furthermore, the process of appointing members to the Board of Directors of the FPC was less election and more selection by the NGO field staff. The women chosen were those who, by the implication of being part of an SHG and thus already actively "participating," were considered more available, educated, and (relatively) free to attend meetings and travel to the NGO field offices, sometimes on very short notice. This group included women who already had some sort of asset holdings in terms of human capital (education, skills, knowledge), social capital (membership in a group that can provide childcare/complete household tasks while she is away), or physical capital (transportation). Thus, the selection process reinforced the status of women who already had access to greater asset holdings than most, leading to elite capture of the FPC. On the other hand, women who may fit these selection criteria but do not want to join could be pressured by household members who want to capture ownership of any assets she may gain by being a governing member of the FPC, thus reducing her decision-making capacity.

During a two-day joint training program held by the NGO for the Board of Directors and village-level NGO field staff (called Village Resource Persons), participants (9 women and 5 men) were educated on a number of topics related to the FPC. They were instructed on agricultural best practices, the necessity of collectivizing farmers, the roles and responsibilities of the Board, and how the benefits of being part of a producer company would reach members in terms of income. Not surprisingly, a large part of the ensuing questions and discussions revolved around the last topic, that of income. One such question concerned forms of identification required to collect profit (bank checks) once products have been sold in the market. The trainer responded that as per FPC rules, bank information provided must be in the name of the shareholder, except in the case of married women who are permitted to provide their husbands' information. Any other male family member must have prior approval from the shareholder in order to provide their bank information. While such provisions may seem logical since many women do not have bank accounts or official identification required to open bank accounts, it leads directly to male capture of any income gained through the FPC.

As a development strategy that targets women for empowerment, a producer company should neither reinforce existing asset inequalities among women, nor should they put in place asset-based barriers such as "over-simplistic criteria for program participation."[45] Trying to increase a certain type of asset without corresponding complementary inputs can only result in empowerment at a superficial level or on paper. The insistence on women's participation by the state and development practitioners without any real thought as to what participation and involvement might mean for the women themselves is reflective of a shallow understanding of the mainstreaming gender narrative. Thus, despite taking steps to rectify some common failures of cooperatives, producer companies in India are still reproducing the problems of elite capture, exclusion of the poor, and promotion of inequity (between women, as well as men and women).

The inadvertent consequences of this are many, one of which is subscription to the mandatory inclusion narrative by the target community themselves. Rather than creating a space within which women are able to meaningfully participate and represent themselves, instead women often end up being inadvertently coerced into attending meetings by their families (male and female members). This is largely due to a perception on the part of their families that simply by attending meetings, these women, and by extension her family, may gain some monetary or development advantage.[46] This assumption is commonly made by both, beneficiaries of development as well as NGO personnel, that women recipients of development benefits will automatically and selflessly extend those benefits to her children and family.[47] While it may be true that participating in SHGs, and by extension producer companies, does accord some women greater decision-making capacities, and they may also gain from knowledge of projects leading to better access to its benefits, yet, taking time off from household and agricultural duties to attend meetings is not a priority for many of these women. In fact, as is commonly known, participation in development quite often adds to women's already burdened daily activities.[48]

Participation and empowerment are not two sides of the same coin. By conflating the two, stakeholders of development risk over-burdening women while at the same time negating the idea of women's agency. During fieldwork, NGO staff were often implicated in confusing participation with agency. A staff member unintentionally revealed this while explaining to me the changes that have occurred within the community in terms of gender ideology. He said that at first, men would refuse to let women from their families attend meetings in public spaces. They would instead offer their own labor and participation for whatever the NGO required. But today, as soon as NGO staff say, "send your wife," the men say "yes." He continued: "He (the husband or father) might not come but she will definitely attend. This is the biggest change that has happened. That they (men) used to say, 'No Sir, you sit here because our women will not come, or tell me what the work is'… now the difference is '…okay Sir, I will not come but my wife will.' So this much confidence is there [in women]… they are making their own decisions by coming to the meetings. They (women) plan what work needs to be done, how it needs to be done." Revealingly, in the very same sentence he contradicts himself by mentioning that men are the ones who "send their women" to participate and then stating that this is how women have become more confident in "making their own decisions." This is the paradox inherent in "participation-as-empowerment" strategies of development. It throws into question the idea of meaningful empowerment through gender mainstreaming narratives that populates current development discourse in India and abroad. Even women express frustration with the constant demand on their time simply to pay lip service to development agenda. Ultimately, issues of participation and empowerment are tied to practicality. As another Bhil woman interviewee questions in annoyance, "If there is someone from the house going to the meeting then why do I need to go?"

Agro-Ecological Impacts

The Western region of the state of Madhya Pradesh is an arid, drought-prone ecological zone, with generally low rainfall. Much of the land area is composed of hard rock which is characterized by low replenishment of the groundwater contained in them. Majority of the population in this region lives in rural areas and is agriculture dependent. The district of Jhabua is considered one of the most impoverished districts in the country and has the lowest Human Development Index in the entire state.[49] The anthropologist Amita Baviskar describes the district of Jhabua as "notorious in development circles as a disaster, a drought-prone moonscape from which people migrate in hordes in search of a livelihood."[50]

A large percentage of India's tribal population, including the Bhil, lives in Madhya Pradesh. These are minority groups with limited access to government extension services, including in agriculture. The Bhil are a largely agricultural community, although in many villages most families can be found to migrate seasonally to nearby cities in search of manual labor. A typical agricultural cycle sees Bhil farmers grow maize, lentils, rice, soybean, peanuts, and cotton from July to October. They harvest and plow the fields for one month for which most migrants return. Some farmers are then able to grow a second crop of chick-peas and wheat over the winter months, from November/December to February/March. March to May is the festival and marriage season for the Bhil. No agriculture work is done, neither is there any farming done during the summer months. While some big farmers are able to get enough yield to sell in markets, most Bhil practice subsistence agriculture. Many households also cultivate vegetable gardens adjacent to their homes for immediate consumption. Cash income from manual labor supplements income from the fields, often being the primary source of income for landless villagers.

Debt and small land holdings are deemed to be key reasons for sustained seasonal migration.[51] Typically, all able-bodied members in the family migrate, including women, leaving behind young children and older members to look after the home and family fields. Often migrants remain outside of the village year-round, except for in harvest season and spring. Thus, they are easy to overlook while planning development programs. Manual labor can include jobs in construction, as security guards, office workers, or even farming for large landowners—any labor for which they are paid in cash. Cities in Madhya Pradesh like Indore or the neighboring state of Gujarat are common sites of migration. Many of my informants mentioned that migrants usually do not enjoy coming back to villages, after having lived in cities with *pakka* (cement) houses, electricity, bathrooms, and other modern amenities such as television sets.

With increasing reliance on cash, Bhil villagers are aware that subsistence farming will not sustain them in a capitalist market economy. They maintain that migration will not stop even after agricultural interventions aimed at farming because cash is a pressing need. Specifically, for villages that are remote, with no industry or employment opportunity nearby, migration will remain a reality. Even for those households with high-yielding fields, small land holdings are an obstacle. No more than two or three members of the family are required for agricultural work for a majority of the year. The rest migrate because "money is needed even if we have food."

Migration and ecological degradation are inextricably connected. The Green Revolution that started in the 1960s exacerbated groundwater use with limited corresponding increase in agricultural productivity. The move to high-yield variety and hybrid seeds drained local water resources contained in hard rock aquifers. Since renewability of groundwater is limited in this region, excessive water use and irrigation has led to water scarcity and extreme drought-like conditions. At the same time, a shift away from low-value food crops and local varieties of water-efficient cereals to high-value cash crops (particularly oilseeds like soybean) further exacerbated groundwater usage. Low-yield fields are compounded with growing pressure from population increase resulting in a proliferation of small (1–2 hectares) and marginal (less that 1 hectare) land holdings in the region. This leads to an increase in "landed" agricultural laborers and increased migration to urban centers.[52,53] Smaller landholdings mean less agricultural yield which pushes more families into endless cycles of debt and migration.

Theoretically, producer companies are meant to be able to address ecological degradation as well as curb high rates of migration to urban centers. According to Trebbin and Hassler, "The emphasis on the collective spirit of these new producer companies stems from the idea that groups of stakeholders (that is, primary producers) are best suited to commonly and sustainably manage and develop community resources such as land and water... [because] farmers' organizations are... concerned with a wider range of activities, such as environmental conservation, in addition to their overall business goals."[54] However, the question remains that if economic liberalization has intensified resource extraction in the peripheries (or rural areas) for the benefit of urban centers, marginalizing farmers in the process, then why should the onus of conservation fall on these same farmers?

The Green Revolution largely contributed to groundwater depletion and a shift away to cash crops to the benefit large-scale farmers and capitalist interests. Similarly, the White Revolution (dairy revolution) in the 1970s contributed to large-scale livestock farming, significantly increasing methane production which severely impacts the environment. As Meena Khandelwal asserts, "The poor drink relatively little milk, because of its high market value."[55] The question that must be asked then is why these marginalized communities are charged with protecting the environment. Scholars[56] have long commented on the asymmetry inherent in the relationship between core and peripheries with regard to conservation efforts. Often it is the small farmer or landless laborer located at the periphery who produces commodities for the consumption of the middle or upper classes in the centers. Yet they are the ones shouldering responsibilities for curbing deforestation, partaking in soil and water conservation, and "safeguarding the environment for future generations".[57]

Elsewhere, ecofeminist scholars[58] have argued that women are natural carers of the environment by virtue of being women. The ecofeminist discourse suggested that women enjoyed a "special" relationship with the environment[59] based on the premise of "natural" and bio-physical connectedness. It posited that women interact with the environment more closely than men on a daily basis through activities that can be considered "reproductive" in nature, such as gathering fuel and fodder, collecting water for household use, and food production.[60] Taking their cue from such literature, the Indian Joint Forest Management program of the 1990s "decided that involving women [in conservation efforts] was not only desirable but necessary since they would be more committed to protecting the forests due to their dependence on its resources more so than men."[61] Such essentialist thought is unfortunately reproduced by studies on producer companies and farmer collectivities when they make assumptions about rural communities', specifically women's, natural inclination toward environmental conservation rather than exploitation. While astutely pointing out the current trend toward feminization of agriculture in India due to increased male migration, Bina Agarwal[62] also advocates for women's collectivities as the road to empowerment for women farmers. However, she neglects to nuance women's participation, agency, or willingness to become members of such collectivities, nor questions why women would be selfless carers of the environment. On the other hand, Baviskar notes in her ethnography of the Bhil an instance where she observes an (woman) informant cutting down a living tree rather than collecting dead wood for fuel. She says that such deforestation is common and "part of a series of practices which tend to treat the forest as a given…[and]… resources seem to be used without any qualms about waste; there is no attempt at conserving for the future."[63] It is my assertion that studies of producer companies must be wary of romanticizing the notion of "selfless" rural farmers who will not engage in exploitative practices by virtue of some higher metaphorical "connection" to their land.[64]

Conclusion

There are certain flaws inherent in the logic of neoliberal development. The primary assertion of neoliberalism in the context of development is that "human well-being can best be advanced by liberating individual entrepreneurial freedoms and skills."[65] Firstly, this conception shifts the responsibility of development onto the "subjects" themselves and moves scrutiny away from the real causes of poverty and disenfranchisement. Unequal socioeconomic and political structures biased toward upper and middle classes are not considered. Rather, poverty is understood a symptom of individual failure.[66] Secondly, "the neoliberal doctrine of limited, small, and participatory government is premised on decentralized power and self-regulating citizens who are not coerced to follow certain regimens but voluntarily submit to – as Barbara Cruikshank phrases it, a 'tutelary power' – such as a social worker, a program, or a therapist, because it is in their self-interest to do so."[67] Producer companies subscribe to the same logic by implying that farmers are responsible for their own upliftment out of poverty despite being integrated into an inherently exploitative modern capitalist system.

A key advantage of producer companies has been that they are meant to operate with minimal government intervention as opposed to cooperatives where political interference and corruption, among other issues, were major reasons for failure.[68] In contrast, most producer companies are set up with support from civil society organizations, non-profits, NGOs, and less frequently, private entities. However, many scholars believe that the state should do more to support the formation and operation of producer companies such as: providing financial support and knowledge dissemination; offering subsidies; encouraging banks to advance credit linkages; and rigorously promoting private sector investment in the companies.[69] Further, others like Tushaar Shah[70] posit that without adequate backing from the state and investment in technical and expertise inputs, producer companies will go the way of earlier cooperatives. He notes that no producer company has as yet been able to match the success of the dairy or sugar cooperatives in India. However, state involvement is never as simple as it may seem. The extent of the damage caused by increased state intervention is aptly demonstrated by the example of the FPC annual general meeting presented in this chapter. Analyzing the current situation through the framework provided by James Ferguson and Akhil Gupta,[71] the Indian state, in its pursuit of participatory and decentralized development, is practicing a different form of governance. Extending Michel Foucault's groundbreaking theory on self-governance and conduct-of-conduct, Ferguson and Gupta have called this "a neoliberal governmentality." Rather than "rolling back" the state in operations of development, the Indian government has instead distributed its responsibilities among non-state (and sometimes state-controlled) entities, along with implicating the targets of development in their own well-being. Poverty alleviation and development narratives in India are therefore far from state-free; rather, they are infused with bureaucratic practices that often nullify the intended consequences of community action and participation.

Since their inception in the early 2000s, producer companies in India have undoubtedly done much to forward the idea of collective action as being beneficial to small-scale farmers. Many of its central principles can, on paper and in practice, greatly help alleviate farmer immiseration and exploitation. Nevertheless, it can be argued that producer companies today are expanding agricultural frontiers in the rural areas of India, along with the negative associations that invariably accompany capitalist expansion. As yet, the ultimate goal of empowerment via producer companies has not been reached by (women) farmers at the agricultural frontiers. Rural communities continue to remain in a zone of production/surplus extraction for the benefit of urban centers, and are impacted by ecological degradation and changes in labor patterns. In a nation plagued by routine farmer suicides, producer companies can prove invaluable to their empowerment, and the agricultural sector as a whole, *if* implemented thoughtfully, with a healthy skepticism of stereotypical assumptions regarding communities located in the peripheries of the global economy.

Notes

1. Jason W. Moore, "Sugar and the Expansion of the Early Modern World-Economy: Commodity Frontiers, Ecological Transformation, and Industrialization," *Review* 23, no. 3 (2000): 412.
2. Ibid., 412.
3. Anika Trebbin, "Linking Small Farmers to Modern Retail Through Producer Organizations—Experiences with Producer Companies in India," *Food Policy* 45 (April 2014). https://doi.org/10.1016/j.foodpol.2013.12.007.
4. Ibid., 35.
5. Ibid.
6. Historian David Washbrook (1990) dates the incorporation of South Asia in the global economy as occurring around 1750, according to Wallerstein's world-system model.
7. P. S. V. Shankar, "Four Decades of Agricultural Development in MP: An Agro-Ecological Sub-Region Approach," *Economic and Political Weekly* 12 (2005): 5014–24.
8. Refer to Bina Agarwal (2010) and other ecofeminist literature.
9. David Lewis, "Anthropology and Development: The Uneasy Relationship" (London: LSE Research Online, 2005), http://eprints.lse.ac.uk/253/.
10. Ibid.
11. Ibid.
12. Sugata Bose, "Instruments and Idioms of Colonial and National Development: India's Historical Experience in Comparative Perspective," in *International Development and the Social Sciences: Essays on the History and Politics of Knowledge*, ed. Frederick Cooper and Randall Packard (Berkeley: University of California Press, 1997), 45–63; David Lewis, "Anthropology and Development: The Uneasy Relationship."
13. David Ludden, "India's Development Regime," in *Colonialism and Culture*, ed. Nicholas B. Dirks (Ann Arbor: University of Michigan Press, 1992), 249.
14. Bose, "Instruments and Idioms of Colonial and National Development: India's Historical Experience in Comparative Perspective," 49.
15. Bose, "Instruments and Idioms of Colonial and National Development: India's Historical Experience in Comparative Perspective"; Partha Chatterjee, *The Nation and Its Fragments: Colonial and Postcolonial*

Histories (Princeton: Princeton University Press, 1993); Akhil Gupta, *Postcolonial Developments: Agriculture in the Making of Modern India* (Durham and London: Duke University Press, 1998); Sudipta Kaviraj, *The Imaginary Institution of India: Politics and Ideas* (New York: Columbia University Press, 2010); and Ludden, "India's Development Regime."

16. Madhav Gadgil and Ramachandra Guha, *Ecology and Equity: The Use and Abuse of Nature in Contemporary India* (London: Routledge, 1995).
17. Gupta, *Postcolonial Developments: Agriculture in the Making of Modern India*.
18. Amita Baviskar, *In the Belly of the River: Tribal Conflicts Over Development in the Narmada Valley* (New York: Oxford University Press, 1995); Gadgil and Guha, *Ecology and Equity*; and Gupta, *Postcolonial Developments*.
19. "Planning Commission, Government of India: Five Year Plans," accessed May 28, 2018, http://planningcommission.gov.in/plans/planrel/fiveyr/welcome.html.
20. Ibid.
21. He went on to become the prime minister of India in 2004.
22. Akhil Gupta, *Red Tape: Bureaucracy, Structural Violence, and Poverty in India* (Durham and London: Duke University Press, 2012).
23. Ibid.
24. See Akhil Gupta (2012) for an enlightening ethnography on how pre-liberalization programs transformed in the wake of liberalization according to neoliberal governmentality.
25. Ibid., 242.
26. Aradhana Sharma, *Logics of Empowerment: Development, Gender, and Governance in Neoliberal India* (Minneapolis: University of Minnesota Press, 2008), 2.
27. Baviskar, *In the Belly of the River*, 26.
28. Trebbin, "Linking Small Farmers to Modern Retail Through Producer Organizations—Experiences with Producer Companies in India."
29. The immense success of dairy cooperatives set up in Western India in the 1970s gave rise to the term "white revolution." These cooperatives turned India from a milk-deficient nation to one of the largest milk producers in the world.
30. Tushaar Shah, "Farmer Producer Companies: Fermenting New Wine for New Bottles," *Economic and Political Weekly* 51, no. 8 (2016): 15–20; Sukhpal Singh and Tarunvir Singh, *Producer Companies in India: A Study of Organization and Performance*, Centre

for Management in Agriculture, IIM, Ahmedabad (2013); and R. Venkattakumar and B.S. Sontakki, "Producer Companies in India-Experiences and Implications," *Indian Research Journal of Extension Education Special Issue* 1 (2012): 7.

31. Tushaar Shah, "Farmer Producer Companies: Fermenting New Wine for New Bottles," *Economic and Political Weekly* 51, no. 8 (2016): 17.
32. Trebbin, "Linking Small Farmers to Modern Retail Through Producer Organizations—Experiences with Producer Companies in India," 38.
33. Anika Trebbin and Markus Hassler, "Farmers' Producer Companies in India: A New Concept for Collective Action?" *Environment and Planning A* 44, no. 2 (February 2012): 413, https://doi.org/10.1068/a44143.
34. Singh and Singh, *Producer Companies in India: A Study of Organization and Performance.*
35. Trebbin and Hassler, "Farmers' Producer Companies in India," 413.
36. Ibid., 415.
37. Ibid.
38. NGO Publication, "Watershed Development Program Manual (Second Amendment)," April 2010.
39. The data presented in this paper is part of a larger dissertation project by Tandon (2019).
40. Sukhpal Singh, "Producer Companies as New Generation Cooperatives," *Economic and Political Weekly* 43, no. 20 (2008): 22–24; Singh and Singh, *Producer Companies in India: A Study of Organization and Performance.*
41. Shah, "Farmer Producer Companies: Fermenting New Wine for New Bottles."
42. *Mahila Kisan Sashaktikaran Yojana* roughly translates to Women Farmers' Empowerment Scheme.
43. Singh and Singh, *Producer Companies in India: A Study of Organization and Performance.*
44. Venkattakumar and Sontakki, "Producer Companies in India-Experiences and Implications."
45. International Food Policy Research Institute (IFPRI), "Gender, Assets, and Agricultural Development Programs: A Conceptual Framework" (Washington, DC: International Food Policy Research Institute, 2011), 17, https://doi.org/10.2499/CAPRiWP99.
46. Maryann R. Cairns, Cassandra L. Workman, and Indrakshi Tandon, "Gender Mainstreaming and Water Development Projects: Analyzing

Unexpected Enviro-Social Impacts in Bolivia, India, and Lesotho," *Gender, Place & Culture* 24, no. 3 (March 4, 2017): 325–42, https://doi.org/10.1080/0966369X.2017.1314945.

47. Srilatha Batliwala and Deepa Dhanraj, "Gender Myths That Instrumentalise Women: A View from the Indian Frontline." *IDS Bulletin* (Special Issue *Repositioning Feminisms in Gender and Development*) 35, no. 4 (2004): 11–18; Kalpana Wilson, "'Race', Gender and Neoliberalism: Changing Visual Representations in Development." *Third World Quarterly* 32, no. 2 (March 2011): 315–31. https://doi.org/10.1080/01436597.2011.560471.
48. Srilatha Batliwala and Deepa Dhanraj, "Gender Myths That Instrumentalise Women: A View from the Indian Frontline." *IDS Bulletin* (Special Issue *Repositioning Feminisms in Gender and Development*) 35, no. 4 (2004): 11–18.
49. Government of Madhya Pradesh, "Madhya Pradesh Human Development Report 2007," 2007, http://www.dif.mp.gov.in/MPHDR2007.htm.
50. Amita Baviskar, "The Dream Machine: The Model Development Project and the Remaking of the State," in *Growth, Equity, Environment and Population: Economic and Sociological Perspectives*, ed. Kanchan Chopra and C.H. Hanumantha Rao (New Delhi: Thousand Oaks: Sage, 2008), 288.
51. See Mosse (2005), Mosse et al. (2002), Mosse et al. (2005) for more on Bhil migration.
52. Shankar, "Four Decades of Agricultural Development in MP: An Agro-Ecological Sub-Region Approach."
53. My own fieldwork in Jhabua supports this data. The village where I conducted research is considered a relatively impoverished village due to its population size and relatively smaller land holdings.
54. Trebbin and Hassler, "Farmers' Producer Companies in India," 417.
55. Meena Khandelwal, "Cooking with Firewood: Deep Meaning and Environmental Materialities in a Globalized World," in *Mapping Feminist Anthropology in the Twenty-First Century*, ed. Ellen Lewin and Leni M. Silverstein (New Brunswick, NJ: Rutgers University Press, 2016), 222.
56. Baviskar, *In the Belly of the River*; Gadgil and Guha, *Ecology and Equity*.
57. Felix Padel and Samarendra Das, "Cultural Genocide and the Rhetoric of Sustainable Mining in East India," *Contemporary South Asia* 18, no. 3 (September 2010): 338, https://doi.org/10.1080/09584935.2010.503871.

58. Maria Mies and Vandana Shiva, *Ecofeminism* (London: Zed Books, 1993).
59. Melissa Leach and Cathy Green, "Gender and Environment History: From Representation of Women and Nature to Gender Analysis of Ecology and Politics," *Environment and History* 3, no. 3 (1997): 343–70.
60. Indrakshi Tandon, "The Women-Nature Correlation: Mapping the Legacy of Ecofeminism," *Voices* 12, no. 1 (2012): 15–22.
61. Ibid., 17.
62. Bina Agarwal, "Rethinking Agricultural Production Collectivities," *Economic and Political Weekly* 45, no. 9 (2010): 64–78.
63. Baviskar, *In the Belly of the River*, 148.
64. Anthropologists have long warned against the tendency to "romanticize the local." See Alvard (1993), Diamond (1986), Ellingson (2001), Hames (2007), Redford (1991), and Smith et al. (1983) for more on the "Noble Savage" debate.
65. David Harvey, *A Brief History of Neoliberalism* (Oxford: Oxford University Press, 2007), 2.
66. Sharma, *Logics of Empowerment*.
67. Ibid., 17.
68. Singh, "Producer Companies as New Generation Cooperatives."
69. Singh; Trebbin, "Linking Small Farmers to Modern Retail Through Producer Organizations—Experiences with Producer Companies in India"; Venkattakumar and Sontakki, "Producer Companies in India-Experiences and Implications."
70. Shah, "Farmer Producer Companies: Fermenting New Wine for New Bottles."
71. James Ferguson and Akhil Gupta, "Spatializing States: Toward an Ethnography of Neoliberal Governmentality," *American Ethnologist* 29, no. 4 (2002): 981–1002.

Bibliography

Agarwal, Bina. "Rethinking Agricultural Production Collectivities." *Economic and Political Weekly* 45, no. 9 (2010): 64–78.

Alvard, Michael S. "Testing the 'Ecologically Noble Savage' Hypothesis: Interspecific Prey Choice by Piro Hunters of Amazonian Peru." *Human Ecology* 21, no. 4 (December 1993): 355–87. https://doi.org/10.1007/BF00891140.

Batliwala, Srilatha, and Deepa Dhanraj. "Gender Myths That Instrumentalise Women: A View from the Indian Frontline." *IDS Bulletin* (Special Issue *Repositioning Feminisms in Gender and Development*) 35, no. 4 (October 1, 2004): 11–18. https://doi.org/10.1111/j.1759-5436.2004.tb00150.x.

Baviskar, Amita. *In the Belly of the River: Tribal Conflicts Over Development in the Narmada Valley*. New York: Oxford University Press, 1995.

———. "The Dream Machine: The Model Development Project and The Remaking of the State." In *Growth, Equity, Environment and Population: Economic and Sociological Perspectives*, edited by Kanchan Chopra and C.H. Hanumantha Rao, 287–307. New Delhi; Thousand Oaks: Sage Publications, 2008.

Bose, Sugata. "Instruments and Idioms of Colonial and National Development: India's Historical Experience in Comparative Perspective." In *International Development and the Social Sciences: Essays on the History and Politics of Knowledge*, edited by Frederick Cooper and Randall Packard, 45–63. Berkeley: University of California Press, 1997.

Cairns, Maryann R., Cassandra L. Workman, and Indrakshi Tandon. "Gender Mainstreaming and Water Development Projects: Analyzing Unexpected Enviro-Social Impacts in Bolivia, India, and Lesotho." *Gender, Place & Culture* 24, no. 3 (March 4, 2017): 325–42. https://doi.org/10.1080/0966369X.2017.1314945.

Chatterjee, Partha. *The Nation and Its Fragments: Colonial and Postcolonial Histories*. Princeton: Princeton University Press, 1993.

Diamond, Jared M. "The Environmentalist Myth." *Nature* 324, no. 6092 (November 1, 1986): 19–20. https://doi.org/10.1038/324019a0.

Ellingson, Ter. *The Myth of the Noble Savage*. Berkeley: University of California Press, 2001.

Ferguson, James, and Akhil Gupta. "Spatializing States: Toward an Ethnography of Neoliberal Governmentality." *American Ethnologist* 29, no. 4 (2002): 981–1002.

Gadgil, Madhav, and Ramachandra Guha. *Ecology and Equity: The Use and Abuse of Nature in Contemporary India*. London: Routledge, 1995.

Government of Madhya Pradesh. "Madhya Pradesh Human Development Report 2007," 2007. http://www.dif.mp.gov.in/MPHDR2007.htm.

Gupta, Akhil. *Postcolonial Developments: Agriculture in the Making of Modern India*. Durham and London: Duke University Press, 1998.

———. *Red Tape: Bureaucracy, Structural Violence, and Poverty in India*. Durham and London: Duke University Press, 2012.

Hames, Raymond. "The Ecologically Noble Savage Debate." *Annual Review of Anthropology* 36 (September 2007): 177–190. https://doi.org/10.1146/annurev.anthro.35.081705.123321.

Harvey, David. *A Brief History of Neoliberalism*. Oxford: Oxford University Press, 2007.

Kaviraj, Sudipta. *The Imaginary Institution of India: Politics and Ideas*. New York: Columbia University Press, 2010.

Khandelwal, Meena. "Cooking with Firewood: Deep Meaning and Environmental Materialities in a Globalized World." In *Mapping Feminist Anthropology in the Twenty-First Century*, edited by Ellen Lewin and Leni M. Silverstein, 211–33. New Brunswick, NJ: Rutgers University Press, 2016.

Leach, Melissa, and Cathy Green. "Gender and Environment History: From Representation of Women and Nature to Gender Analysis of Ecology and Politics." *Environment and History* 3, no. 3 (1997): 343–70.

Lewis, David. "Anthropology and Development: The Uneasy Relationship." London: LSE Research Online, 2005. http://eprints.lse.ac.uk/253/.

Ludden, David. "India's Development Regime." In *Colonialism and Culture*, edited by Nicholas B. Dirks. Ann Arbor: University of Michigan Press, 1992.

Mies, Maria, and Vandana Shiva. *Ecofeminism*. London: Zed Books, 1993. https://www.cabdirect.org/cabdirect/abstract/19941800191.

Moore, Jason W. "Sugar and the Expansion of the Early Modern World-Economy: Commodity Frontiers, Ecological Transformation, and Industrialization." *Review* 23, no. 3 (2000): 409–33.

Mosse, David. "Cultivating Development: An Ethnography of Aid Policy and Practice." *Anthropology, Culture, and Society*. London; Ann Arbor, MI: Pluto Press, 2005.

Mosse, David, Sanjeev Gupta, Mona Mehta, Vidya Shah, Julia fnms Rees, and KRIBP Project Team. "Brokered Livelihoods: Debt, Labour Migration and Development in Tribal Western India." *The Journal of Development Studies* 38, no. 5 (June 1, 2002): 59–88. https://doi.org/10.1080/00220380412331322511.

Mosse, David, Sanjeev Gupta, and Vidya Shah. "On the Margins in the City: Adivasi Seasonal Labour Migration in Western India." *Economic and Political Weekly* 40, no. 28 (2005): 3025–38.

NGO Publication. "Watershed Development Program Manual (Second Amendment)," April 2010.

Padel, Felix, and Samarendra Das. "Cultural Genocide and the Rhetoric of Sustainable Mining in East India." *Contemporary South Asia* 18, no. 3 (September 2010): 333–41. https://doi.org/10.1080/09584935.2010.503871.

"Planning Commission, Government of India: Five Year Plans." Accessed May 28, 2018. http://planningcommission.gov.in/plans/planrel/fiveyr/welcome.html.

Redford, Kent H. "The Ecologically Noble Savage." *Cultural Survival Quarterly* 15, no. 1 (January 31, 1991): 46.

Research Institute (IFPRI), International Food Policy. "Gender, Assets, and Agricultural Development Programs: A Conceptual Framework." Washington, DC: International Food Policy Research Institute, 2011. https://doi.org/10.2499/CAPRiWP99.

Shah, Tushaar. "Farmer Producer Companies: Fermenting New Wine for New Bottles." *Economic and Political Weekly* 51, no. 8 (2016): 15–20.

Shankar, P.S.V. "Four Decades of Agricultural Development in MP: An Agro-Ecological Sub-Region Approach." *Economic and Political Weekly* 12 (2005): 5014–24.

Sharma, Aradhana. *Logics of Empowerment: Development, Gender, and Governance in Neoliberal India*. Minneapolis: University of Minnesota Press, 2008.

Singh, Sukhpal. "Producer Companies as New Generation Cooperatives." *Economic and Political Weekly* 43, no. 20 (2008): 22–24.

Singh, Sukhpal, and Tarunvir Singh. *Producer Companies in India: A Study of Organization and Performance*. Centre for Management in Agriculture, IIM Ahmedabad, 2013.

Smith, Eric Alden, Robert L. Bettinger, Charles A. Bishop, Valda Blundell, Elizabeth Cashdan, Michael J. Casimir, Andrew L. Christenson, et al. "Anthropological Applications of Optimal Foraging Theory: A Critical Review [and Comments and Reply]." *Current Anthropology* 24, no. 5 (December 1983): 625–51. https://doi.org/10.1086/203066.

Tandon, Indrakshi. "The Women-Nature Correlation: Mapping the Legacy of Ecofeminism." *Voices* 12, no. 1 (2012): 15–22.

Tandon, Indrakshi. "'We Get Nothing': An Ethnography of Participatory Development and Gender Mainstreaming in a Water Project for the Bhil of Central India." PhD diss., University at Albany SUNY, 2019.

Trebbin, Anika. "Linking Small Farmers to Modern Retail Through Producer Organizations—Experiences with Producer Companies in India." *Food Policy* 45 (April 2014): 35–44. https://doi.org/10.1016/j.foodpol.2013.12.007.

Trebbin, Anika, and Markus Hassler. "Farmers' Producer Companies in India: A New Concept for Collective Action?" *Environment and Planning A* 44, no. 2 (February 2012): 411–27. https://doi.org/10.1068/a44143.

Venkattakumar, R., and B.S. Sontakki. "Producer Companies in India-Experiences and Implications." *Indian Research Journal of Extension Education Special Issue* 1 (2012): 7.

Washbrook, David. "South Asia, the World System, and World Capitalism." *The Journal of Asian Studies* 49, no. 3 (August 1990): 479–508. https://doi.org/10.2307/2057768.

5

Ecosystems as Commodity Frontiers—Challenges Faced by Land Set Aside as Protected Areas (PAs) in the Dubai Emirate, United Arab Emirates (UAE)

Brigitte Howarth, Tamer Khafaga, Greg Simkins and Sabrina Joseph

Introduction

Land development in the UAE rapidly expanded with the arrival of oil wealth in the late 1950s in the Emirate of Abu Dhabi.[1] The rise of the oil economy brought with it the increasing commodification of land. The first manifestation of this was with the introduction of modern agriculture in the mid-twentieth century. British colonial authorities working closely with coastal rulers took a keen interest in developing land and water resources during this period, partly in the hopes that this would improve local people's standard of living, support emerging urban centres, and allow for the spread of modern agriculture. The emergence of protected areas (PAs) as commodity frontiers must be looked at in the context of the history of land commercialization in the country.

B. Howarth (✉) · T. Khafaga · G. Simkins · S. Joseph
Dubai, United Arab Emirates
e-mail: brigitte.howarth@zu.ac.ae

S. Joseph
e-mail: sjoseph@aud.edu

S. Joseph (ed.), *Commodity Frontiers and Global Capitalist Expansion*,
Palgrave Studies in Economic History, https://doi.org/10.1007/978-3-030-15322-9_5

In their study of nature tourism and forest conservation in South India, Daniel and Ursula Munster argue that the commodification of nature and landscape is the continuation of an earlier process of capitalist transformation instigated by the spread of modern agriculture. According to this perspective, nature tourism is simply a new opportunity for accumulation.[2] This is all the more relevant in the United Arab Emirates (UAE) given the harsh environmental conditions that work against agricultural expansion and necessitate other 'marketable' uses of land. Ultimately, the rise of capitalist agriculture in the region transformed customary farming practices (which were more communal in nature), spurred land privatization, altered labour arrangements on farms, and impacted the desert ecology itself. With the establishment of the United Arab Emirates in 1971, the new government built on earlier efforts by the British to introduce modern agriculture, including for instance fodder production and cash crop farming. From 1978 to 1980, the government supported various agricultural trials.[3] With the spread of cultivated areas also came the spread of forestry plantations. State discourses have highlighted how such 'greening the desert' initiatives promote economic diversification and combat desertification.[4] In practice, however, such cultivation has depleted groundwater resources and threatened biodiversity.

Customary practices of sharing natural resources among tribes gave way to boundaries, private property, and centralized state control over natural desert lands and water resources.[5] Using Jason Moore's concept of the 'commodity frontier' to understand the development and function of PAs in Dubai allows us to situate the emergence of these areas within the broader context of capitalist expansion in the region.[6] Furthermore, while environmental degradation has certainly been a consequence of capitalist expansion, the latter has also given rise to conservation agendas, which in turn have reinforced processes of land commodification that were already in place.

Further diversification into tourism has grown in the past two decades, and currently, Dubai is bracing itself for the arrival of crowds from around the globe as it hosts Expo in 2020. The population of the UAE has grown exponentially in the past few decades (both expatriate and local), as has the country's infrastructure including road networks, residential areas, schools, academic institutions, industrial facilities, airports, seaports, commercial outlets, and land reclamation creating megastructures such as the offshore island projects. While many of the terrestrial projects have modified existing strata, some terrestrial remodelling has altered the land utterly such as the recently completed Dubai Canal. In deserts, such advancement is seen as the development of apparently barren landscapes. Such development has resulted in ecological degradation, which in turn has instigated a significant shift in recent years towards environmental protection with the creation of PAs. The Emirate of Fujairah declared a mountain wadi (Wadi Wurayah) a PA in 2009. This site is listed as an IUCN category II PA as well as having the recognition of being a Ramsar site of international importance.[7] While the creation of PAs in the UAE should mitigate the impact of development, there are significant challenges to be overcome.

The UAE's land surface is mostly a sand desert.[8] Despite the appearance of sparsely vegetated sandy expanses, sand dunes and their related microhabitats, and gravel plains are diverse both in habitat type[9] as well as being home to innumerable amounts of species biodiversity, most of which are very specialized in order to survive the extreme heat of the summer, and the relative coolness of the winter months. Lying within the approximate geographical range of latitude 22–26° N and longitude 51–56° E, and being situated in the Northern Hemisphere, the deserts of the UAE experience seasons although transitional seasonal changes are subtle, whereas the extremes are noticeable such as intense heat during April to October with relatively cold winter months. During 2017, the hottest day in Dubai was recorded to be July 19th reaching 47 °C, and the coldest temperatures during the winter season were registered as 18 °C on February 3rd diurnally, and a night-time temperature of 11 °C on February 4th according to Weather Underground data collected at Dubai Airport.

Life in the Desert—An Example

Organisms living in such environments have specific adaptations to survive; many reptiles and small mammals are nocturnal, spending most of their time awake during the night, and many trees, shrubs, and other annual/perennial plants have either no leaves, reduced leaves, or leaves that are grey or sport other mechanisms of reflection of harmful UV rays. Other organisms (e.g. insects) have life cycles whereby they occur as adults during the colder months, remaining either as juvenile or pupal stages in the ground during the hotter months. Despite the challenges faced by desert fauna and flora, they exist in high numbers. Rather than describe all taxa that occur, we illustrate species richness using a proxy taxon, namely arthropods, and of those mainly insects, and how recent studies have added to the overall knowledge of this taxon in the UAE. Insects are an integral part of ecosystems contributing vast amounts of ecosystem services. Ecosystem services are intricately linked processes that are exceedingly difficult to quantify and evaluate due to their complexity.[10] A tangible and frequently discussed ecosystem service is the contribution of social bees as pollinators. However, there are many other bees and other insects such as flies, butterflies, beetles, and ants to name a few that are active and essential pollinators.[11]

Until 2005, the information on insects in the UAE was scattered in the literature, and the first publication to bring together insect records was a checklist of published records.[12] Subsequently, in 2008, a further publication drew on records from the literature, data held by the entomology section of the Environment Agency—Abu Dhabi (EAD), and data held by the authors in their private collections.[13] At this stage, a total of 1528 insects had been recorded from the UAE.[14] While there are further scattered records in the literature that have been added to the total number of species since then, with some being significant in their contributions, a systematic approach to create an insect/arthropod inventory culminated in the publication of six volumes of arthropod fauna from 2008 to 2016, the data of which are summarized in Table 5.1.[15] These publications have added an additional 2507 species to the total count, of which 434 were records 'new to science'. The records that are classified as 'new to science' are species that have thus far been recorded from the UAE only, and therefore their status is currently 'endemic'. This means that almost 11% of the known arthropod fauna of the UAE is endemic and, to date, no further studies exist to understand the individual habitat requirements and contributions of each of the recently added endemic species, and it is unknown

Table 5.1 Consolidated data published in 6 volumes of arthropod fauna of the UAE between 2008 and 2016

Publication	Arthropods new to the UAE	Arthropods new to science
van Harten, Volume 1	570	87
van Harten, Volume 2	390	85
van Harten, Volume 3	400	71
van Harten, Volume 4	469	90
van Harten, Volume 5	341	45
van Harten, Volume 6	337	56
Total	**2507**	**434**

what the impact would be on the ecosystems they are a part of if these organisms became extinct.

As is the case in habitats around the world, the likelihood is that endemic species are significant contributors in the complex food chains and food webs and the loss of any of these species would signify a negative change in the respective ecosystems. In many areas of the Dubai Emirate, development has brought about habitat reduction, fragmentation, modification, and destruction, reducing species biodiversity significantly to the point that habitats are becoming 'impoverished'. Impoverished and fragmented ecosystems no longer fulfil their ecological roles resulting in diminished ecosystem services.[16]

The Birth of PAs in the Dubai Emirate

In recent years, the UAE has ratified a number of international conventions (e.g. Ramsar; Convention on Biological Diversity [CBD]). The UAE has been involved in documenting the state of the environment (e.g. State of the Environment Report, The Executive Council, Dubai; Biodiversity Strategy [federal Ministry of Climate Change and Environment, formerly the Ministry of Environment and Water]) and has made a number of protection provisions in federal laws (e.g. Federal Law No. [24] of 1999 for the Protection and Development of the Environment). In addition, the Dubai Emirate, and specifically the government of Dubai, declared six PAs as 'natural reserves' in 2014 (Decree No. [22] of 2014 which details the establishment of reserves based on the provisions of Law No. [11] of 2003 on Nature Reserves within the Dubai Emirate).[17] As it is the government that takes the lead in the development of Dubai,[18] it is not surprising that this includes decision-making surrounding PAs. After the initial six regions being protected, two more reserves were added, bringing the total to eight PAs with specific names for each (see Table 5.2).

Given that the area of the Dubai Emirate is 4114 km^2, with the entire UAE area occupying approximately 83,600 km^2, it means that the Dubai Emirate has set aside 31% of its surface area as PAs. The intention of setting aside land for protection is articulated in the objectives (Article 4) of Law No. (11) of 2003 on Nature Reserves within the Emirate of Dubai (https://www.ddcr.org/en/board-sponsors.aspx?Menu=1):

- Protecting the natural environment, preserving their original states, and ensuring the maintenance of their aesthetics in any development thereof.
- Preserving the natural resources and the biodiversity of life within the PAs, including the preservation of vegetation, animals and migrant and resident birdlife.
- Protection of the geology and geographic features of the reserves.
- Actively manage the reserves in a manner which assists in the propagation of rare and endangered species, and their reintroduction.

Table 5.2 List of protected areas in the Dubai Emirate

Protected area	Size (km^2)	% of Emirate of Dubai
Al Marmoum Conservation Reserve	990	24
Al Wohoosh Desert Conservation Reserve	15.1	0.4
Dubai Desert Conservation Reserve	225	5.4
Ghaf Nazwa Conservation Reserve	0.1	0.002
Hatta Mountain Conservation Area	27.4	0.67
Jebel Ali Marine Sanctuary[a]	21.9	0.53
Jebel Nazwa Conservation Reserve	1.1	0.03
Ras Al Khor Wildlife Sanctuary	6.2	0.15
Total	**1286.8**	**31.18**

[a]It should be noted that JAMS mostly comprises a marine protected area off-shore, with a reduced surface area being protected on land

- The monitoring of wildlife and naturally occurring species, their numbers, areas of breeding, the growth of populations, and the natural habitats in which they occur.
- The protecting of locations that are considered the natural range and environment of the species, whether animal or plant and specifically protecting areas critical to the breeding, growth or development of the populations.
- Contributing to the development of ecologically based tourism in the emirate.

Pressures on the PAs

Deserts in the UAE are utilized or exploited in many ways, which include farming (livestock and agriculture), residential, and commercial development that translates into urban sprawl (e.g. Dubailand, Academic City Dubai, Academic City Abu Dhabi, etc.). Also, commercial safari tour operators that are either based in camps set up in patches of desert, with activities that radiate out into the dunes such as camel riding, and 'dune bashing', or visiting tour operators, offering desert drive experiences also impact the desert greatly. While some of the camps usually operate during the cooler months, skeleton staff and the infrastructure remain throughout the year, and other camps remain fully operational, though with fewer tourists visiting them. During peak times, camps receive hundreds of guests per day. These types of activities occur within the PAs. One of the PAs (Dubai Desert Conservation Reserve or DDCR) which has a total of four tour operators using base camps within the reserve and one visiting tour operator offering desert nature drives receives 250,000–300,000 tourists per year. Another PA (Al Wohoosh Desert Conservation Reserve) includes several camps in the Northern part of the reserve, with the authors recording five during their October 2017 field survey. Patches of PA deserts have also been used to grow artificially irrigated plantations of mainly native and regional trees, but also including exotic species (i.e. species that do not naturally occur in the UAE). Unlike naturally occurring groves, e.g. ghaf (*Prosopis cineraria*), plantations of any sort in the UAE require regular irrigation as root systems of trees artificially planted usually can't tap into the groundwater. The addition of water to the sandy ecosystem changes the nature of desert ecosystems. Recreational uses of the PA deserts include gatherings for BBQs, off-road driving, cycling tracks, horse endurance tracks, camping, and peripheral impacts due to traditional falconry (e.g. off-road driving on gravel plains and dunes). All the activities above impact the natural ecosystem of the desert in many ways, all of which can be classified into habitat fragmentation and destruction. As was first discussed in 1967 by MacArthur and Wilson in their article on island biogeography, habitats can be compared to habitat 'islands', and as such, habitats that are smaller and more isolated support fewer species, and several large-scale studies have provided empirical evidence to support this theory.[19]

The eight PAs are not immune to development that continues to grow and impact the reserves. To understand the pressures currently associated with the PAs, some of the eight PAs are examined more closely. Data are presented for three of the four sandy desert and dune habitat PAs (Al Wohoosh Conservation Area; Al Marmoum Conservation Reserve; DDCR) as these share similarities.

As each infrastructure on the reserves represents fragmentation of or a threat to the habitat in question, infrastructure recorded is therefore referred to as 'fragmentation type' in Table 5.3. Threats are also added to Table 5.3 insofar as they impact on biodiversity on the reserves.

It should be noted that the list provided is not exhaustive and that further fragmentation types and threats are likely to be present on both reserves, but not recorded by the authors to date.

Perhaps the most destructive activity impacting the sandy desert PAs is related to camels. In its 2017 Abu Dhabi State of the Environment Report, EAD state that '*Over-grazing has been a significant threat to natural desert vegetation over the past few decades, leading to the degradation of some of these areas. Grazing by camels and other livestock is a major issue and limits regeneration in overgrazed areas*'.[20] Camel farms are found throughout the UAE in every Emirate. An example of a camel farm can be seen in Fig. 5.1.

Although total numbers of camels are not available for the whole of the UAE, data presented for the Abu Dhabi Emirate by EAD in 2017

Table 5.3 Fragmentation types and threats recorded at Al Marmoum Conservation Reserve and Al Wohoosh Desert Conservation Reserve

Fragmentation type/threat	Description
Groundwater abstraction (wells and manhole covers)	Wells usually comprise two structures, a pump and a metre. Manhole covers take up the same amount of space as wells as a concrete infrastructure has to be built in the sand
Groundwater abstraction (pump house)	Larger buildings, occasionally with a fence
Plantations	Include irrigated local and exotic plant species
Fencing	Fences are either for farms (e.g. camel farms, temporary or permanent fencing), protected area boundaries, or to fence off private and military land
Roads and tracks	Some of the tracks are compacted sand tracks, others are asphalted roads and/or bicycle tracks
Developed areas	Include military areas, solar parks, hotels, shops, desert safari camps, stables, and recreational areas
Habitat re-modelling	E.g. man-made lakes, plantation of oasis, crop plantations in irrigated fenced areas
Off-road driving	Off-road driving on both reserves includes large 4 × 4 vehicles, as well as lighter four-wheel dune buggies or motorbikes
Over-grazing	Grazers such as camels, and to a lesser extent two species of gazelle. Oryx is considered to contribute minimally to grazing pressure
Littering (small scale and large scale)	Large-scale littering includes disused structures such as wells, farms, fences, shacks, houses, whereas small-scale littering includes domestic waste left by campers/visitors to the reserves or safari parks, as well as domestic waste from the work force that tends the farms and safari parks

estimated that there were a total of 25,200 camel farms, with a total of 408,470 camels.[21] Camel farms can be divided into four types as follows:

- Grazing camel farms
- Racing camel farms

Fig. 5.1 A typical camel farm at the Al Wohoosh Conservation Reserve. The pen holds a large amount of camels, with a fencing structure that interrupts the natural habitat also. It should be noted that pens are often located along gravel plains in sandy habitats making access to the farms easier, causing negative impacts on the ecology of gravel plains

- Breeding farms (including camels, goats, sheep)
- Camel milk farms

Narratives collected from a local Emirati camel owner indicate that camels in racing, breeding, and milk farms are generally not released from the farms for grazing, whereas camels kept as grazing herds rely on both, feeding with subsidized imported, and sometimes locally grown fodder, as well as grazing of natural vegetation in the vicinity of the camel farms, in whatever habitat the farm may be (e.g. while camel farms are mainly found on flat surfaced habitats (sand and/or gravel plains), camel farms are also found at the foothills of mountains; camels will roam in rocky terrain, even though they are usually a sandy desert dweller). The impact of grazing camels cannot be underestimated, especially given the large number of camels in the UAE. To an untrained eye, sandy deserts can often have an outward appearance of being sparsely vegetated, and frequently the descriptions of arid and hyper-arid sandy deserts that occur in the UAE portray the landscape as 'barren'. There can be arid years where rainfall has been sparse, and annuals[22] usually seen in March and April following sufficient winter rains remain absent. However, the sands of the UAE are in fact a seed bank that house both annual and perennial seeds that can remain dormant for many years and then germinate under the right conditions. Camel grazing mainly affects small perennials, e.g. perennial grasses,[23] though camels feed on annuals as well as larger perennials. Perennial seeds that germinate will not grow into larger plants unless their roots reach a permanently wet layer before the beginning of the dry season.[24] In addition, many of the perennial plants that may appear to be desiccated often have live roots that will resurrect during good rainy seasons. This in part is due to many perennial shrubs having extensive root systems below the surface. In a description of the shrub *Leptadenia pyrotechnica*, a shrub commonly found in many of the PAs, its roots were found to extend to approximately 12 m below the surface, with a radius of 10 m.[25] To find out whether grazing impacted the recovery of the flora, one of the studies conducted within the DDCR involved excluding grazers by building fences of 250 × 250 m in two different habitats within the reserve during September 2011 (www.ddcr.org). The two habitats included a sand dune enclosure as well as a sandy gravel plain. While the study is still ongoing, recovery of vegetation has already been observed when compared to outside of the fence. The improvement can be seen in Fig. 5.2 of the sand dune enclosure.

Given the above, many stakeholders gain to benefit from their operations in the PAs discussed, and as such, the pressure on biodiversity in the reserves is high. Al Marmoum Conservation Reserve comprises a non-fenced reserve, and as such, fragmentation types/threats listed above occur throughout the Al Marmoum designated area. Al Wohoosh Desert Conservation Area is fenced; however, there is no access control, and apart from the southern part of the reserve which includes large dunes and is, therefore, less accessible, the remainder of the reserve is severely degraded, and thus impoverished, due to the fragmentation types/threats mentioned in Table 5.3. The authors make a note of the massive water abstraction infrastructure observed at Al Wohoosh Desert Conservation Area. Within the 15.1 km^2 area, more than 70 double structures and pump houses were recorded, many of which appear to be no longer in use (Fig. 5.3).

It is suspected that initially further development for livestock farming and possibly commercial and residential development was planned and that this might account for the high number of wells/utility hole covers/metres/pump houses that exist on the reserve.

Fig. 5.2 The sand dune enclosure at the DDCR shows the difference in vegetation cover between the outer unfenced area in comparison with the fenced area. Excluding grazers, including ungulates and camels, allows the natural seed bank in the ground to germinate under the right conditions with both annuals and perennials then recovering due to not being grazed

One of the main differences between the last two reserves is the encouragement at Al Marmoum Conservation Reserve for the survival of some of the larger desert fauna by supplementary feeding (e.g. spiny-tailed lizards, ungulates). Supplemental feeding becomes necessary when populations of grazers exceed carrying capacity on a reserve. As such, a large number of feeding stations were recorded scattered throughout the reserve totalling 67 (Fig. 5.4, white circles), to enhance or supplement feeding. During fieldwork, a census of the ungulates was carried out, with 615 Arabian Oryx, 1098 Arabian Gazelle, and 650 Sand Gazelle counted.[26] Furthermore, Fig. 5.4 clearly shows how Al Marmoum Conservation Reserve is fragmented by roads, infrastructure, plantations and other impacts discussed above.

Fig. 5.3 Water abstraction includes a number of structures such as the one depicted photographed by the authors on the Al Wohoosh Desert Conservation Area

In essence, the PA desert ecosystems are thought of as 'commodities', much as was stated by Worster in his explanation of land becoming commodified. In his discussion of the beginnings of environmental history, Worster describes how 'historians' have often recounted the use of natural resources without including an ecological perspective. What actually happened, though, was the transformation of natural environments into 'agroecosystems', described by Worster as '*an ecosystem reorganized for agricultural purposes – a domesticated ecosystem*'.[27] This, essentially, is habitat fragmentation, which, together with habitat destruction, reduces the overall biodiversity of ecosystems and as such, ecosystems are not 'functioning' as they should, leading to further degradation and impoverishment of the environment. While experts have suggested possible mitigation measures,[28] many of the measures have not been researched in the UAE context to date. Management planning of the PAs is crucial in ensuring the negative

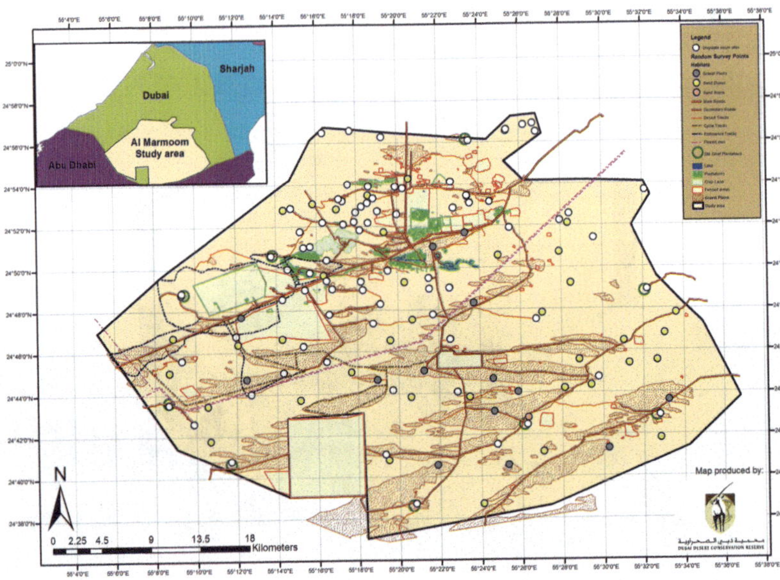

Fig. 5.4 Socio-economic infrastructure of the Al Marmoum Conservation Reserve (*Source* Al Marmoom Desert Conservation Reserve, Preliminary Internal Report, Greg Simkins and Tamer Khafaga, Dubai Desert Conservation Reserve, 30 August 2016, created using ArcMap software)

impact on biodiversity is halted, and one of the eight reserves has made great strides in conservation and highlights of the transformation are discussed below.

The DDCR as an Effective Management Model

As highlighted, impacts on PA desert ecosystems are linked to many anthropogenic activities that directly or indirectly reduce biodiversity. In the late 1990s in the very southern part of the Dubai Emirate, an area of the desert was commodified for the construction of an exclusive resort and spa complex that was opened by Emirates Airlines (Al Maha Desert Resort and Spa) on land allocated to them by Dubai Government. The concept of this hotel was to offer visitors a unique wildlife and desert experience in natural surroundings. The southern part of Dubai was primarily home to camel farms and activities impacting the desert in much the same way as has been described above. To build the resort, an area comprising 27 km^2 was fenced, excluding grazing camels. From the time of opening of the resort, 5% of the profits have been invested in conservation projects. Following an environmental audit carried out by resort managers of the surrounding area adjacent to the resort in 2001, current and potential threats to the desert ecosystem were highlighted. This led to a proposal of a more comprehensive conservation area to be created around the resort and was presented by the owner of Emirates Airlines to the Ruler of Dubai. The Ruler of Dubai approved the proposal and allocated a total of 225 km^2, which includes the land occupied by the resort. The initial steps of creating the DDCR included the establishment of a governing board originally comprising of the head of Emirates Airlines and other influential leaders of governmental organizations (e.g. utility organizations). The board outlined the goals and values that continue to be the main remit of the reserve, which are listed below:

- To create a permanent PA which ensures the future of the region's desert habitats and biodiversity managed according to sound scientific ecological principles, aimed at protecting natural resources (water being the most obvious one, but extending to many others as well), and maintaining original desert landscapes.
- To ensure that the community and visitors have access to the Reserve through the sustainable and responsible development of commercial practices that would not impact on the primary role of conservation and habitat protection.
- To protect the heritage of traditional activities which have become a part of the region's history and culture and maintain the identity of Dubai's tribal beginnings.
- To register and gain international recognition for the Reserve under the United Nations' PAs Management principles, amongst others and to ensure that the DDCR is adequately protected under law.[29]

In 2003, a fence surrounding the whole reserve was built, along with a perimeter track inside of the fence comprising 92 km. This excluded activities and people entering, however, at that time nine tourist camps belonging to four tour operators remained operational inside of the reserve, as well as ten camel (grazing) farms, the latter significantly impacting the aims and goals of the newly established reserve. Over a period of five years, the camel farms were relocated to areas outside of the reserve. The tour operators remained within the reserve and to date have to adhere to strict conduct regulations implemented by a newly appointed reserve management team that first became operational in 2003. Tour operators contribute towards conservation projects by paying a per capita nominal fee for each visitor they bring to the DDCR.

The day-to-day activities (both conservation and administration) on the reserve are managed by senior conservation managers who have established the reserve's rules such as no off-road driving except on designated paths, with fines imposed for violators. Ongoing research and monitoring are providing evidence that the management practices at the DDCR have helped restore the desert ecosystem over the past 15 years of intense management.

Following extensive clean-up operations ridding the reserve of old farm buildings, construction, and other anthropogenic debris, the management approach of the senior conservation team involve the following:

- On-site presence. The DDCR has three security-controlled gates that record and control access to the reserve and the resort. The DDCR office is located on the reserve, with a 24-hour presence of staff to deal with emergencies after working hours. The senior conservation officers actively patrol the reserve during working hours, which are flexible with an on-site presence for 9 hours minimum per conservation officer daily. Occasionally, evening and night surveys mean the team is on the reserve after hours. In addition to the senior conservation officers, the team comprises of reserve artisans (technical and mechanical support), animal helpers, and casual workers.

- Succession without interference. The reserve actively conserves endangered large mammals. However, the ecosystems included within the area are left to recover at their own rate.
- Supplemental feeding to preserve natural vegetation. Over-grazing by the large mammals is not observed in the reserve due to the maintenance of feeding points that are frequently relocated to enhance natural roaming behaviour of the ungulates. Also, feeding occurs once a day in the morning and feed is not replenished which further encourages natural roaming behaviour.
- The integrity of the reserve through holistic practices. Fragmentation, as mentioned above, causes many negative impacts on the habitats and the biodiversity it supports. Ecosystems are interconnected with food chains and food webs that are complex. The reserve has a modest 'track' infrastructure of underlying gravel tracks covered by sand that have been placed strategically to connect tour operator activities, with narrower tracks traversing sensitive habitats. The sand-covered tracks, therefore, create a continual habitat with the surrounding sand sea.
- Conservation through collaboration. One of the strategic initiatives of the DDCR is to interface with local higher education institutions and researchers, pursuing research activities in collaboration with the senior conservation officers. In addition, volunteers and internship students support the research agenda. Research topics include ecological, botanical, and zoological studies, most of which help inform conservation management practices. Senior conservation officers also interface with national and international organizations to share their accumulated knowledge and experience in conservation.

To date, of the three sandy desert and dune habitat PAs, the DDCR represents the most natural environment which was achieved through the implementation of basic management interventions, including controlled tourism. Success at the DDCR required the fencing of the reserve. One of the social impacts often reported as a result of reducing access to land for conservation purposes is discontent among the local population with frequently the poorest people being impacted.[30] While this angle would be problematic if livelihoods depended on income from camel farms, farmers who were relocated to areas outside of the DDCR received equal land as they had occupied within the reserve.

Discussion and Conclusion

The main difference between the DDCR and other PAs is that clearly articulated objectives informed the commodification of nature, with the primary goal being conservation. Given that the conservation objectives of the DDCR are dissimilar to the activities discussed that impact the PAs ecosystems, in essence, the conservation model implemented by the DDCR is an example of green capitalism whereby aspects of the natural world are being brought into the economic sphere.[31] The difference at the DDCR in comparison to other PAs is that a balance is maintained between profit gained from the commodity (PA) and implementation of ecologically friendly measures aimed at mitigating degradation of the environment. In a rapidly developing country with a relatively modest surface area in comparison with other countries, land is commodified in several ways, including infrastructure building, urban sprawl, the expansion of industry and other commercial expansions that are in direct competition with conservation agendas. The government has recognized this, and thus the PAs were created. However, the intent to protect is interpreted in a variety of conflicting ways by stakeholders, specifically those that intend to pursue wealth accumulation through projects within the PAs that do not enhance the conservation aspects, but also by a variety of interpretations of the intent of the PAs protective status.

In an article published in the local newspaper *The National* in early 2018, the launch of the '*Marmoom Desert Conservation Reserve*' is announced, along with the types of activities that are planned for the reserve.[32] These include some of the activities one might associate with a nature reserve (e.g. bird observation platforms), but it also mentions other initiatives (e.g. cultural; sports and sport events; lakes; plant nursery),[33] many of which will bring their own impacts on the reserve alone for the infrastructure they will require. The law that establishes the nature reserves in Dubai states the following, '*Protecting the natural environment, preserving their original states, and ensuring the maintenance of their aesthetics in any development thereof*'[34] where protection of the natural environment is placed alongside the development of the PA. The use of the word 'development' in the context of the maintenance of the aesthetics of the natural environment in any development thereof could be argued to assume development will take place in the PAs. This could be an indication of PAs being seen as reserved land for development. It should be noted that on closer inspection of the English translation of Law No. (11) of 2003 on Nature Reserves within the Emirate of Dubai, there appears to be a discrepancy between the original Arabic text and the English translation thereof, e.g. the word 'propagation' in the English text, does not occur in the Arabic version. With the inclusion of this word in the context of '*actively manage the reserves in a manner which assists the propagation of rare and endangered species, and their reintroduction*', it shifts the aim towards propagation and reintroduction, negating the conservation agendas.

In his article discussing the commodification of nature, Scales[35] alludes to the taming of nature through technologies, and several examples of this are seen in proposed developments for the PAs (e.g. hydro-electric power production in the Hatta Mountain Reserve).[36] Within the PAs discussed, there is a risk that the implementation of projects will adversely affect species biodiversity and therefore ecosystem services they render as well as overall ecosystem health. Moore eloquently dissects the friction of capitalism, nature, and its interface in his essay 'The Capitalocene, Part 1: On the Nature and Origins of Our Ecological Crisis'.[37] Quite frequently, capitalism is placed at the centre of the reasoning behind the current ecological crisis. However, in ancient history, it was not unusual for areas of land to be protected for reasons other than protecting the natural environment altruistically, but for safeguarding common land or resources for instrumental reasons, e.g. hunting for food, in parts of the world.[38] In more recent years, activities such as tourism have played a vital role alongside species protection in PAs globally.[39] However, it is essential that effective management practices are put in place as there have been many examples of PAs not meeting their conservation targets due to inadequate management, resulting in the loss of species biodiversity.[40] The PAs in the Dubai Emirate are not unusual in facing pressures from economic development, the difference being that without a clear articulation of conservation targets, the PAs are in danger of only being seen as new profitability frontiers.

Acknowledgements The authors wish to thank Dr. Gary Brown for discussion and supplementary information. BH also acknowledges grateful thanks to Zayed University for the use of the research vehicle during fieldwork.

Notes

1. Frauke Heard-Bey, "The Beginning of the Post-imperial Era for the Trucial States from World War 1 to the 1960s," in *United Arab Emirates: A New Perspective*, ed. Ibrahim Al Abed and Peter Hellyer (London: Trident Press, 2001), 119.
2. Daniel Munster and Ursula Munster, "Consuming the Forest in an Environment of Crisis: Nature Tourism, Forest Conservation, and Neoliberal Agriculture in South India," *Development and Change* 43, no. 1 (2012): 205–27.
3. Sabrina Joseph and Brigitte Howarth, "Fertile Sands: Colonial Politics and the Development of Land and Water Resources in the Trucial States, Mid to Late 20th Century," *The Arab World Geographer* 18, no. 3 (2015): 156–57.
4. UAEinteract, "Agricultural Policy Has Been Successful: Humaid," April 16, 2002, accessed July 7, 2015, http://www.uaeinteract.com/docs/Agricultural_policy_has_been_successful_Humaid/3818.htm; UNCCD Secretariat, *Summary of the Second United Arab Emirates National Report to the UNCCD* (Bonn: UNCCD Secretariat, 2002).
5. Sabrina Joseph, "Farming the Desert: Agriculture in the Oil Frontier, the Case of the United Arab Emirates, 1940s to 1990s," *British Journal of Middle Eastern Studies* 45, no. 5 (2018): 678–694, https://doi.org/10.1080/13530194.2017.1320977.
6. Jason W. Moore, "Sugar and the Expansion of the Early Modern World-Economy: Commodity Frontiers, Ecological Transformation, and Industrialization," *Review: A Journal of the Fernand Braudel Center* 23, no. 3 (2000): 409–33.
7. http://uae.panda.org/our_work/fresh_water/wadi_wurayah/, accessed August 16, 2018.
8. Gary Feulner, "Geological Overview," in *The Emirates: A Natural History*, ed. Peter Hellyer and Simon Aspinall (London: Trident Press, 2005), 46.

9. Gary Brown and Benno Böer, "Terrestrial Habitats," in *The Emirates: A Natural History*, ed. Peter Hellyer and Simon Aspinall (London: Trident Press, 2005), 99–102.
10. Nicolás Kosoy and Esteve Corbera, "Payments for Ecosystem Services as Commodity Fetishism," *Ecological Economics* 69 (2010): 1231–33.
11. Romina Rader, Bartomeus Ignasi, Lucas A. Garibaldi, Michael P.D. Garratt, Brad G. Howlett, Rachael Winfree, Saul A. Cunningham, et al., "Non-Bee Insects Are Important Contributors to Global Crop Pollination," *Proceedings of the National Academy of Sciences* 113, no. 1 (2016): 2.
12. Antonius van Harten, *Insects of the UAE: A Checklist of Published Records* (Abu Dhabi: Dar Al Ummah, 2005).
13. Brigitte Howarth and Michael P.T. Gillett, "The Terrestrial and Freshwater Arthropods of Abu Dhabi Emirate," in *Terrestrial Environment of Abu Dhabi Emirate*, ed. Richard Perry (Abu Dhabi: Environment Agency-Abu Dhabi, 2008).
14. Ibid.
15. Antonius van Harten, ed., *Arthropod Fauna of the UAE Volume 1* (Abu Dhabi: Dar Al Ummah, 2008); Antonius van Harten, ed., *Arthropod Fauna of the UAE Volume 2* (Abu Dhabi: Dar Al Ummah, 2009); Antonius van Harten, ed., *Arthropod Fauna of the UAE Volume 3* (Abu Dhabi: Dar Al Ummah, 2010); Antonius van Harten, ed., *Arthropod Fauna of the UAE Volume 4* (Abu Dhabi: Dar Al Ummah, 2011); Antonius van Harten, ed., *Arthropod Fauna of the UAE Volume 5* (Abu Dhabi: Department of the President's Affairs, 2014); Antonius van Harten, ed., *Arthropod Fauna of the UAE Volume 6* (Abu Dhabi: Department of the President's Affairs, 2017).
16. Forest Isbell, David Tilman, Stephen Polasky, and Michel Loreau. "The Biodiversity-Dependent Ecosystem Service Debt," *Ecology Letters* 18, no. 2 (2015): 119.
17. The law is issued in Arabic with an English translation and can be found on the DDCR webpage, https://www.ddcr.org/en/board-sponsors.aspx?Menu=1.
18. Martin Hvidt, "The Dubai Model: An Outline of Key Components of the Development Process in Dubai," *International Journal of Middle Eastern Studies* 41, no. 3 (2009): 401.

19. Of the various studies, the following study provides good empirical evidence: Richard O. Bierregaard, Jr., Thomas E. Lovejoy, et al. "The Biological Dynamics of Tropical Rainforest Fragments," *Bioscience* 42, no. 11 (1992): 859–66.
20. *Abu Dhabi State of the Environment Report* (Abu Dhabi: EAD, 2017), 98.
21. EAD presentation.
22. 'Annuals' are plants that complete a life cycle in one year and are opposed to perennials that persist for many years.
23. David J. Gallacher and Jeffrey P. Hill, "Effects of Camel Grazing on the Ecology of Small Perennial Plants in the Dubai (UAE) Inland Desert," *Journal of Arid Environments* 66, no. 4 (2006): 738–50.
24. Kamal Batanouny, *Adaptations of Desert Organisms—Plants in the Deserts of the Middle East* (Heidelberg: Springer, 2001), 47.
25. Ibid., 50–51.
26. Greg Simkins and Tamer Khafaga, *Al Marmoom Desert Conservation Reserve Preliminary Report* (Dubai Desert Conservation Reserve Internal Report, 2016).
27. Donald Worster, "Transformations of the Earth: Toward an Agroecological Perspective in History," *The Journal of American History* 76, no. 4 (1990): 1093.
28. Andrew S. Gardner and Brigitte Howarth. "Urbanisation in the United Arab Emirates: The Challenges for Ecological Mitigation in a Rapidly Developing Country," *BioRisk* 3 (2009): 27–38.
29. DDCR website at www.ddcr.org, accessed August 16, 2018.
30. Caroline Seagle, "Inverting the Impacts: Mining, Conservation and Sustainability Claims Near the Rio Tinto/QMM Ilmenite Mine in Southeast Madagascar," *The Journal of Peasant Studies* 39, no. 2 (2012): 457; Ivan R. Scales. "Paying for Nature: What Every Conservationist Should Know About Political Economy," *Oryx* 49, no. 2 (2015): 229..
31. Ibid., 227.
32. "Dubai Ruler Launches Marmoom Desert Conservation Reserve," *The National*, January 16, 2018, accessed August 12, 2018, https://www.thenational.ae/uae/environment/dubai-ruler-launches-marmoom-desert-conservation-reserve-1.696015.
33. Ibid.
34. Law No. (11) of 2003 on Nature Reserves within the Emirate of Dubai. https://www.ddcr.org/en/board-sponsors.aspx?Menu=1.

35. Scales, "Paying for Nature," 228.
36. "First of Its Kind: Hatta Hydroelectric Plant Study Underway," *Gulf News*, October 3, 2017, accessed August 15, 2018, https://gulfnews.com/business/energy/first-of-its-kind-hatta-hydroelectric-plant-study-underway-1.2099948.
37. Jason W. Moore, "The Capitalocene, Part I: On the Nature and Origins of Our Ecological Crisis," *The Journal of Peasant Studies* 44, no. 3 (2017): 601–2.
38. James E.M. Watson, Nigel Dudley, Daniel B. Segan, and Marc Hockings, "The Performance and Potential of Protected Areas," *Nature* 515, no. 7525 (2014): 67.
39. Ibid.
40. Ibid., 69.

Bibliography

Batanouny, Kamal. *Adaptations of Desert Organisms—Plants in the Deserts of the Middle East*. Heidelberg: Springer, 2001.

Bierregaard, Richard O., Jr., Thomas E. Lovejoy, Valerie Kapos, Angelo Augusto dos Santos, and Roger W. Hutchings. "The Biological Dynamics of Tropical Rainforest Fragments." *Bioscience* 42, no. 11 (1992): 859–66.

Brown, Gary, and Benno Böer. *Interpretation Manual of the Major Terrestrial Natural and Semi-natural Habitat Types of Abu Dhabi Emirate*. Abu Dhabi: ERWDA Internal Research Report, 2004.

———. "Terrestrial Habitats." In *The Emirates: A Natural History*, edited by Peter Hellyer and Simon Aspinall, 93–107. London: Trident Press, 2005.

Decree No. (22) of 2014. https://www.ddcr.org/media/Ruler_Decree_Number_22-2014.pdf.

Environment Agency—Abu Dhabi (EAD). *State of the Environment Report 2017*. Abu Dhabi: EAD, 2017. https://www.ead.ae/Publications/Abu%20Dhabi%20State%20of%20Environment%20Report%202017/EAD-full-report.pdf#search=camel.

Federal Law No. (24) of 1999 for the Protection and Development of the Environment. http://extwprlegs1.fao.org/docs/pdf/uae67811E.pdf.

Feulner, Gary. "Geological Overview." In *The Emirates: A Natural History*, edited by Peter Hellyer and Simon Aspinall, 41–63. London: Trident Press, 2005.

Gallacher, David J., and Jeffrey P. Hill. "Effects of Camel Grazing on the Ecology of Small Perennial Plants in the Dubai (UAE) Inland Desert." *Journal of Arid Environments* 66, no. 4 (2006): 738–50.

Gardner, Andrew S., and Brigitte Howarth. "Urbanisation in the United Arab Emirates: The Challenges for Ecological Mitigation in a Rapidly Developing Country." *BioRisk* 3 (2009): 27–38.

Gulf News. "First of Its Kind: Hatta Hydroelectric Plant Study Underway." *Gulf News*, October 3, 2017. Accessed August 15, 2018. https://gulfnews.com/business/renewables/first-of-its-kind-hatta-hydroelectric-plant-study-underway-1.2099948.

Heard-Bey, Frauke. "The Beginning of the Post-imperial Era for the Trucial States from World War I to the 1960s." In *United Arab Emirates: A New Perspective*, edited by Ibrahim Al-Abed and Peter Hellyer, 117–20. London: Trident Press, 2001.

Howarth, Brigitte, and Michael P.T. Gillett. "The Terrestrial and Freshwater Arthropods of Abu Dhabi Emirate." In *Terrestrial Environment of Abu Dhabi Emirate*, edited by Richard Perry, 379–463. Abu Dhabi: Environment Agency-Abu Dhabi, 2008.

Hvidt, Martin. "The Dubai Model: An Outline of Key Components of the Development Process in Dubai." *International Journal of Middle Eastern Studies* 41 (2009): 397–418.

Isbell, Forest, David Tilman, Stephen Polasky, and Michel Loreau. "The Biodiversity-Dependent Ecosystem Service Debt." *Ecology Letters* 18, no. 2 (2015): 119–34.

Joseph, Sabrina. "Farming the Desert: Agriculture in the Oil Frontier, the Case of the United Arab Emirates, 1940s to 1990s." *British Journal of Middle Eastern Studies* 45, no. 5 (2018): 678–694. https://doi.org/10.1080/13530194.2017.1320977.

Joseph, Sabrina, and Brigitte Howarth. "Fertile Sands: Colonial Politics and the Development of Land and Water Resources in the Trucial States, Mid to Late 20th Century." *The Arab World Geographer* 18, no. 3 (2015): 156–57.

Kosoy, Nicolás, and Esteve Corbera. "Payments for Ecosystem Services as Commodity Fetishism." *Ecological Economics* 69 (2010): 1231–36.

Law No. (11) of 2003 on Nature Reserves Within the Emirate of Dubai. https://www.ddcr.org/en/board-sponsors.aspx?Menu=1.

MacArthur, Robert H., and Edward O. Wilson. *The Theory of Island Biogeography*. Princeton, NJ: Princeton University Press, 1967.

Moore, Jason W. "The Capitalocene, Part I: On the Nature and Origins of Our Ecological Crisis." *The Journal of Peasant Studies* 44, no. 3 (2017): 594–630. https://doi.org/10.1080/03066150.2016.1235036.

———. "Sugar and the Expansion of the Early Modern World-Economy: Commodity Frontiers, Ecological Transformation, and Industrialization." *Review: A Journal of the Fernand Braudel Center* 23, no. 3 (2000): 409–33.

Munster, Daniel, and Munster, Ursula. "Consuming the Forest in an Environment of Crisis: Nature Tourism, Forest Conservation, and Neoliberal Agriculture in South India." *Development and Change* 43, no. 1 (2012): 205–27.

Rader, Romina, Ignasi Bartomeus, Lucas A. Garibaldi, Michael P.D. Garratt, Brad G. Howlett, Rachael Winfree, Saul A. Cunningham, et al. "Non-Bee Insects Are Important Contributors to Global Crop Pollination." *Proceedings of the National Academy of Sciences* 113, no. 1 (2016): 146–51.

Scales, Ivan R. "Paying for Nature: What Every Conservationist Should Know About Political Economy." *Oryx* 49, no. 2 (2015): 226–31. https://doi.org/10.1017/s0030605314000015.

Seagle, Caroline. "Inverting the Impacts: Mining, Conservation and Sustainability Claims Near the Rio Tinto/QMM Ilmenite Mine in Southeast Madagascar." *The Journal of Peasant Studies* 39, no. 2 (2012): 447–77. https://doi.org/10.1080/03066150.2012.671769.

Simkins, Greg, and Tamer Khafaga. *Al Marmoom Desert Conservation Reserve Preliminary Report*. Dubai: Dubai Desert Conservation Reserve Report, 2016.

The National. "Dubai Ruler Launches Marmoom Desert Conservation Reserve." *The National*, January 16, 2018. Accessed August 12, 2018. https://www.thenational.ae/uae/environment/dubai-ruler-launches-marmoom-desert-conservation-reserve-1.696015.

UAEinteract. "Agricultural Policy Has Been Successful: Humaid," April 16, 2002. Accessed July 7, 2015. http://www.uaeinteract.com/docs/Agricultural_policy_has_been_successful_Humaid/3818.htm.

UNCCD Secretariat. *Summary of the Second United Arab Emirates National Report to the UNCCD*. Bonn: UNCCD Secretariat, 2002.

van Harten, Antonius, ed. *Arthropod Fauna of the UAE Volume 1*. Abu Dhabi: Dar Al Ummah, 2008.

———, ed. *Arthropod Fauna of the UAE Volume 2*. Abu Dhabi: Dar Al Ummah, 2009.

———, ed. *Arthropod Fauna of the UAE Volume 3*. Abu Dhabi: Dar Al Ummah, 2010.

———, ed. *Arthropod Fauna of the UAE Volume 4*. Abu Dhabi: Dar Al Ummah, 2011.

———, ed. *Arthropod Fauna of the UAE Volume 5*. Abu Dhabi: Department of the President's Affairs, 2014.

———, ed. *Arthropod Fauna of the UAE Volume 6*. Abu Dhabi: Department of the President's Affairs, 2017.

———, ed. *Insects of the UAE: A Checklist of Published Records*. Abu Dhabi: Dar Al Ummah, 2005.

Watson, James E.M., Nigel Dudley, Daniel B. Segan, and Marc Hockings. "The Performance and Potential of Protected Areas." *Nature* 515, no. 7525 (2014): 67+ (Health Reference Center Academic). Accessed August 15, 2018.

Worster, Donald. "Transformations of the Earth: Toward an Agroecological Perspective in History." *The Journal of American History* 76, no. 4 (1990): 1087–106.

www.ddcr.org.

http://uae.panda.org/our_work/fresh_water/wadi_wurayah/.

6

From the Amazon to the Congo Valley: A Comparative Study on the Violent Commodification of Labour During the Rubber Boom (1870s–1910s)

Louise Cardoso de Mello and Sven Van Melkebeke

Introduction

This chapter presents a comparative historical analysis of the processes of labour commodification during the rubber boom period in two major rubber producing regions between the 1870s and the 1910s: Western Amazonia and the Congo Free State. Two regions and one global trade system interconnected by a commodity that came to be notably invoked as "red gold" or "red rubber", in clear reference to the violence and bloodshed it prompted. Therefore, the primary purpose of this chapter is to tackle the issue of the expansion of commodity frontiers and its social repercussions on the native populations.

L. Cardoso de Mello (✉)
Universidad Pablo de Olavide, Seville, Spain

Universidade Federal Fluminense, Rio de Janeiro, Brazil

S. Van Melkebeke
Ghent University, Ghent, Belgium

S. Joseph (ed.), *Commodity Frontiers and Global Capitalist Expansion*, Palgrave Studies in Economic History, https://doi.org/10.1007/978-3-030-15322-9_6

According to the Cambridge English Dictionary, the term "commodity" is defined as "*a substance or product that can be traded, bought, or sold*".[1] This fairly simple definition manages, however, to highlight an underlying feature of the commodity: its exchangeability. According to Appadurai,[2] this exchangeability is not only the commodity's most relevant social aspect, but it is also the source of its economic value. In his acclaimed work, *The Social Life of Things*, the anthropologist stresses the social potential of the commodity, which is considered rather as a situation or a phase always subject to the surrounding context.

This idea is further developed by Kopytoff,[3] who looks at it as a process, in which anything or even any person can experience commodification and become de-commodified. The anthropologist further theorises on the expansion of commodification, which according to him may happen both at a micro-level, whereby the commodity progressively becomes exchangeable for more and more things, and at a macro one, insofar as more and more different things become progressively more exchangeable.[4] In line with this reasoning, we argue that the commodification of rubber followed by the expansion of this commodity frontier prompted the coercive commodification of indigenous workforce both in the Latin American and African scenarios.

As far as the specialised literature is concerned, much has been written about the rubber boom in Amazonia. It is true that in the past decade, more and more scholars have been dedicating their research to the social aspects of this rubber fever and the indigenous groups that were affected by it.[5] Nonetheless, this period in Amazonian history has been addressed from a predominantly economic perspective. Such is the case of ground-breaking works by Roberto Santos[6] and Barbara Weinstein,[7] to name but a few examples. One of the major contributions of Weinstein's work was to point out the persistence of pre-capitalist relations of production and exchange during the rubber boom.[8] Although Weinstein recognises the demographic repercussions of the rubber trade in Amazonia, she reinforces the assertion that "*the rubber boom did not give rise to a basic transformation of Amazonian society*".[9]

As opposed to this interpretation that stresses the persistence of pre-capitalist relations of production, we further argue that the rubber trade system engendered an alienation of labour relations, which degraded from patron–client bonds into enhanced forms of chattel slavery and peonage. This coercion into labour took different shapes: in the Amazonian case, by revisiting non-monetary ways of compelling labour through the enslavement by debt, and in the Congo Free State, by establishing a different form of self-perpetuating enslavement that is hereby defined as "enslavement by tax". In order to demonstrate that, this chapter assesses the changes and continuities within social and work relations both in Amazonia and the Congo Free State in regard to their colonial background and neo-colonial context. With this approach, more relevance is given both to colonial dynamics and indigenous inheritance in terms of persisting practices, as well as to the roles played by the native peoples in the changing contexts.

Concurrently, works on the rubber trade and policy in the Congo Free State are unquestionably vast. To such an extent that it would not be exaggerated to claim that basically every study that deals with colonialism in the Congo Free State touches upon rubber exploitation, due to the centrality of rubber in this period. In addition, current scholarship tends to remain confined within colonial boundaries and fails to place the Congo Free State into a broader (comparative and global) perspective, with very few exceptions. To name some, Harms used a continental lens to compare rubber exploitation in colonial Africa, and more recently, Clarence-Smith has compared rubber production in the Belgian Congo and Indonesia, but for the period after the rubber boom (1910s–1950s).[10]

In this sense, this chapter proposes a rather original outlook by placing the regional social outcomes of the rubber boom in Western Amazonia and the Congo Free State into a global comparative perspective, in a humble attempt to better comprehend them in relation to global processes and transformations in social and labour relations. In other words, what Beckert observes for the cotton commodity may equally apply to this study on rubber: "*(...) only a global viewpoint allows us to understand the great realignment that each of these local stories was part of (...)*".[11] To fulfil this goal, we make use of the incorporated comparison method, in which comparisons are subordinated to diverse historical processes, rather than used conventionally to establish a causal relationship that is generalising regardless of specific temporal and spatial frameworks.[12]

By applying this analytical tool, we expect not only to unravel similarities, but also to capture variations across practices of violent workforce recruitment, labour control, harsh working conditions, as well as forms of enslavement and abuse. Additionally, we also aim at pointing out the varied strategies of resistance and endurance carried out by the native peoples in the light of the violent territorialisation of the rubber trade system. In doing so, we ultimately hope to shed some light on the violent repercussions that underlaid the expansion of capitalism and globalisation, as well as the persistence of coloniality in the context of developmentalist policies and predatory neo-extractive activities both in the Amazonian and Congo regions to this day.

The Commodification of Rubber

On 1 May 1851, London's famous Hyde Park hosted the first international exhibition, whose main theme was none other than industrialisation itself. The Great Exhibition brought together manufactured goods and the latest industrial technology and inventions from all over the world. Amongst its most notable exhibits were innovative India rubber products, such as storm-resisting shoes, gloves, cloth, raincoats,[13] cushions, life jackets, buoys and even an inflatable boat. According to Harp,[14] rubber underlaid the expansion of both European and North American industrialisation. As a matter of fact, rubber was a raw material present across all industrial sectors, such as in factories' machinery and engines, in steamships, in railway engines and other industrial parts such as hoses, gaskets, sprockets, belts, as an isolator for electricity production and distribution and telegraphic communication, as well as medical materials such as latex gloves and in the manufacturing of prophylactics.

Nevertheless, it was not until the 1880s and 1890s that a big turn of events would take place, led by inventors and entrepreneurs whose names resonate amongst drivers across the globe, such as Dunlop, Michelin, Firestone. Once again, the revolution started with the wheel; surprisingly, not the car wheel, but the bicycle wheel. The equally-sized-wheel bicycle, marketed by Dunlop, came along in 1888 with an even greater innovation: the pneumatic tyre. Less than a decade later, the pneumatic tyre was implemented in automobiles by the Michelin brothers, replacing the solid tyre and greatly boosting the demand for natural rubber in the international market.

In point of fact, the weight of the automobile industry in the rubber market is directly reflected on Amazonian exports, which began to take off after 1888, starting with a 50% growth with regard to the previous year in Brazil.[15] In the first decade of the twentieth century, Brazilian rubber exports surpassed the annual amount of 30,000 tons. In 1910, they reached their peak at 40,000 tons, representing up to 40% of the total amount of national exports—second to coffee only—directed mainly to the UK and the USA.[16] In Bolivian Amazonia, the peak of rubber exportation was reached one year later, in 1911, registering 3.637 tons; although it should be noted that a great deal of rubber from landlocked Bolivia was sent into Brazil and exported as Brazilian rubber, so the real numbers might have been considerably higher.[17] The rubber exported from the Putumayo Basin started to properly compete in the international market around 1907, consolidating its share of the market in 1912 to later outrank Brazilian exports towards 1924.[18]

Similarly, Africa's rubber production also experienced a huge leap from a mere 5% in the 1880s to more than 30% of global rubber production in 1900. Zooming in on the continent reveals that the Congo Free State's rubber export rate grew faster than that of other African colonies (such as the Gold Coast and Angola). From 1890 to 1904, exports multiplied by 40 to reach a total of almost 5500 tons, equalling 10% of the global amount of rubber produced in 1904.[19] Nonetheless, after 1912, due to Asian competition—which came to control over 90% of global exports—prices of rubber dropped dramatically, leading to the decay of the activity in both regions. Up until then, the

Amazonian Basin was the most important rubber producing region in the world, followed by the Congo Free State.

The flourishing of the rubber production in Southeast Asia at the beginning of the twentieth century, especially in British Malaya and Ceylon, is credited to Henry Wickman, who is nowadays considered a "bio-pirate" due to having smuggled thousands of *hevea* tree seeds from Brazil in the 1870s. Having said that, it is important to note that rubber is obtained from the latex extracted from different types of trees, mostly native to Latin America. Different types of trees produce different rubber types and qualities. For instance, the *Castilloa Elastica* and *Siphonia Elastica*, mostly present in Peruvian and Bolivian Amazonia, produce the "*caucho*", whereas the *Hevea Brasiliensis*, native to the Amazonian biome and predominantly found in its western area, produces the "*seringa*" or "*goma elástica*",[20] which is considered the finest kind of rubber. As opposed to Amazonia, the Congolese rubber was extracted from vines. The *Landolphia* vines, with its more than 50 varieties of species, were native to tropical West and Central Africa and grew wildly in vast areas of the Congo Valley in particular. The extraction of latex from these different rubber plants meant different work methods and relations to the land, as will be discussed further ahead.

The Expansion of the Rubber Commodity Frontier

By introducing the concept of "commodity frontiers", Jason W. Moore examines the restructuring of geographical spaces at the margins of the world-system.[21] Increased agricultural production (including rubber) on a global scale from the 1870s onwards resulted in the expansion of the so-called tropical frontier, which was based on allegedly abundant new supplies of labour (and land), and resulted in the incorporation of vast rural zones in the Global South into the global economy.[22]

As far as Western Amazonia is concerned, it encompasses at least three then-recently consolidated republics and one Empire, respectively,

Bolivia, Peru, Colombia and Brazil, even though the Amazonian region currently spans across a total of 9 nations, including Ecuador, Venezuela, Guyana, Suriname and French Guiana (see Fig. 6.1). This undefined continent-wide transnational frontier zone had remained on the fringes of both colonial and State control up until the rubber boom period (1850s–1910s). Nevertheless, the natural rubber trade really started to develop after some important technological innovations, such as the vulcanisation method, developed by Charles Goodyear in 1839,[23] and especially with the arrival of the first steamer in Amazonia, in 1853. Fifty years later, there were already 1601 steamboats operating on the Amazon River[24] and more than 20 overseas companies managing the rubber trade in the Brazilian Amazonia alone. These international companies were mainly owned by North American and European capital, which included Belgium. Therefore, the rubber frontier expansion would foster a sort of "second colonisation" in the region, converting it into the largest rubber exporter in the world, and thus forcing its way into the first globalisation.[25]

As for the Congo Free State, empirical evidence also suggests that in both the south-western and north-western Congo, Africans gathered and traded rubber prior to colonialism.[26] However, before the rubber boom, ivory was basically the only Congolese export commodity. By the end of the nineteenth century, the Congo Free State had failed to export sufficient ivory in order to balance the budget of its expanding colonial State. Therefore, the presence of wild rubber in combination with a rising demand for it on the global market ended up saving the Congo Free State from bankruptcy.[27] The introduction of an in-kind rubber tax from the early 1890s onwards proved to be the solution to increase revenue and to make the colony economically viable. Although rubber extraction was not a novelty introduced by the Congo Free State, this huge increase in exports received by in-kind taxation would result in severe and violent labour mobilisations and would cause devastation throughout the Congolese countryside, as we will see next.

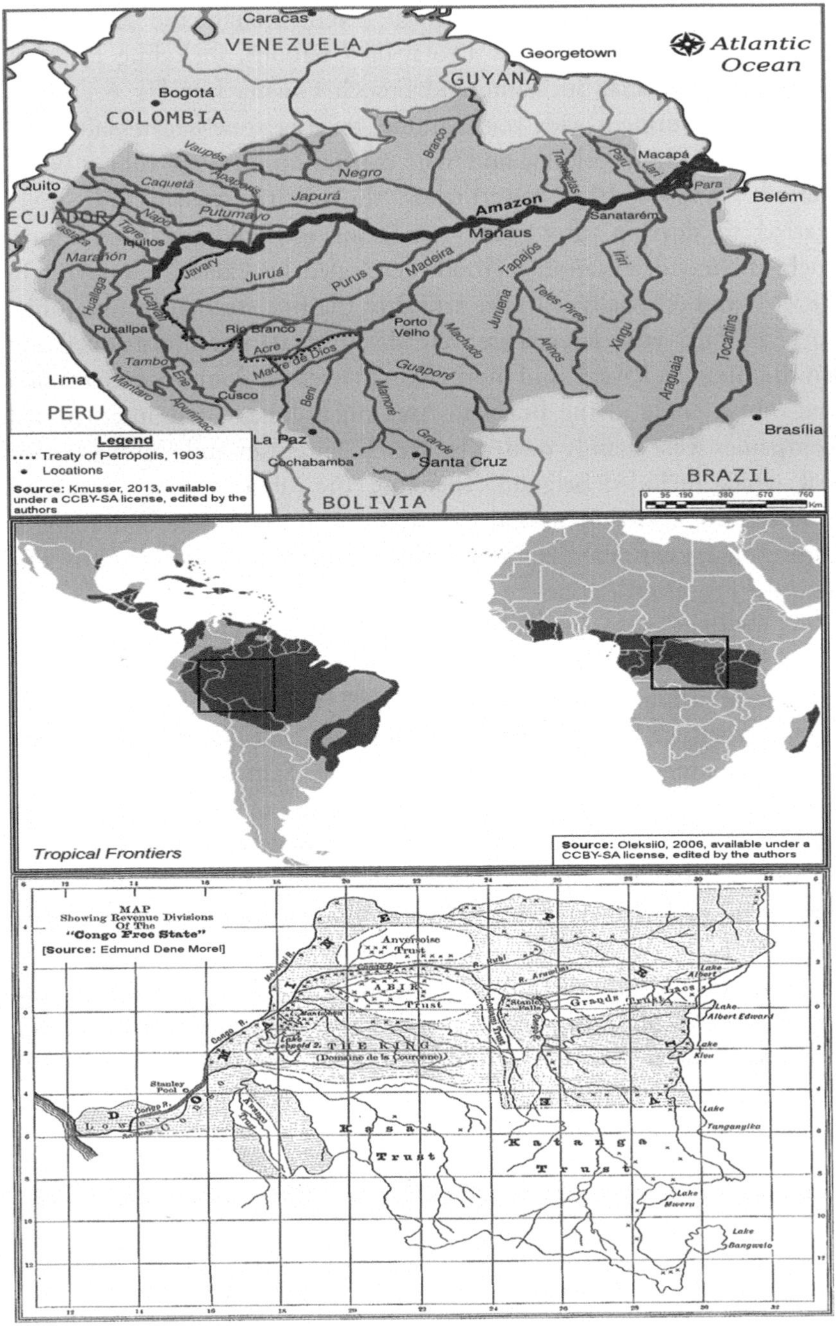
Caracas
VENEZUELA
Georgetown
Atlantic Ocean
GUYANA
Bogotá
COLOMBIA
Quito
ECUADOR
Macapá
Belém
Amazon
Manaus
Negro
Japurá
Putumayo
Caquetá
Vaupés
Branco
Trombetas
Paru
Jari
Para
Sanatarém
Iquitos
Marañón
Javary
Juruá
Purus
Madeira
Tapajós
Juruena
Teles Pires
Iriri
Xingu
Araguaia
Tocantins
Huallaga
Ucayali
Pucallpa
Rio Branco
Acre
Porto Velho
Machado
Madre de Dios
Guaporé
Arinos
Tambo
Ene
Lima
Mantaro
Apurímac
Cusco
PERU
Beni
Mamoré
Grande
La Paz
Cochabamba
Santa Cruz
Brasília
BRAZIL
BOLIVIA
Legend
Treaty of Petrópolis, 1903
Locations
Source: Kmusser, 2013, available under a CCBY-SA license, edited by the authors
0 95 190 380 570 760 Km
Tropical Frontiers
Source: Oleksii0, 2006, available under a CCBY-SA license, edited by the authors
MAP Showing Revenue Divisions Of The "Congo Free State"
[Source: Edmund Dene Morel]
Anversoise Trust
A B I R Trust
Congo R.
Stanley Pool
Stanley Falls
Lake Albert
Lake Albert Edward
Lake Kivu
Lake Tanganyika
Lake Mweru
Lake Bangwelo
THE KING (Domaine de la Couronne)
Kasai Trust
Katanga Trust

◀ **Fig. 6.1** Maps showing the Amazon Basin (above), tropical frontiers and study regions (middle) and the Congo Free State with concessionary companies (below) (*Sources* [respectively, top to bottom]: Kmusser, Map of the Amazon River drainage basin with the Amazon River highlighted. License: Creative Commons Attribution-Share Alike 3.0 Unported. In Wikimedia Commons contributors, "File:Amazonrivermap.svg," Wikimedia Commons, the free media repository, 2013. https://commons.wikimedia.org/w/index.php?title=File:Amazonrivermap.svg&oldid=266045857. Accessed on 16 July 2018. Edited by authors; Oleksii0. 2006. Tropical rainforest map. License: GFDL. In Wikimedia Commons contributors, "File:Tropical rainforest map.png," Wikimedia Commons, the free media repository. https://uk.wikipedia.org/w/index.php?title=%D0%A4%D0%B0%D0%B9%D0%BB:Tropical_rainforest_map.png&oldid=329016. Accessed on 16 July 2018. Edited by authors; and Edmund D. Morel, *Red Rubber: The Story of the Rubber Slave Trade Flourishing on the Congo in the Year of Grace 1906* [New York: Negro Universities Press, 1906], s.p.)

The Territorialisation of the Rubber Trade

The framing of the rubber trade's labour relations within broader models such as capitalist or pre-capitalist—albeit very helpful—might have failed to unveil the nuances and variations that took place within them. On the one hand, wage labour also expanded, especially for the hiring of labour agents, work enforcers and slavers. On the other hand, for the majority of the indigenous workers "employed", the predominant scenario was one of forced labour and/or slavery. Ullán de la Rosa talks about neo-feudalism and neo-slavery to refer to the different forms of labour relations developed within the rubber trade system in the Amazon Basin.[28] As we will try to demonstrate, in an "inherited" context marked by the coloniality of power followed by a consistently feeble presence of the State in both regions, the existing pre-capitalist labour relations would intensify and degenerate from patron–client bonds into enhanced forms of chattel slavery and peonage, characterised by bondage and coercion.[29]

The Congolese Rubber Frontier

Up until the end of the rubber boom in the 1910s, rubber was gathered rather than produced.[30] The Congolese were forced to collect rubber in often hostile forests, either by concessionary companies, backed by the colonial State, or by the State itself. Even though the Berlin act of 1885 stipulated free trade in the Congo, by expropriating all alleged vacant land—land not effectively tilled by Africans—and claiming that this land (including its natural resources) belonged to the colonial State, King Leopold II managed to circumvent the principles of free trade.[31] From 1891 onwards, vast areas were considered property of the State, but the infrastructure of said nascent State was arterial rather than capillary.[32] The presence of the State was concentrated and largely limited to administrative and military posts. One important consequence of this is that villages located near such posts suffered more from forced rubber collection than villages situated further away.[33] The lack of governmental presence was compensated by granting huge concessions to private firms in order to economically exploit and financially revive the colony, as well as to anticipate the rising global demand for rubber.

In 1892, two major rubber exploiting companies were established and granted full property of their concession (including harvesting natural products) and the right to collect in-kind taxes on behalf of the State for a period of 30 years. To the south of the Congo River, the *Anglo-Belgian India Rubber Company* (ABIR) was granted a concession of 160,000 km^2, whereas to the north of the river, the *Société Anversoise de Commerce au Congo* (*Anversoise*) exploited an area covering the same size (see Fig. 6.1).[34] The Congo Free State possessed half of the share of both companies which means that when rubber exports started to take off, profits and dividends started to pour in.[35]

The ways private companies and the State operated to collect rubber were largely similar. In order to get a deeper understanding of the *modus operandi*, a brief focus on the eastern Congo at the end of the nineteenth century is required. From about 1870 onwards, Arab troops commanded by Tippu Tip occupied large parts of eastern Congo and attempted to establish a commercial empire during the raids of slave traders from eastern Africa—this became known as the Zanzibari colonisation. While advancing throughout the region, the Zanzibari caused material damage by burning down houses and changing existing labour dynamics. People were captured and enslaved, usually men, but also women, who were incorporated into the raiders' harems. Those slaves were then employed as porters, servants, soldiers or food plantation (rice for example) workers exposed to harsh labour conditions.[36]

There is consensus in the literature that both private enterprises (in their respective concessions) and the State (in the *domaine privé* and in King Leopold's personal *domaine de la couronne*) continued Zanzibari methods.[37] Expeditions often ended up in plunder, destruction of villages and capturing of people: initially, to collect ivory (by the Congo Free State) and subsequently, to collect rubber (by the Congo Free State and private sector).

In the context of sustained high demand and increasing exhaustion of rubber vines (from about 1903 to 1904), Africans not only had to travel further into forests to collect rubber, but sentries also used more force in order to achieve their quotas, which in turn resulted in villagers killing 142 sentries in 1905.[38] In an attempt to increase production, labourers often chopped off vines—which was illegal. But cutting off and extensive tapping of the same vines caused their exhaustion and ultimately death. The Congo Free State was well aware of this issue and initially ordered concessionary companies to plant new rubber plants, which was to no avail.[39] After Belgium took over the Congo Free State (1908), agronomists experimented with new varieties, not only to diversify the botanical family, but especially to reinforce production, albeit also unsuccessfully.[40]

The Amazonian Rubber Frontier

Many authors coincide in describing the Amazonian rubber economy as being one of relatively low levels of production, very high prices,[41] a labour-scarce scenario and thus, a high-wage cost structure.[42] Due to a general scarcity of labour, the rubber boom relied a great deal on indigenous workforce, and in some regions, such as the Peruvian and Bolivian Amazonia, it was carried out mostly by lowland Amerindians[43] and to a lesser extent by migrants from the Andean Altiplano. In other areas such as the Brazilian Amazonia, it was mostly performed by Amerindians, but also by mestizos, blacks, mulattos and from the end of the 1870s, also by migrants from the north-east of Brazil. Both in the Brazilian and Peruvian Amazonia, Afro-Caribbean immigrants also started to be recruited in the first decade of the twentieth century under rather shady terms; they were all generally referred to as Barbadians. Anyways, it is important to highlight that the indigenous peoples were the backbone of the rubber trade in Amazonia, not only as valuable workforce, but also as inhabitants of its lands and bearers of the knowledge regarding the extraction of rubber and survival techniques in the Amazonian forests (as to what and when to hunt, what to collect and cultivate, how to treat tropical diseases and snakebites, etc.).

The great majority of the rubber production was managed by rubber patrons and creditor companies by means of a financing and supply-credit system (*aviamento*, in Portuguese). The creditor companies (*casas aviadoras*), usually based in the port cities of Belém and Manaus, were externally financed mainly by British and North American capital. The obtainment of credit enabled rubber patrons to pay for the rubber transportation costs and the workforce recruitment, as well as for the necessary provisions for their maintenance in the rubber fields (*seringais*). At the other end of this long credit chain were the rubber tappers (*seringueiros*), who also by means of a credit, were able to finance their relocation costs and furnish themselves with the necessary working tools and basic goods such as foodstuff, which were forcibly acquired at the rubber patron's storehouse or station (*barracão* or *barraca*). The rubber tapper was, therefore, not only the patron's employee, but also his client; and it is not by chance that in Portuguese he would be called "*freguês*" (or "customer").[44]

The payment of this credit, or rather, this debt, was made by the rubber tappers in goods, namely in rubber, whose price, as well as that of the provisions acquired, was tampered with by the patron in a highly unfavourable way. For instance, for the Peruvian Amazonian region of the Putumayo River, there is evidence of lists of trade goods showing their real values and the exorbitant prices charged to the indigenous rubber tappers by the local commissioned enforcers.[45] Hence, in order to perform the rubber tapping labour, workers were most commonly forced to engage in a debt-peonage system (or *enganche*), which meant they were tied to the rubber patrons by a patron–client bond. Oftentimes these client-like relations were subscribed by means of fidelity ties, symbolic gifts (including the granting of non-indigenous names) and fictitious bonds of kinship, such as godfathership.[46] As put forward by Appadurai,[47] it may be observed that with this manipulation of the price of rubber, the value of this commodity varied according to the context and the commodity phase, which was determined by the level of production on the credit chain. In other words, in this pyramid-like credit system, surplus ended up being retained at the top by the creditor groups and a handful of rubber barons.

Much like in the Congo, in some parts of the Amazonian region the rubber trade crisis was inflated by the depletion of rubber trees, which started to be perceived by the turn of the century. This is the case of the Peruvian Amazonia, where in 1905, governmental officers were already denouncing this resource emptying in the areas around Iquitos and the Madre de Dios Valley.[48] This was due to the predatory extraction of the *caucho* rubber, which consisted of cutting down trees—a measure that had been forbidden both in Brazil and Bolivia in the early 1900s, but sadly not in Peru.[49] Other causes that have contributed to this market crisis include the lack of governmental incentives, the inexistence of plantation techniques for an intensive production and the general deficiency of capital.[50] In spite of the collapse of what is known as the first rubber cycle, the economic activity of rubber tapping along with its labour relations would continue throughout Amazonia, experiencing peaks and downfalls, but surviving up to this day.

The Violent Commodification of Indigenous Workforce

During his expedition to the Amazon River in the 1860s, British explorer Henry Bates[51] was astonished to find that practically every indigenous person or mestizo was indebted, either in terms of money or labour. Many authors have drawn attention to the fact that during the rubber boom period, the Amazonian economy lacked cash flow and that it was rather based on the exchange of goods. Some go as far as maintaining that the shortage of cash flow was the reason why rubber patrons kept their workers in debt. Amongst these, Van Valen joins Weinstein and Barham and Coomes to sustain that debt-peonage in rubber-boom Amazonia may not be equated with slavery, with the exception of the Putumayo Basin, as he notes, insofar as:

> patrones could not really oppress their workers, as labor was scarce and workers could easily run away… Nor could patrones keep an eye on the activities of their highly dispersed workforce.[52]

In this section, we question this assumption by proposing an alternative and broader look at the nuances of slavery regardless of whether it is practised within or outside a legitimising legal framework. In so doing, we highlight the many forms of slavery that were forged as the backbone of the rubber trade system, by means of the (coerced) commodification of indigenous workforce, which would take different shapes in different rubber frontiers, ranging from autonomy captivity, to enslavement by debt and chattel slavery. In the same way that we consider direct and indirect forms of coercing labour that go beyond those of oppression and control, we give special attention to plural forms of indigenous resistance and resilience other than flight.

The Many Forms of Enslavement

Defined as the "captivity of autonomy" by Ramos Núñez[53], the *enganche* contract is a form of work recruitment that is considered to be typical of the Andean region.[54] However, primary sources indicate that it was also common practice in the Portuguese colonial experience in Amazonia. There's documental evidence that shows that Amerindians who deserted from the Spanish Moxos missions, crossing the Portuguese border through the Guaporé River, for instance, were also engaged in a credit system, through which apart from "asylum", they were given food, clothing and tools in exchange for their work.[55]

In keeping with colonial practices, the indigenous workforce was often mediated by the tribal chiefs themselves. In addition, physical coercion in the recruitment of indigenous workforce was, more often than not, perpetrated by labour agents (or *enganchadores*, in Spanish) or rubber tappers that worked on commission and directly recruited them. As for recruitment, it varied: both indigenous and non-indigenous workers were voluntarily recruited, *enganchados*, bought and sold or captured and sold. The kidnapping of indigenous infants was yet another "recruitment strategy" put into practice—these children represented the booty obtained by perverse hunting expeditions (or *correrias*, in Portuguese), and they were to be raised within the families of enforcers or patrons to work in the rubber fields. In the Peruvian Amazonia, in the Putumayo Basin, it was common praxis to have indigenous youths "civilised", which actually meant arming and training them into becoming work enforcers themselves, perpetrating violence and causing death to their still "savage" peers.[56]

In point of fact, indigenous captivity not only continued in Western Amazonia throughout the colonial period since the seventeenth century, but it even grew in the latter half of the 1800s. Recently discovered British diplomatic correspondence between the Foreign Office and their representatives and consuls in Brazil, Bolivia, Peru and Ecuador suggests the existence of transnational networks of trafficked indigenous peoples from the major Amazonian ports of Iquitos[57] and Manaus.[58] There's also evidence of Amerindians being bodily branded as property with the rubber patron's initials in the Peruvian lowlands, a practice that may be traced to as early as the sixteenth century and that was extensively applied both in colonial America and the Iberian Peninsula to claim as property both Amerindians and Africans that had been enslaved, whether legally or not.[59] In the Putumayo Basin, indigenous peoples were further coerced into working on crops for the provision of foodstuff, into transporting loads and building infrastructures for the rubber stations and their staff.[60] In the case of Bolivian Amazonia, Walle points out that the recruited indigenous workers were:

> simply a slave whom the master could retain in his service indefinitely under the pretext of more or less imaginary debts, and that he could even transfer to other employers through sale or exchange.[61]

All of this exemplifies the process of commodification undergone by the indigenous workforce, in which they were brand-marked on the one hand, and on the other, they could not only be sold, but also exchanged for the discharge of debts. Therefore, slavery was what kept the engines of the whole rubber trade/credit system functioning in Amazonia. Slavery in Amazonia, most specifically in the Peruvian–Colombian frontier, is a constant source of comparison with the Congo Free State in Roger Casement's works and diary.[62] Casement was an Irish member of the British Foreign Office, who was commissioned in Congo in 1903 and later sent to Peru in 1910 to investigate the atrocities committed against the native peoples in light of the rubber trade. He comes to the ever-arguable conclusion that slavery in the Putumayo region was a graver crime than in the Congo Free State, because contrary to the African case, it was lawless and thus merciless, in spite of the fact that in Congo people were affected by the millions, whereas in the Putumayo these numbers ran into the thousands, as he notes.[63]

Further inspection of Casement's diary on the Peruvian Putumayo region allows us to dig deeper and expand these parallels. For instance, Casement describes the seasonal rubber production cycle carried out by indigenous rubber tappers.[64] As he observed, every fifteen days, they were escorted by armed enforcers to weigh the collected rubber at the rubber station's headquarters. Each rubber tapper was expected to collect a quarterly amount of over 30 kilos of natural rubber. If the quantity brought by them was insufficient, they might have got whipped or chained and kept in captivity for a certain amount of time. Those who did manage to meet quantity expectations were not exactly paid; instead, they received an advancement for the following production season, figuring in the patron's books as "debtors" rather than "employees". In other parts of Western Amazonia, mostly in Brazil, the rubber tapping activity was a more seasonal one. It would take place during the dry season, being hindered by floods in the wet season, when trees were left to rest and recover; this production mode further reinforced reliance on the credit and debt system as a way to endure throughout the wet season.

In parallel with the Peruvian Amazonian scenario, in the Congo Free State, from the early 1890s onwards, local administrative agents were allowed to determine the amount of rubber Africans had to collect. Even though there were regional and time variations, the goal was to achieve about six to eight kilograms per person every two weeks, regardless of the time required to collect this amount of rubber.[65] This would mean a quarterly average of at least 36 kilos per person, which is approximately the same amount required in Peruvian Amazonia, albeit slightly higher.

In order to perform the rubber collection, workers built a shelter where they resided until they gathered enough rubber. In these temporary camps, workers often had to resort to a restricted diet which could result in starvation, and they could be exposed to harsh weather conditions and the threat of wild animals.[66] Once the tapping was over, escorted by sentries (and sometimes soldiers), workers had to transport the collected rubber to either private or State stations, where all the rubber was assembled, checked for quantity and quality, and prepared for exportation. In these stations, workers were oftentimes not paid for their work at all, and when they did receive some sort of remuneration, this was usually in-kind (salt, knives, beads, textiles, etc.).[67] This further perpetuated the enslavement by tax system, in which workers could never achieve to pay taxes if not through their own work.

Ensuring that Africans gathered the required quantities was a task that both concessionary firms and the State consigned to African middlemen (sentries or forest guards, sometimes accompanied by soldiers of the *Force Publique*). Similar to mobilisations for the *Force Publique*, these middlemen were either former Zanzibari slaves now forced to work as sentry or requisitioned African villagers or farmers.[68] Guards were heavily armed and resided in or near rubber-gathering villages. Concessionary firms received weapons, bullets and sometimes even soldiers to assist sentries, from the State.[69]

Moreover, ABIR and the *Anversoise* both were granted *droits de police*. Both firms had the right to mobilise armed guards, to enforce rubber collection and to act as if their concession was their own private territory.[70] Sentries were charged to meticulously control the method, quality and quantity of rubber harvests. In the event that guards failed to achieve quotas imposed on them, they were fined, dismissed, beaten or imprisoned by European administrative and/or company agents.[71] It was not until November 1903 onwards that the colonial State officially limited the amount of time men (and women) had to work to collect rubber to 40 hours per month.[72] Moreover, as local colonial agents[73] were granted bonuses in relation to production figures (and not production methods), "*(…) the expansion in export production became increasingly dependent on the use of force and terror*".[74]

Even though Anglo-Saxons, in particular, heavily criticised King Leopold's rubber regime in the early twentieth century, the reaction of the Congo Free State was rather half-hearted: "*As they have no money, a contribution in the shape of labour is required from them. It has been said that, if Africa is ever to be redeemed from barbarism, it must be by getting the negro to understand the meaning of work by the obligation of paying taxes*".[75] Not only in the 1890s, but even after severe criticism did the Congo Free State still depict forced labour as taxation.[76]

Nevertheless, criticism continued, and King Leopold was left with no choice but to allow an investigative commission to look into rubber exploitation (1904–1905). This commission confirmed extreme atrocities committed against Congolese workers which, in turn, resulted in Belgium taking over the Congo Free State in 1908 and in the establishment of a new political system. The colony was no longer the personal property of one individual, instead, it was administered by a State. Supported by a series of laws, a new colonial policy that aimed at replacing King Leopold's despotic rule was implemented and subject to Parliamentary control.

In Western Amazonia, on the other hand, British report and criticism against rubber atrocities would not result in a major political twist. On the contrary, although the Anglo-Peruvian Amazon Rubber Co., responsible for the atrocities on the Putumayo River, was forced to shut down and over sixteen of its labour enforcers were arrested (out of the 215 arrests warrants issued),[77] its managing partner in Peru, rubber baron Julio Cesar Arana, would end up as a Member of Parliament and a respected Peruvian entrepreneur and patriot.

The Many Forms of Abuse

Despite the sudden economic bonanza brought about by the rubber boom, it drastically affected native peoples, not only on account of the exploitation of their workforce and land, but also in terms of violence and mass murder, wherever one chooses to look, be it in Amazonia or the Congo Free State. There are numerous first-hand accounts of the violent cruelty perpetrated, amongst which whipping, chaining, rape, decapitation, mutilation, drowning, branding, torture, torching, beatings, crucifixion, murder, starvation, malnourishment, plunder, blackmailing, kidnapping, infanticide, confiscation, destruction and burning down villages were just some of the many forms of abuse. A source that deserves our special attention is the previously cited Roger Casement's reports and diaries. His accounts are rich and revealing, yet they are even more brutal and rough.

For instance, in the Putumayo Basin alone, Casement's report depicts an appalling scenario, in which he estimates that, between 1900 and 1911, at least 30,000 Amerindians had either been murdered or deliberately starved to death by crop destruction, in exchange for gaining 4000 tons of rubber.[78] Amongst said indigenous peoples were the Yahua, Ticuna, Muraes, Huitoto, Miraña, Orejones,[79] Bora and many more. The labour conditions encountered in the Peruvian Amazonian have been qualified by Casement as being worse than slavery, since these slaves were not even fed or taken care of so they could continue to fulfil their masters' will.[80] At least, Casement's *Putumayo Black Book* along with Hardenburg's report entitled *Putumayo: The Devil's Paradise* managed to divulge the alienation and atrocities committed against indigenous rubber tappers in Amazonia, causing outrage amidst the seemingly also alienated consumers and investors in the rubber market overseas.

In the bordering Colombian Amazonia, the rubber boom also brought severe demographic consequences for the Amerindians of the Caquetá (or Japurá) and Putumayo regions. Such is the case of the Andoke, whose group was reduced by half and completely dispersed after the first fifteen years of the twentieth century, reaching 130 individuals in the 1970s.[81] According to anthropologist Guzmán, the word the Andoke use to refer to white men probably dates back to these times, meaning "burners" (or "*quemadores*").[82]

In the Bolivian Amazonia, by the end of the nineteenth century, the Pauserna Indians, who inhabited the middle course of the Guaporé (or Iténez) River, were being hunted and sold in the rubber fields of Beni and in Santa Cruz de la Sierra.[83] The Sirionó, who were an autonomous indigenous group of hunter-gatherers inhabiting the interfluve of the Mamoré River, were said to be shot on sight by rubber enforcers, as they were considered inappropriate for labour.[84] Primary sources denounce some of the punishments and mistreatments endured by the Moxo

Indians, who were commonly recruited as paddlers on the treacherous stretch of Brazil's Madeira River, such as lashing them for stealing alcohol or feeding them rotten meat.[85]

Thanks to sharp criticism and condemnatory publications by the aforementioned Roger Casement, as well as Edmund D. Morel, Mark Twain and others, the atrocities committed against the Congolese have also been vividly described.[86] As an American missionary wrote in 1905: "*The dreadful form of rubber collecting has (…) introduced a form of slavery of the worst possible kind*".[87] Africans who (deliberately or not) disobeyed rules or who refused or failed to collect sufficient rubber were punished in manifold ways. Sentries strictly inspected rubber tappers, but it was the indigenous chiefs' responsibility to recruit sufficient village labour in order to collect the imposed rubber quantities. When workers failed to achieve these goals for whatever reason—such as chiefs failing to mobilise sufficient labourers or villagers refusing to gather rubber, chiefs refusing to cooperate with Europeans, etc.—chiefs were penalised. There is ample evidence that in such cases, chiefs were severely punished by sentries and/or European administrative agents: in the best-case scenario they were replaced by others that were more faithful allies, but in most scenarios, chiefs were beaten (and/or whipped), chained, imprisoned, or in some cases, murdered.[88] A common method to enforce rubber tapping was to hold chiefs hostage until the imposed quantity was delivered, as the following lengthy quote from 1903 illustrates:

> On the 17th August (…): They had taken the usual tax of eight baskets of rubber (…), and the white man (…) said the baskets were too few, and that they [villagers] must bring other three; meanwhile, they put the chain round his [chief] neck, the soldiers beat him with sticks, he had to cut firewood, to carry heavy junks, and to haul logs in common with others. Three mornings he was compelled to carry the receptacle from the white man's latrine and empty it in the river. On the third day (sickening to relate) he was made to drink therefrom by a soldier named Lisasi. (…) When the three extra baskets were produced he was set at liberty. He was ill for several days after his return.[89]

In-kind rubber taxation and collection was enforced by the State and the unremitting obligation to tap imposed rubber quantities, even when vines were exhausted, resulted in dramatic working conditions for Africans subjected to this regime. Chiefs were not the only ones who suffered from severe misconduct, rubber workers themselves suffered at least as much, on both concessionary and State-controlled land, either by sentries and/or colonial agents.

A common and well-known feature related to Congolese rubber gathering was cutting off hands of men, women and children. Officially, cutting off hands was not a punishment for the refusal or failure to deliver sufficient rubber and, contrary to what the Congo Free State argued, it was not a continuation of pre-existing practices.[90] The origins of this practice are unclear, but other forms of violence (murder, captivation, mutilation, rape) were informed by precolonial praxis. A recent study argues that abuses even increased in the early colonial period (1885–1890) in an attempt by African leaders to remedy their disintegrated existing political-military authority.[91] That said, cut-off hands had to be shown to the colonial administration as proof of used munition. Consequently, cutting off hands was, officially, only allowed on people who had been killed. According to Hochschild, some administrative agents even considered cut-off hands as serving a "humanitarian" purpose: making an example of murdered victims for the benefit of others.[92] However, living Congolese victims with cut-off hands have been taken on record.

This indicates that either some people survived crimes committed against them or that African guards and/or lower-ranked local administrators ignored higher-ranked officials. The fact that lower-ranked officials often turned a blind eye is confirmed by the following quote; it refers to the *Anversoise* and manifestly indicates that during the rubber boom, exports were all that mattered, not the indigenous Congolese population:

> (...) the chiefs of the Concession Company have, if not by formal orders, at least by their example and their tolerance, induced their agents to take no account whatever of the rights, property, and lives of the natives; to use the arms and soldiers which should have served for their defence and

> the maintenance of order to force the natives to furnish them with produce and to work for the Company (...). That, above all, the fact that the arrest of women and their detention, to compel the villages to furnish both produce and workmen, was tolerated and admitted even by certain of the administrative authorities of the region.[93]

Indigenous Agency and the Social Repercussions of the Rubber Boom

Faced with the aforementioned harsh and often inhuman labour conditions, Africans reacted in various ways. The Congolese initially considered Europeans as trading partners, but that changed rapidly when the Congo Free State imposed the coercive rubber regime in the early 1890s.[94] From then on, Africans generally resisted and rebelled against European imperialism—although some also collaborated in order to extend social and economic wealth.[95] However, this does not mean that the tactics employed by the native peoples were not as varied and diverse as the groups themselves. They responded to different types of resistance, endurance and adaptation strategies. By looking closely both at the Congolese and Amazonian regions, one may observe how some groups would hire out their services to rubber traders and labour agents, while others would trade their own collected rubber for tools and manufactured goods, and others would rebel, attack, flee, tamper with the fashioned rubber slabs and even engender millenarian exodus movements.

Attacks, Rebellions and Exterminations

In the Brazilian–Bolivian Amazonia, the Karipuna Indians are known to have adopted multiple strategies. They used to inhabit the treacherous section of the upper Madeira River. Both colonial and nineteenth-century sources have usually described rather pacific encounters with the Karipuna, in which they often helped travellers cross the rapids and traded goods with them.[96] However, with the beginning of the rubber boom, primary sources display increasingly violent relations during contacts with the Karipuna. In 1893, for example, an armed party of 50 men managed to exterminate a whole tribe on the Abunã River.[97] The rubber boom's final blow to the Karipuna came with the construction of the Madeira-Mamoré Railway (1907–1912), implemented as an outflow solution for the transport of Bolivian rubber. The constant robberies and attacks led by the natives at the workers' camp gave way to extermination raids, which would have them shot on sight or killed by electrocution fences.[98]

The Moré Indians, from the middle Guaporé Valley, also entered into conflict with rubber tappers and traders, carrying out attacks with more than one hundred men. In the lower Bolivian Beni area, the Ese Ejja are also known to have opposed resistance and attacked rubber tappers and enforcers,[99] having later dispersed and moved up river and towards the Madre de Dios area. Furthermore, the aforementioned Andoke Indians orchestrated a rebellion in 1917 on a tributary of the Putumayo River, where they assaulted the area's main station, sieging it for several days.[100]

Much like in Amazonia, native resistance had a profound effect on the development of the rubber boom in the Congo Valley. Many villages openly revolted against the rubber tax, and in some regions, revolt would persist until 1908.[101] In his report, Casement recounts a "rubber-war" that lasted for seven years around Lake Mantumba (*domaine privé* in the north-west).[102] In 1893, the war started because villages had lost many people due to mobilisations for the *Force Publique*, and hence, had failed to meet rubber quotas. But the Congo Free State continued to impose high labour demands on villages, enforced by the *Force Publique*. This resulted in the murder of two Europeans and several African soldiers. The Congo Free State reacted by sending more soldiers (unhampered in the execution of their tasks), by killing villagers and burning down houses. The battle between the *Force Publique* on behalf of the Congo Free State and villages around the lake would continue until the State supposedly stopped compelling the Congolese to gather rubber in 1900.

Flight, Exodus and Demographic Decline

The above example illustrates that African resistance against the rubber extractive regime could result in even more oppression.[103] That is why most resistance against the rubber tax consisted of small-scale day-to-day resistance, the otherwise called "weapons of the weak".[104] Amongst these "weapons", flight was the most common. People tried to evade rubber taxation, either by fleeing into regions with less rubber vines and/or State/company presence, by fleeing into nearby forests or by crossing the colonial border. Other "weapons" commonly used by Congolese rubber tappers were foot-dragging, deliberately sabotaging or cutting down vines, faking illness, adding water into rubber slabs in order to increase its weight, etc. Due to inadequate control of rubber harvests, some Congolese even managed to trick assembly station employees by adding rubber with inferior quality or other substances to the rubber they were forced to gather,[105] a strategy that was also applied in Amazonia.

As far as Western Amazonia is concerned, the rubber boom period saw both organised and spontaneous mass migration waves that would have an enormous impact on the regions' demographic and social structure. In the late 1870s, a large migration wave, which was estimated at over 260,000 workers, originated from the north-east of Brazil bound for innermost Amazonia. This veritable diaspora was caused not only by the "rubber fever" but also by what was considered one of the most severe droughts of the century. The cultural and demographic impact of this mass migration to Amazonia has undoubtedly contributed to paint the region's current demographic picture. On the other hand, if not a diaspora, the word "exodus" could apply for the mass migration experienced by some indigenous groups, such as the Tacana in the Bolivian Amazonia, being forced to abandon their ancestral territories.[106] Many, if not most indigenous groups that participated with or came into contact with the rubber trade, such as the Movima, the Toromona, the independent Chácobo, the Cayuvava, Baures and Canichana, eventually fled to more remote areas.

It was not only flight that impacted population sizes, but also decimation. "*Betofe Bole Iwa*" ("Rubber is our death")[107] and "*Ipanga Ngunda*" ("He who destroys the country")[108] are Congolese proverbs that not only refer to the atrocities committed, but also to the demographic consequences of the coercive labour regime. Both contemporary observers and present-day scholars agree on rural depopulation and decimation of the Congolese. In his report, Casement cites numerous cases of depopulated villages.[109] Van Groenweghe argues that, compared to the period before the rubber regime, some villages in the *domaine de la couronne* lost up to 80% of their population.[110]

However, there is still much debate regarding the actual "body count". Some scholars claim that ten million or more Congolese died due to rubber exploitation.[111] Others have downplayed this number and stressed that population declined not only due to rubber atrocities, but also due to hunger, diseases (sleeping sickness, smallpox, dysentery) and to low natality rates.[112] It is nevertheless undoubtful that at least some of these "alternative explanations" can be linked to the rubber regime.[113] Due to a lack of censuses, it is impossible to quantify demographic changes in this period. It is therefore reasonable to argue that millions of Congolese directly or indirectly died as a consequence of forced rubber exploitation.

The demographic repercussions brought about by the rubber boom in Amazonia may also be thought of as catastrophic, considering the decrease of the general ethnic diversity and the reduction of numerous ethnic groups to near extinction. In general terms, the demographic post-boom scenario is marked by the emptying of villages or whole regions, being caused either by workforce recruitment, the resulting unsustainable livelihood, death by diseases, ethnocide, demographic replacement and miscegenation or encroachment.

In the Peruvian upper Ucayali region, primary sources have registered the migration of entire indigenous groups.[114] In other areas of the Peruvian lowlands, such as the Madre de Dios River, estimations go as high as to 1/3 of the region's population being emptied, with main centres like Puerto Maldonado being on the verge of disappearing.[115] According to Walle, the recruitment of indigenous workforce in Santa Cruz de la Sierra by labour agents was provoking a severe situation of depopulation.[116] It actually came to a point where the Bolivian Government was so worried about the depopulation of the Beni department that in 1882, indigenous trafficking and workforce recruitment to Brazilian rubber fields were made illegal.[117]

Furthermore, diseases such as rubella, dysentery, smallpox, malaria, yellow fever, catarrh and beriberi had devastating effects both on the natives and on migrants from other regions of Brazil, Bolivia and Peru. In the Brazilian region of Acre alone, Roux estimates that beriberi is accountable for having decimated over half of its population.[118] In the Japurá and Putumayo regions, anthropologist Guzmán encountered many groups in the 1970s that had been left on the verge of extinction, such as the Huitoto, Muinane, Miraña and Nonuya.[119] Worse was the situation of the Sinabo Indians, who inhabited the confluence of the Mamoré and Madeira rivers and were ultimately brought down to extinction.[120] Finally, the Wanyam group (or Migueleno), from a tributary on the right bank of the middle course of the Guaporé River, were thought to be extinct by Vallvé,[121] but they have actually managed to survive, being estimated in 267 people in 2014.[122] Nevertheless, sadly in 19 January 2008, this ethnic group lost the last speaker of their Txapakuran language.[123]

Closely linked to demography are the effects of imposed rubber collection on pre-existing economies. Scholars agree on the disruptive repercussions of the forced rubber regime on subsistence activities in the Congo.[124] Yields from agriculture, hunting and fishing declined. This was caused by the absence of men who temporarily resided in forests, while women were often put in a compromised position as they were forced to produce food, both for their families and for European posts, when they were not being kept hostage as a way to coerce their families into gathering rubber. This situation led to scarcity, hunger and diseases. As well as undermining agriculture, rubber exploitation also led to disturbances and decay in craft production and regional trade.

A rather analogous situation would have also been found in Western Amazonia. As debt increased, rubber tappers became increasingly more tied to the stations and storehouses, to such an extent that they were forced to abandon their own farming activities. In line with this, in the Bolivian Amazonia there are registered complaints by rubber tappers expressing their reluctance towards farming on account of not having access to seeds, and of the constant risk of suddenly being relocated to another rubber field without any compensation for the land investments that had been made.[125] Other sources document further "preventive" measures implemented by rubber patrons and enforcers, such as crop destructions[126] and holding the rubber tappers' wives and children hostage, as they did in the Congolese rubber frontier, while they were away collecting rubber.[127] Consequently, the rubber boom also led to a self-sufficiency crisis in many parts of Amazonia.

Cultural Transformation, Hybridity and Millenarian Movements

Upon studying the Andoke Indians in the 1970s, along with other groups from the Japurá and Putumayo areas in the Colombian Amazonia, bordering Peru, Guzmán describes what he defines as the "cultural adaptations"[128] undergone by these groups in order to survive the effects of the rubber boom, during which many had been recruited and captured to work on the rubber fields, a great deal of whom while still infants. These resistant adaptation strategies included, amongst others, the prohibition of polygamy, changes in settlement patterns and rules of kinship, reorganisation of the production unit—with the substitution of the extended family by the nuclear one—and the incorporation of foreigners in the group (especially women).[129]

There's evidence that indicates how these strategies were applied by many indigenous groups from different parts of Amazonia, to which we must add the fission and fusion of groups, interethnic alliances by means of marital bonds and even diasporic millenarian movements. In the Congo for instance, the rubber regime not only affected social relations within families, but also within and between communities. Contact between communities increased, not only because people migrated, but also because workers eventually had to travel further to seek new vines. This resulted either in conflict or, in some cases, in cooperation between hitherto competing groups.[130] Moreover, it was not infrequent to have chiefs dismissed and replaced by others who lacked authority.[131]

In the Bolivian Amazonia, many chieftains intermarried with non-indigenous rubber traders or patrons from Santa Cruz de la Sierra or elsewhere, becoming part of the regional elite.[132] Even though these alliances may have been beneficial for Amerindians in the beginning, it should be noted that this led to the eventual disappearance of the traditional chieftain figures.[133] Therefore, it may be observed how Amerindians developed new strategies and "recycled" old ones, since many of them had already been resorted to during the colonial period.[134] This time, however, they struggled to resist against the disrupting deracination process that was being imposed by the rubber trade system and the resulting precarious life conditions—which is further evidence of how coloniality not just underlaid, but drove the expansion of capitalism in the Global South.

Final Remarks

After analysing the process of commodification of rubber and the territorialisation of this commodity frontier in Western Amazonia and in the Congo Free State, we were able to assess the resulting process of commodification of indigenous workforce in its different forms of enslavement. In this sense, by taking into consideration both their colonial background and neo-colonial context, it was possible to perceive an alienation in labour relations that were forged in the forms of enslavement by debt and enslavement by tax—two socio-economic frameworks permeated by the same thread of coloniality. Likewise, it allowed us to observe both new and renovated forms of violence and abuse. Besides, upon placing the social repercussions of the rubber boom of both regions into a global comparative perspective, we managed to weigh up the impact of the process of capitalist expansion in the Global South and further to put into consideration its real price for native peoples.

On the other hand, the endurance and resistance of indigenous peoples against the many forms of enslavement and abuse brought about by the rubber trade system both in Amazonia and the Congo Free State have managed not only to raise awareness within the international community, giving birth to what is considered to be the "modern humanitarianism", but also to consolidate their struggle in organised forms of institutional and political resistance carried out by local community leaders. Although the Congo Free State trivialised and basically denied rubber crimes committed against Africans, Anglo-Saxon criticism was the first mass movement for human rights. Casement, Morel, Twain and others have contributed to and enhanced the underlying idea of equal rights and fundamental freedoms for all human beings, that present-day organisations such as Amnesty International, Human Rights

Watch or the Kinshasa-based *Voix des Sans Voix* fight for. Promoting human rights and revealing abuses in present-day Democratic Republic of the Congo as soon as possible is the main objective of such organisations; an objective that at least tries to restrict new forms of forced labour and predatory neo-extractive activities.

If we look at Western Amazonia, within the Brazilian territory for instance, the advancement of the agricultural and cattle-raising industries, particularly since the 1970s under the military dictatorship, led most rubber patrons to either switch to the agribusiness or have their lands transferred to large-scale farmers and ranchers, leaving most rubber tappers deprived of their main livelihood. Hence, it was in this context that the syndicalist struggle of rubber tappers emerged as an institutionalised voice led by the acclaimed activist *seringueiro* Chico Mendes, who ended up being tragically murdered by Acre's landed gentry. His legacy, however, was the creation of Extractive Reserves, which are protected public areas that are sustainably exploited by traditional communities and indigenous groups whose livelihood depends on an extractive economy. Nowadays, these reserves may also be credited for the preservation of the ecosystem and its natural resources.

The social repercussions of the rubber boom are, therefore, not only undeniable but also long-standing. When the Congo Free State ceased to exist (1908), one of the goals of the new regime was to end the brutal exploitation of the Congolese people. Colonial policies were readjusted and made more acceptable for national and international observers.[135] Despite legal changes, labour relations (albeit redefined) showed more continuity than change, which resulted in concealed forms of coerced labour. Starting in 1917—and lasting until the end of the colonial period in 1960—the colonial administration implemented the *cultures obligatoires*: a system by means of which peasants were forced to produce an imposed quantity of a certain crop (cotton for example). In addition, recent research argues that violence and coercion were also widespread in the plantation economy, at least until the end of the Second World War.[136]

Despite being out of the scope of this paper, it was difficult not to note the rather feeble role played by the State both in Western

Amazonia and the Congo Free State during the first rubber cycle up until the 1910s. Since then, especially after the Second World War, which gave way to a brief revival of the natural rubber trade until it was mostly displaced by synthetic rubber, governments started to react and increasingly intervene in regional economies. Unfortunately, in the case of Amazonia, this enhanced State presence has been mainly marked by an everlasting coloniality approach and a developmentalist model, with enormous investments and land concessions still being made for mineral prospecting and hydroelectric power plants, solely driven by economic interests as opposed to what should be environmental and social priorities.

Unfortunately, in the last two years, this situation has severely worsened, with the conservative regression of Brazil's political and judicial scenarios, marked by the retreat of the State in detriment of the interests of the private sectors and the landed gentry, who overtly rule by means of coerced land expropriations and even by threatening, attacking and murdering resisting community leaders and members. For those who still may question whether we can speak of slavery during the rubber boom, it is relevant to point out how this period is remembered both by the Congolese and some Amazonian groups. While some Amerindians recall the "Rubber Fields Era" (or "*Era do seringal*") as one defined by enslavement, death by disease and family fragmentation,[137] in the Congolese collective memory, working for Europeans is still perceived as a form of slavery.[138]

Acknowledgements We would like to extend our gratitude to the organisers and publishers of this volume, as well as to the Commodities of Empire Research Project and all of those involved in the Commodity Frontiers Workshop held in Zayed University, Dubai in December 2017. The remarks and inputs made by our colleagues and fellow presenters were very useful. Furthermore, we would like to thank the institutions that have funded and/or supported this research, namely, the Rio de Janeiro Research Foundation (FAPERJ) and the Economies, Comparisons, Connections (ECC) research group at Ghent University.

Notes

1. Cambridge English Dictionary. Cambridge University Press [Online Version], accessed October 29, 2017, https://dictionary.cambridge.org/dictionary/english/commodity.
2. Arjun Appadurai, "Introduction: Commodities and the Politics of Value," in *The Social Life of Things: Commodities in Cultural Perspective*, ed. Arjun Appadurai (Cambridge: Cambridge University Press, 1986), 13, 56.
3. Igor Kopytoff, "The Cultural Biography of Things: Commoditisation as Process," in *The Social Life of Things: Commodities in Cultural Perspective*, ed. Arjun Appadurai (Cambridge: Cambridge University Press, 1986), 69, 73.
4. Ibid., 73.
5. See Alberto Chirif and Manuel Cornejo Chaparro, eds., *Imaginario e imágenes de la época del caucho: los sucesos del Putumayo* (Lima: CAAAP/IWGIA/UPC, 2009); Frederic Vallvé, "The Impact of the Rubber Boom on the Indigenous Peoples of the Bolivian Lowlands (1859–1920)" (PhD, Georgetown University, 2010); Gary Van Valen, *Indigenous Agency in the Amazon: The Mojos in Liberal and Rubber-Boom Bolivia 1842–1932* (Tucson: The University of Arizona Press, 2013); and David E. Gilbert, "Territorialization in a Closing Commodity Frontier: The Yasuní Rainforests of West Amazonia," *Journal of Agrarian Change* 18 (2018): 229–48.
6. Roberto Santos, *História Econômica da Amazônia (1800–1920)* (São Paulo: T. A. Queiroz, 1980).
7. Barbara Weinstein, *The Amazon Rubber Boom: 1850–1920* (Stanford: Stanford University Press, 1983).
8. Ibid., 263.
9. Ibid., 267–68.
10. Robert Harms, "The End of Red Rubber: A Reassessment," *Journal of African History* 16, no. 1 (1975); William Gervase Clarence-Smith, "Rubber Cultivation in Indonesia and the Congo from the 1910s to the 1950s: Divergent Paths," in *Colonial Exploitation and Economic Development: The Belgian Congo and the Netherlands Indies Compared*, ed. Ewout Frankema and Frans Buelens (London and New York: Routledge, 2013).
11. Sven Beckert, *Empire of Cotton: A New History of Global Capitalism* (London: Penguin Books, 2015), xxi.

12. Philip McMichael, "World-Systems Analysis, Globalization and Incorporated Comparison," *Journal of World-Systems Research* 4, no. 3 (2000): 668–99; "Incorporating Comparison Within a World-Historical Perspective: An Alternative Comparative Method," *American Sociological Review* 55, no. 3 (1990): 385–97.
13. Also called "Macintoshes", on account of its inventor, British chemist, Charles Macintosh (Stephen L. Harp, *A World History of Rubber: Empire, Industry, and the Everyday* [Wiley. ProQuest Ebook Central, 2015], 13, accessed October 30, 2017, https://ebookcentral.proquest.com/lib/bupo-ebooks/detail.action?docID=4205815).
14. Harp, *A World History of Rubber*, 14.
15. Melisa Janet Luc, "Recursos naturales y delimitación de fronteras en América Latina en la primera globalización: una aproximación desde la Guerra del Acre," *tiempo&economía* 2, no. 1 (2015): 83.
16. Ibid.
17. Paul Walle, *Bolivia: Its People, Its Resources, Its Railways, Maines and Rubber-Forests* (London: T. Fisher Unwin, 1914), 281.
18. Preston Wallace Barker, *Rubber Statistics 1900–1957* (Washington, DC: Ministerio de Comercio de los EE.UU., 1938).
19. For these figures, see Samuel H. Nelson, *Colonialism in the Congo Basin, 1880–1940* (Athens, OH: Center for International Studies, 1994), 82.
20. Roger Casement sarcastically explains why rubber is also known in Peru as "goma de la India," as it erases indigenous peoples from the map (Roger Casement, *Diario de la Amazonía*, edition by Angus Mitchell, translation by Sonia Fernánde Ordás (La Coruña: Ediciones del viento, 2011 [1910]), 33).
21. Jason W. Moore, "Madeira, Sugar, and the Conquest of Nature in the 'First' Sixteenth Century, Part II: From Regional Crisis to Commodity Frontier, 1506–1530," *Review (Fernand Braudel Center)* 33, no. 1 (2010): 1–24.
22. Edward B. Barbier, *Scarcity and Frontiers: How Economies Have Developed Through Natural Resource Exploitation* (Cambridge and New York: Cambridge University Press, 2011), 418.
23. The vulcanisation method consisted of adding sulphur to natural rubber so as to increase its mechanical properties and render it more temperature-stable.
24. Paul Walle, *Au pays de l'or noir: Para, Amazonas, Matto Grosso* (Paris: E. Guilmoto Éditeur, 1909), 80–81.

25. Luc, "Recursos naturales y delimitación de fronteras en América Latina en la primera globalización: una aproximación desde la Guerra del Acre"; Vallvé, "The Impact of the Rubber Boom on the Indigenous Peoples of the Bolivian Lowlands (1859–1920)," 374.
26. See Jan Vansina, *Being Colonized: The Kuba Experience in Rural Congo, 1880–1960* (Madison: University of Wisconsin Press, 2010), 61; Daniël Vangroenweghe, *Rood Rubber: Leopold II En Zijn Kongo* (Brussel: Elsevier, 1985), 33–41.
27. Bas De Roo, "Colonial Taxation in Africa: A Fiscal History of the Congo Through the Lens of Customs (1886–1914)" (PhD, Ghent University, 2016), 78.
28. Francisco Javier Ullán de la Rosa, "La era del caucho en el Amazonas (1870–1920): modelos de explotación y relaciones sociales de producción," *Anales del Museo de América* 12 (2004): 183–204.
29. Marcel Van der Linden, *Workers of the World: Essays Toward a Global Labor History* (Leiden and Boston: Brill, 2008), 33–35.
30. Production of rubber, both by smallholders and on estates started during the First World War, see Clarence-Smith.
31. Piet Clement, "The Land Tenure System in the Congo, 1885–1960: Actors, Motivations and Consequences," 90.
32. Terminology used by Frederick Cooper, "Conflict and Connection: Rethinking Colonial African History," *American Historical Review* 99, no. 5 (1994): 1533.
33. Nelson, *Colonialism in the Congo Basin, 1880–1940*, 97; Jean Stengers, *Le Congo, Mythes Et Réalités. 100 Ans D'histoire* (Gembloux: Duculot, 1989), 100.
34. To give an impression of the size of the workforce: the ABIR-concession counted 36,189 rubber tappers in 1903 (Vangroenweghe, 105).
35. Frans Buelens, *Congo 1885–1960. Een Financieel-Economische Geschiedenis* (Berchem: EPO, 2007), 133–39.
36. David Northrup, *Beyond the Bend in the River: African Labor in Eastern Zaire 1865–1940* (Athens, OH: Center for International Studies, 1988), 23–36.
37. David M. Gordon, "Precursors to Red Rubber: Violence in the Congo Free State, 1885–1895," *Past & Present* 236, no. 1 (2017): 133–68; Jean Stengers and Jan Vansina, "King Leopold's Congo 1886–1908," in *The Cambridge History of Africa, Volume VI, c.1870–1905*, ed. Roland Oliver and G.N. Sanderson (Cambridge:

Cambridge University Press, 1985), 344; and Jean-Luc Vellut, "La Violence Armée Dans L'etat Indépendant Du Congo," *Cultures et Développement* 16, no. 3–4 (1984): 480–517.

38. Harms, "The End of Red Rubber: A Reassessment," 85.
39. Ibid., 82. Both ABIR and the *Anversoise* lacked enthusiasm and withdrew from rubber exportation, which resulted in the Congo Free State absorbing both enterprises in 1906.
40. Edmond Leplae, "Les Grandes Cultures Coloniales Au Congo Belge: Café, Cacao, Caoutchouc, Coton," *Bulletin Agricole du Congo Belge* 8, no. 3–4 (1917): 181.
41. According to Frank and Musacchio (2008), the average price of rubber from 1880 to 1884 was of 401 pounds/ton; and from 1900 to 1904, with the beginning of the establishment of the first Asian plantations, it was of 459 pounds/ton.
42. Bradford L. Barham and Oliver T. Coomes, "Reinterpreting the Amazon Rubber Boom: Investment, the State, and Dutch Disease," *Latin American Research Review* 29, no. 2 (1994): 73–109; Zephyr Frank and Aldo Musacchio, *The International Natural Rubber Market, 1870–1930*, EH.Net Encyclopedia, ed. Robert Whaples, accessed October 29, 2017, http://eh.net/encyclopedia/the-international-natural-rubber-market-1870-1930/; Weinstein, 2008.
43. Vallvé, "The Impact of the Rubber Boom on the Indigenous Peoples of the Bolivian Lowlands (1859–1920)," 296.
44. Claude Lévi-Strauss, *Tristes trópicos* (Barcelona: Paidós, 1988), 407.
45. John Loadman, *Tears of the Tree: The Story of Rubber—A Modern Marvel* (Oxford: Oxford University Press, 2005), 159.
46. Márcio C. Henrique and Laura T. Morais, "Estradas líquidas, comércio sólido: índios e regatões na Amazônia (século XIX)," *Revista História* (São Paulo) 171 (2014): 49–82. http://dx.doi.org/10.11606/issn.2316-9141.rh.2014.89007.
47. Appadurai, "Introduction: Commodities and the Politics of Value," 13–15.
48. Jean Claude Roux, "El reino del oro negro del Oriente peruano; una primera destrucción del medio amazónico, 1880–1910," in *La construcción de la amazonía andina (siglos XIX–XX)*, ed. Pilar García Jordán (Quito: Ediciones Abya-Yala, 1995), 141, 146.
49. Ibid., 139–40.
50. José María Valcuende, coord., *História e Memórias das Três Fronteiras: Brasil, Peru e Bolívia* (São Paulo: PUC-SP, 2009), 87.

51. Henry W. Bates, *O naturalista no rio Amazonas* (Belo Horizonte: Itatiaia, 1979 [1863]), 160.
52. Gary Van Valen, *Indigenous Agency in the Amazon: The Mojos in Liberal and Rubber-Boom Bolivia 1842–1932* (Tucson: The University of Arizona Press, 2013), 86.
53. Carlos Ramos Núñez, *Historia del derecho civil peruano: siglos XIX y XX*. Vol. 5 (2) (Peru: PUCP/Fondo Editorial; Roux, 2006), 101.
54. Ibid., 121.
55. D. Maldi Meireles, *Guardiães da Fronteira Rio Guaporé, século XVIII* (Petrópolis: Editora Vozes, 1989), 173–75.
56. Casement, *Diario de la Amazonía*, 67.
57. Peru. Annual report. Mr. des Graz to Sir Edward Grey. Lima, January 5, 1914. No. 8 [9318] p. 9. In "Confidential Print: South and Central America and Caribbean General (Folder 6)." (Government Papers, The National Archives, Kew, FO 118/331, 1913), accessed March 19, 2019, http://www.archivesdirect.amdigital.co.uk/Documents/Details/FO_118_331.
58. Brazil. Annual report. Sir W. Haggard to Sir Edward Grey. Petropolis, June 19, 1913. No. 54 [32229] p. 28. In "Confidential Print: South and Central America and Caribbean General (Folder 5)." (Government Papers, The National Archives, Kew, FO 118/317, 1912), accessed March 19, 2019, http://www.archivesdirect.amdigital.co.uk/Documents/Details/FO_118_317.
59. Casement, *Diario de la Amazonía*, 72–73.
60. Ibid., 127, 131–32.
61. Walle, *Bolivia: Its People, Its Resources, Its Railways, Mines and Rubber-Forests*, 286.
62. Casement, *Diario de la Amazonía*, 74–75, 101, 126, 206.
63. Ibid., 101, 206.
64. Ibid., 70–71.
65. Vangroenweghe, *Rood Rubber: Leopold II En Zijn Kongo*, 117.
66. Morel, *Red Rubber: The Story of the Rubber Slave Trade Flourishing on the Congo in the Year of Grace 1906*, 132–33.
67. Vangroenweghe, *Rood Rubber: Leopold II En Zijn Kongo*, 104–5, 110, 239; Harms, "The End of Red Rubber: A Reassessment," 81. An exception to these "modes of remuneration" was Kasai, where rubber workers were usually paid in copper crosses (Vansina, *Being Colonized: The Kuba Experience in Rural Congo, 1880–1960*, 90). Furthermore, before atrocities started in the early 1890s, the Congolese who traded rubber

with Europeans were pleased to receive sufficient payment (textiles and beads), see Roger Anstey, "The Congo Rubber Atrocities—A Case Study," *African Historical Studies* 4, no. 1 (1971): 67.
68. Vangroenweghe, *Rood Rubber: Leopold II En Zijn Kongo*, 44.
69. Ibid., 48.
70. Roger Casement, "Correspondence and Report from His Majesty's Consul at Boma Respecting the Administration of the Independent State of the Congo," *Africa*, no. 1 (1904): 43, accessed June 28, 2018, https://archive.org/details/CasementReport.
71. Robert Harms, "The World Abir Made: The Maringa-Lopori Basin, 1885–1903," *African Economic History* 12 (1983): 133.
72. Nelson, *Colonialism in the Congo Basin, 1880–1940*, 89.
73. For instance: administrative agents active in the ABIR-concession received a 2% commission on the rubber collected, see Harms, "The World Abir Made: The Maringa-Lopori Basin, 1885–1903," 132.
74. Nelson, *Colonialism in the Congo Basin, 1880–1940*, 92.
75. Note from the Court of Appeal at Boma, 13/2/1901, quoted by Casement, "Correspondence and Report from His Majesty's Consul at Boma Respecting the Administration of the Independent State of the Congo," 11.
76. Aldwin Roes, "Towards a History of Mass Violence in the Etat Indépendant Du Congo, 1885–1908," *South African Historical Journal* 62, no. 4 (2010): 639.
77. Consul Huckin to Sir Edward Grey, Iquitos, January 21, 1914. [9192], p. 62. In "South and Central America: Further Correspondence (Folder 3)." (Government Papers, The National Archives, Kew, FO 420/258, 1914), accessed March 19, 2019, http://www.archivesdirect.amdigital.co.uk/Documents/Details/FO_420_258.
78. Walter Hardenburg, *The Putumayo: The Devil's Paradise* (London: T. Fisher Unwin, 1912), 47.
79. Roux, "El reino del oro negro del Oriente peruano; una primera destrucción del medio amazónico, 1880–1910," 142.
80. Casement, *Diario de la Amazonía*, 73.
81. Manuel José Guzmán González, "Los Andokes: historia, conciencia étnica y explotación del caucho," *Revista Universitas Humanistica* 2 (Bogotá: Pontifícia Universiadad Javeriana, 1971), 75.
82. Ibid., 74.

83. Erland Nordenskiöld and George Ernest Fuhrken, *An Ethno-geographical Analysis of the Material Culture of Two Indian Tribes in the Gran Chaco* (Göteborg: Elanders boktryckeri aktiebolag, 1919).
84. Vallvé, "The Impact of the Rubber Boom on the Indigenous Peoples of the Bolivian Lowlands (1859–1920)," 319.
85. Ibid., 341–42.
86. See for example: Casement, *Diario de la Amazonía*; Morel, *Red Rubber: The Story of the Rubber Slave Trade Flourishing on the Congo in the Year of Grace 1906*; and Mark Twain, *King Leopold's Soliloquy: A Defense of His Congo Rule* (Boston: P.R. Warren Co., 1905).
87. Written by the American missionary Charles H. Harvey in January 1905; quoted by Morel, *Red Rubber: The Story of the Rubber Slave Trade Flourishing on the Congo in the Year of Grace 1906*, 76.
88. Casement, *Diario de la Amazonía*; Morel, *Red Rubber: The Story of the Rubber Slave Trade Flourishing on the Congo in the Year of Grace 1906*, 76; and Harms, "The World Abir Made: The Maringa-Lopori Basin, 1885–1903," 134.
89. Letter from missionary Whitehead to the General Governor of the Congo Free State, 7/9/1903; quoted by Casement, "Correspondence and Report from His Majesty's Consul at Boma Respecting the Administration of the Independent State of the Congo," 68–69.
90. Vangroenweghe, *Rood Rubber: Leopold II En Zijn Kongo*, 70–73.
91. Gordon, "Precursors to Red Rubber: Violence in the Congo Free State, 1885–1895."
92. Adam Hochschild, *De Geest Van Koning Leopold II En De Plundering Van De Congo*, trans. Jan-Willem Bos (Amsterdam: Meulenhoff/Kritak, 1988), 170.
93. Note from the Court of Appeal at Boma, 13/2/1901, quoted by Casement, "Correspondence and Report from His Majesty's Consul at Boma Respecting the Administration of the Independent State of the Congo," 53. Although severe atrocities were sometimes brought before the court, Europeans were rarely sentenced.
94. Allen Isaacman and Jan Vansina, "African Initiatives and Resistance in Central Africa, 1880–1914," in *General History of Africa, VII: Africa Under Colonial Domination 1880–1935*, ed. Albert Adu Boahen (Berkeley: Heinemann, 1985), 176.
95. Nelson, *Colonialism in the Congo Basin, 1880–1940*, 97.
96. Franz Keller, *Exploración del Río Madeira en la parte comprendida entre la cachuela de San Antonio y la desembocadura del Mamoré, por los ingenieros brasileños* (La Paz: Imprenta de la Unión Americana, 1870).

97. Vallvé, "The Impact of the Rubber Boom on the Indigenous Peoples of the Bolivian Lowlands (1859–1920)," 363.
98. Ibid., 364.
99. Valcuende, *História e Memórias das Três Fronteiras*, 72; Vallvé, "The Impact of the Rubber Boom on the Indigenous Peoples of the Bolivian Lowlands (1859–1920)," 311.
100. Guzmán, "Los Andokes: historia, conciencia étnica y explotación del caucho," 72.
101. Vansina, *Being Colonized: The Kuba Experience in Rural Congo, 1880–1960*, 105–8, 332–33; Stengers and Vansina, "King Leopold's Congo 1886–1908."
102. Casement, "Correspondence and Report from His Majesty's Consul at Boma Respecting the Administration of the Independent State of the Congo," 70–76.
103. Roes, "Towards a History of Mass Violence in the Etat Indépendant Du Congo, 1885–1908," 659.
104. Terminology derived from James Scott, *Weapons of the Weak: Everyday Forms of Peasant Resistance* (New Haven and London: Yale University Press, 1985). For examples, see Casement, "Correspondence and Report from His Majesty's Consul at Boma Respecting the Administration of the Independent State of the Congo"; Vangroenweghe, *Rood Rubber: Leopold II En Zijn Kongo*; Isaacman and Vansina, "African Initiatives and Resistance in Central Africa, 1880–1914," 181–82; and Nelson, *Colonialism in the Congo Basin, 1880–1940*, 102–3.
105. Circular from the General Governor of the Congo Free State Wahis, 29/3/1901; enclosed in Casement, "Correspondence and Report from His Majesty's Consul at Boma Respecting the Administration of the Independent State of the Congo," 81–82.
106. Vallvé, "The Impact of the Rubber Boom on the Indigenous Peoples of the Bolivian Lowlands (1859–1920)," 334.
107. Quoted by Vangroenweghe, *Rood Rubber: Leopold II En Zijn Kongo*, 252.
108. Quoted by Osumaka Likaka, *Naming Colonialism: History and Collective Memory in the Congo, 1870–1960* (Madison: University of Wisconsin Press, 2009), 85.
109. Casement, "Correspondence and Report from His Majesty's Consul at Boma Respecting the Administration of the Independent State of the Congo."
110. Vangroenweghe, *Rood Rubber: Leopold II En Zijn Kongo*, 255.

111. For instance: Hochschild, *De Geest Van Koning Leopold II En De Plundering Van De Congo*; Isidore Ndaywel è Nziem, *Histoire Générale Du Congo. De L'héritage Ancien À La République Démocratique* (Paris: Duclot, 1998).
112. For example: Stengers, *Le Congo, Mythes Et Réalités. 100 Ans D'histoire*; Jean-Luc Vellut, "Prestige Et Pauvreté De L'histoire Nationale. A Propos D'une Histoire Générale Du Congo," *Revue Belge de Philologie et d'histoire* 77, no. 2 (1999): 480–517.
113. Roes, "Towards a History of Mass Violence in the Etat Indépendant Du Congo, 1885–1908," 646–47.
114. Roux, "El reino del oro negro del Oriente peruano; una primera destrucción del medio amazónico, 1880–1910," 139–40.
115. Valcuende, *História e Memórias das Três Fronteiras*, 75.
116. Walle, *Bolivia: Its People, Its Resources, Its Railways, Mines and Rubber-Forests*, 286.
117. Marco Antônio D. Teixeira and Dante Ribeiro Fonseca, *História Regional (Rondônia)* (Porto Velho: Rondoniana, 2003), 114–15.
118. Roux, "El reino del oro negro del Oriente peruano; una primera destrucción del medio amazónico, 1880–1910," 136.
119. Guzmán, "Los Andokes: historia, conciencia étnica y explotación del caucho," 90.
120. Vallvé, "The Impact of the Rubber Boom on the Indigenous Peoples of the Bolivian Lowlands (1859–1920)," 390.
121. Ibid., 313.
122. Source: Siasi/Sesai, 2014.
123. Carlos Alberto Ricardo and Fany Ricardo, org., *Povos indígenas no Brasil: 2006/2010* (São Paulo: Instituto Socioambiental, 2011), 556.
124. See: Buelens, *Congo 1885–1960. Een Financieel-Economische Geschiedenis*, 84; Nelson, *Colonialism in the Congo Basin, 1880–1940*, 100–1; Stengers and Vansina, "King Leopold's Congo 1886–1908," 337.
125. Walle, *Bolivia: Its People, Its Resources, Its Railways, Mines and Rubber-Forests*, 284.
126. Loadman, *Tears of the Tree: The Story of Rubber—A Modern Marvel*, 158.
127. Vallvé, "The Impact of the Rubber Boom on the Indigenous Peoples of the Bolivian Lowlands (1859–1920)," 334.
128. Guzmán, "Los Andokes: historia, conciencia étnica y explotación del caucho," 86–87, 90.
129. Ibid.

130. Isaacman and Vansina, "African Initiatives and Resistance in Central Africa, 1880–1914," 177.
131. Nelson, *Colonialism in the Congo Basin, 1880–1940*, 97.
132. Vallvé, "The Impact of the Rubber Boom on the Indigenous Peoples of the Bolivian Lowlands (1859–1920)," 343.
133. Ibid., 348.
134. Louise Cardoso de Mello, "Cosmovisión e identidades indígenas en el suroeste de la Amazonía en la primera mitad del siglo XVIII," in *Abya Yala Wawgeykuna: artes, saberes y vivencias de indígenas americanos*, ed. Beatriz Carrera Maldonado and Zara Ruiz Romero (Acer-VOS. Patrimonio Cultural Iberoamericano, 2016), 120–33. http://www.crespial.org/public_files/1493246658.pdf.
135. Julia Seibert, "More Continuity Than Change? New Forms of Unfree Labor in the Belgian Congo, 1908–1930," in *Humanitarian Intervention and Changing Labor Relations: The Long-Term Consequences of the Abolition of the Slave Trade*, ed. Marcel Van der Linden (Leiden and Boston: Brill, 2011), 374.
136. Sven Van Melkebeke, "'Changing Grounds': The Development of Coffee Production in the Lake Kivu Region (1918–1960/62): The Colonial State, Labor, Land and Production for the World Market" (PhD, Ghent University, 2017), 196–201.
137. Edinaldo B Freitas, "Índios de Rondônia. Vozes da (des)integração e Imaginário da sobrevivência," paper presented at the XXV Simpósio Nacional de História, ANPUH, Florianópolis/SC, July 13–17, 2009.
138. Seibert, "More Continuity Than Change? New Forms of Unfree Labor in the Belgian Congo, 1908–1930," 385.

References

Primary Sources (Printed)

Bates, Henry W. *O naturalista no rio Amazonas*. Belo Horizonte: Itatiaia, 1979 [1863].

Casement, Roger. "Correspondence and Report from His Majesty's Consul at Boma Respecting the Administration of the Independent State of the Congo." *Africa* 1 (1904): 1–84. https://archive.org/details/CasementReport.

———. *Diario de la Amazonía*. Edited by Angus Mitchell. Translation by Sonia Fernánde Ordás. La Coruña: Ediciones del viento, 2011 [1910].
"Confidential Print: South and Central America and Caribbean General (Folder 5)." (Government Papers, The National Archives, Kew, FO 118/317, 1912). http://www.archivesdirect.amdigital.co.uk/Documents/Details/FO_118_317.
"Confidential Print: South and Central America and Caribbean General (Folder 6)." (Government Papers, The National Archives, Kew, FO 118/331, 1913). http://www.archivesdirect.amdigital.co.uk/Documents/Details/FO_118_331.
Hardenburg, Walter. *The Putumayo: The Devil's Paradise*. London: T. Fisher Unwin, 1912.
Leplae, Edmond. "Les Grandes Cultures Coloniales Au Congo Belge: Café, Cacao, Caoutchouc, Coton." *Bulletin Agricole du Congo Belge* 8, no. 3–4 (1917): 171–89.
Morel, Edmund D. *Red Rubber: The Story of the Rubber Slave Trade Flourishing on the Congo in the Year of Grace 1906*. New York: Negro Universities Press, 1906.
Nordenskiöld, Erland, and George E. Fuhrken. *An Ethno-geographical Analysis of the Material Culture of Two Indian Tribes in the Gran Chaco*. Göteborg: Elanders boktryckeri aktiebolag, 1919.
"South and Central America: Further Correspondence (Folder 3)." (Government Papers, The National Archives, Kew, FO 420/258, 1914). http://www.archivesdirect.amdigital.co.uk/Documents/Details/FO_420_258.
Twain, Mark. *King Leopold's Soliloquy: A Defense of His Congo Rule*. Boston: P.R. Warren Co., 1905.
Walle, Paul. *Au pays de l'or noir: Para, Amazonas, Matto Grosso*. Paris: E. Guilmoto Éditeur, 1909.
———. *Bolivia: Its People, Its Resources, Its Railways, Mines and Rubber-Forests*. London: T. Fisher Unwin, 1914.

Bibliography

Anstey, Roger. "The Congo Rubber Atrocities—A Case Study." *African Historical Studies* 4, no. 1 (1971): 59–76.
Appadurai, Arjun. "Introduction: Commodities and the Politics of Value." In *The Social Life of Things: Commodities in Cultural Perspective*, edited by Arjun Appadurai, 3–63. Cambridge: Cambridge University Press, 1986.
Barbier, Edward B. *Scarcity and Frontiers: How Economies Have Developed Through Natural Resource Exploitation*. Cambridge and New York: Cambridge University Press, 2011.

Barham, Bradford L., and Oliver T. Coomes. "Reinterpreting the Amazon Rubber Boom: Investment, the State, and Dutch Disease." *Latin American Research Review* 29, no. 2 (1994): 73–109.
Barker, Preston Wallace. *Rubber Statistics 1900–1957*. Washington, DC: Ministerio de Comercio de los EE.UU., 1938.
Beckert, Sven. *Empire of Cotton: A New History of Global Capitalism*. London: Penguin Books, 2015.
Buelens, Frans. *Congo 1885–1960. Een Financieel-Economische Geschiedenis*. Berchem: EPO, 2007.
Cambridge English Dictionary. Cambridge University Press [Online Version]. https://dictionary.cambridge.org/dictionary/english/commodity.
Cardoso de Mello, Louise. "Cosmovisión e identidades indígenas en el suroeste de la Amazonía en la primera mitad del siglo XVIII." In *Abya Yala Wawgeykuna: artes, saberes y vivencias de indígenas americanos*, edited by Beatriz Carrera Maldonado and Zara Ruiz Romero, 120–33. Acer-VOS. Patrimonio Cultural Iberoamericano, 2016. http://www.crespial.org/public_files/1493246658.pdf.
Chirif, Alberto, and Chaparro, Manuel Cornejo, eds. *Imaginario e imágenes de la época del caucho: los sucesos del Putumayo*. Lima: CAAAP/IWGIA/UPC, 2009.
Clarence-Smith, William Gervase. "Rubber Cultivation in Indonesia and the Congo from the 1910s to the 1950s: Divergent Paths." In *Colonial Exploitation and Economic Development: The Belgian Congo and the Netherlands Indies Compared*, edited by Ewout Frankema and Frans Buelens, 193–210. London and New York: Routledge, 2013.
Clement, Piet. "The Land Tenure System in the Congo, 1885–1960: Actors, Motivations and Consequences." In *Colonial Exploitation and Economic Development: The Belgian Congo and the Netherlands Indies Compared*, edited by Ewout Frankema and Frans Buelens, 88–108. London and New York: Routledge, 2013.
Cooper, Frederick. "Conflict and Connection: Rethinking Colonial African History." *American Historical Review* 99, no. 5 (1994): 1516–45.
De Roo, Bas. "Colonial Taxation in Africa: A Fiscal History of the Congo Through the Lens of Customs (1886–1914)." PhD, Ghent University, 2016.
Frank, Zephyr, and Aldo Musacchio. *The International Natural Rubber Market, 1870–1930. EH.Net Encyclopedia*. Edited by Robert Whaples, 2008. http://eh.net/encyclopedia/the-international-natural-rubber-market-1870-1930/.
Freitas, Edinaldo B. "Índios de Rondônia. Vozes da (des)integração e Imaginário da sobrevivência." Paper presented at the XXV Simpósio Nacional de História. ANPUH, Florianópolis/SC, July 13–17, 2009.

Gilbert, David E. "Territorialization in a Closing Commodity Frontier: The Yasuní Rainforests of West Amazonia." *Journal of Agrarian Change* 18 (2018): 229–48.

Gordon, David M. "Precursors to Red Rubber: Violence in the Congo Free State, 1885–1895." *Past & Present* 236, no. 1 (2017): 133–68.

Guzmán González, Manuel José. "Los Andokes: historia, conciencia étnica y explotación del caucho." *Revista Universitas Humanistica* (Bogotá: Pontifícia Universiadad Javeriana) 2 (1971): 53–97.

Harms, Robert. "The End of Red Rubber: A Reassessment." *Journal of African History* 16, no. 1 (1975): 73–88.

———. "The World Abir Made: The Maringa-Lopori Basin, 1885–1903." *African Economic History* 12 (1983): 125–39.

Harp, Stephen L. *A World History of Rubber: Empire, Industry, and the Everyday*. Wiley, 2015. ProQuest Ebook Central. https://ebookcentral.proquest.com/lib/bupo-ebooks/detail.action?docID=4205815.

Henrique, Márcio C., and Laura T. Morais "Estradas líquidas, comércio sólido: índios e regatões na Amazônia (século XIX)." *Revista História* (São Paulo) 171 (2014): 49–82. http://dx.doi.org/10.11606/issn.2316-9141.rh.2014.89007.

Hochschild, Adam. *De Geest Van Koning Leopold II En De Plundering Van De Congo*. Translated by Jan-Willem Bos. Amsterdam: Meulenhoff/Kritak, 1998.

Isaacman, Allen, and Jan Vansina. "African Initiatives and Resistance in Central Africa, 1880–1914." In *General History of Africa, VII: Africa Under Colonial Domination 1880–1935*, edited by Albert Adu Boahen, 169–93. Berkeley: Heineman, 1985.

Kmusser. Map of the Amazon River drainage basin with the Amazon River highlighted. License: Creative Commons Attribution-Share Alike 3.0 Unported. In Wikimedia Commons contributors, "File:Amazonrivermap.svg," Wikimedia Commons, the free media repository, 2013. Accessed July 16, 2018. https://commons.wikimedia.org/w/index.php?title=File:Amazonrivermap.svg&oldid=266045857.

Kopytoff, Igor. "The Cultural Biography of Things: Commoditisation as Process." In *The Social Life of Things: Commodities in Cultural Perspective*, edited by Arjun Appadurai, 64–91. Cambridge: Cambridge University Press, 1986.

Lévi-Strauss, Claude. *Tristes trópicos*. Barcelona: Paidós, 1988.

Likaka, Osumaka. *Naming Colonialism: History and Collective Memory in the Congo, 1870–1960*. Madison: University of Wisconsin Press, 2009.

Loadman, John. *Tears of the Tree: The Story of Rubber—A Modern Marvel*. Oxford: Oxford University Press, 2005.

Luc, Melisa Janet. "Recursos naturales y delimitación de fronteras en América Latina en la primera globalización: una aproximación desde la Guerra del Acre." *tiempo&economía* 2, no. 1 (2015): 69–88. http://orcid.org/0000-0002-0960-9686.

Maldi Meireles, D. *Guardiães da Fronteira Rio Guaporé, século XVIII*. Petrópolis: Editora Vozes, 1989.

McMichael, Philip. "Incorporating Comparison Within a World-Historical Perspective: An Alternative Comparative Method." *American Sociological Review* 55, no. 3 (1990): 385–97.

———. "World-Systems Analysis, Globalization and Incorporated Comparison." *Journal of World-Systems Research* 4, no. 3 (2000): 668–99.

Moore, Jason W. "Madeira, Sugar, and the Conquest of Nature in the "First" Sixteenth Century, Part II: From Regional Crisis to Commodity Frontier, 1506–1530." *Review (Fernand Braudel Center)* 33, no. 1 (2010): 1–24.

Ndaywel è Nziem, Isidore. *Histoire Générale Du Congo. De L'héritage Ancien À La République Démocratique*. Paris: Duclot, 1998.

Nelson, Samuel H. *Colonialism in the Congo Basin, 1880–1940*. Athens, OH: Center for International Studies, 1994.

Northrup, David. *Beyond the Bend in the River: African Labor in Eastern Zaire 1865–1940*. Athens, OH: Center for International Studies, 1988.

Oleksii0. Tropical rainforest map. License: GFDL. In Wikimedia Commons contributors, "File:Tropical rainforest map.png," Wikimedia Commons, the free media repository, 2006. Accessed July 16, 2018. https://uk.wikipedia.org/w/index.php?title=%D0%A4%D0%B0%D0%B9%D0%BB:Tropical_rainforest_map.png&oldid=329016.

Ramos Núñez, Carlos. *Historia del derecho civil peruano: siglos XIX y XX*. Vol. 5 (2). Peru: PUCP/Fondo Editorial, 2006.

Ricardo, Carlos Alberto, and Fany Ricardo, org. *Povos indígenas no Brasil: 2006/2010*. São Paulo: Instituto Socioambiental, 2011.

Roes, Aldwin. "Towards a History of Mass Violence in the Etat Indépendant Du Congo, 1885–1908." *South African Historical Journal* 62, no. 4 (2010): 634–70.

Roux, Jean Claude. "El reino del oro negro del Oriente peruano; una primera destrucción del medio amazónico, 1880–1910." In *La construcción de la amazonía andina (siglos XIX–XX)*, org. Pilar García Jordán, 107–52. Quito: Ediciones Abya-Yala, 1995.

Santos, Roberto. *História Econômica da Amazônia (1800–1920)*. São Paulo: T. A. Queiroz, 1980.

Scott, James. *Weapons of the Weak: Everyday Forms of Peasant Resistance*. New Haven and London: Yale University Press, 1985.
Seibert, Julia. "More Continuity Than Change? New Forms of Unfree Labor in the Belgian Congo, 1908–1930." In *Humanitarian Intervention and Changing Labor Relations: The Long-Term Consequences of the Abolition of the Slave Trade*, edited by Marcel Van der Linden, 369–86. Leiden and Boston: Brill, 2011.
Stengers, Jean. *Le Congo, Mythes Et Réalités. 100 Ans D'histoire*. Gembloux: Duculot, 1989.
Stengers, Jean, and Jan Vansina. "King Leopold's Congo 1886–1908." In *The Cambridge History of Africa, Volume VI, c.1870–1905*, ed. Roland Oliver and G.N. Sanderson, 315–58. Cambridge: Cambridge University Press, 1985.
Teixeira, Marco Antônio D., and Dante Ribeiro Fonseca. *História Regional (Rondônia)*. Porto Velho: Rondoniana, 2003.
Ullán de la Rosa, Francisco Javier. "La era del caucho en el Amazonas (1870–1920): modelos de explotación y relaciones sociales de producción." *Anales del Museo de América* 12 (2004): 183–204.
Valcuende, José María, coord. *História e Memórias das Três Fronteiras: Brasil, Peru e Bolívia*. São Paulo: EDUC/PUC-SP, 2009.
Vallvé, Frederic. "The Impact of the Rubber Boom on the Indigenous Peoples of the Bolivian Lowlands (1859–1920)." PhD, Georgetown University, 2010.
Van der Linden, Marcel. *Workers of the World: Essays Toward a Global Labor History*. Leiden and Boston: Brill, 2008.
Van Melkebeke, Sven. "'Changing Grounds': The Development of Coffee Production in the Lake Kivu Region (1918–1960/62): The Colonial State, Labor, Land and Production for the World Market." PhD, Ghent University, 2017.
Vangroenweghe, Daniël. *Rood Rubber: Leopold II En Zijn Kongo*. Brussels: Elsevier, 1985.
Vansina, Jan. *Being Colonized: The Kuba Experience in Rural Congo, 1880–1960*. Madison: University of Wisconsin Press, 2010.
Van Valen, Gary. *Indigenous Agency in the Amazon: The Mojos in Liberal and Rubber-Boom Bolivia 1842–1932*. Tucson: The University of Arizona Press, 2013.
Vellut, Jean-Luc. "La Violence Armée Dans L'etat Indépendant Du Congo." *Cultures et Développement* 16, no. 3–4 (1984): 671–707.
———. "Prestige Et Pauvreté De L'histoire Nationale. A Propos D'une Histoire Générale Du Congo." *Revue Belge de Philologie et d'histoire* 77, no. 2 (1999): 480–517.
Weinstein, Barbara. *The Amazon Rubber Boom: 1850–1920*. Stanford: Stanford University Press, 1983.

7

Chilean Expansion and Southern South America's Integration into the Modern Capitalist System, 1879–1931

James Lockhart

Chilean expansion into the Atacama Desert in the north, Araucania in the south, and the Magellan Straits further south drove the construction of the modern Chilean nation, particularly its institutions, political parties, and labor movement, while shaping and conditioning the integration of Chile and southern South America into the capitalist system in the late nineteenth and early twentieth centuries. Much of this expansion was driven by the region's growing mining activities and Chileans' use of force and negotiations to gain control over them and the territories in which they occurred. These closely interrelated political, military, and economic activities helped to unleash new forms of social conflict within the country that took decades to resolve.

For those inclined to interpret this history through the lens of dependency theory or the world-system, which remain focused on Western European and North American financiers and industrialists as the prime movers of global processes that underdeveloped Latin America, this Chilean-centered perspective may seem counterintuitive. But from a

J. Lockhart (✉)
American University in Dubai, Dubai, United Arab Emirates
e-mail: jlockhart@aud.edu

S. Joseph (ed.), *Commodity Frontiers and Global Capitalist Expansion*,
Palgrave Studies in Economic History, https://doi.org/10.1007/978-3-030-15322-9_7

ground-up perspective, such perspectives become compelling. Thus, this chapter shows how Chileans made their own history while contributing to southern South American and world history as well.[1]

Although modern Chilean history began with independence in the early nineteenth century, it quickened during the War of the Pacific in the early 1880s. What followed was a rough and uneven process, not a smooth linear one. Peruvians, Bolivians, and Argentines contested parts of it, as did some Chileans. The US and Chile's early encounters were troubled, too. Chileans nevertheless reified their country as a liberal nation aligned with like-minded liberals in southern South America, the inter-American and transatlantic communities, and the modern capitalist system by the early 1930s.[2]

Chilean Expansion to the War of the Pacific

Chileans remained mired in anarchy and strongman politics until a merchant named Diego Portales settled their disputes in the early 1830s. Portales was interested in practical government, law and order, and a pro-business legal system, not liberal democracy. He inaugurated a pragmatic constitutional order known as the autocratic republic in 1833. It endured for sixty years, until the civil war of 1891.[3]

The autocratic republic had to confront the same issues that complicated inter-American relations everywhere at the time: territorial integrity and border security, which the collapse of Spain's imperial system had left poorly defined, a problem which the Industrial Revolution's need for minerals and other natural resources would exacerbate in the late nineteenth century. Meanwhile, Brazil and Argentina continued Portugal and Spain's older rivalries in what became Uruguay. Mexico City and Lima, once Spain's two most powerful viceroyalties, lost control over areas they had administered since the sixteenth century. Central America moved away from Mexico City and then disintegrated into several smaller, independent nations, as the US swept through what became the American Southwest. Gran Colombia's history followed a similar trajectory, leaving the republics of Ecuador, Colombia, and Venezuela in its aftermath.

Chileans started projecting political, military, and economic power along southern South America's Pacific coast by the mid-1830s. They broke up a potentially threatening Peruvian-Bolivian confederation in 1836. Then, they started expanding north, south, and east.[4]

Chile had remained a small, agricultural nation, confined to the central valley surrounding Santiago, until the 1830s. Its lands extended north to Copiapó and south to the Rio Bío Bío, which demarcated the Indian frontier, known as Araucania. This changed as Chilean exports surged, partly responding to increases in demand in California and Australia, which were experiencing gold rushes, and partly serving industrializing and urbanizing European markets. Chilean wheat and flour exports to California alone rose from 6000 quintals in 1848 to 500,000 in 1850. This booming economy soon encompassed silver, copper, iron, and nitrate exports from the north and coal production in the south.[5]

These exports and lucrative mining areas propelled Chilean expansion, beginning with the agricultural lands of Araucania. The Mapuche Indians had resisted Incan and Spanish rule there for centuries, but they were no match for the Chilean army, which possessed modern weapons and had much shorter lines of communication and supply. Chileans constructed justifications for this that historians versed in the literature on American expansion will no doubt recognize—starting with their increasing military presence in the region. As Chile's chief of naval operations told congressmen in the 1840s, "if you cast a glance over the rest of the world and observe that the two most free and industrious nations are precisely those that possess the greatest naval forces, you will be tempted perhaps to study the intimate relationship between war and merchant fleets, and between merchant fleets and the greatness of a people." Chileans developed sea power, seizing positions along the Araucanian coast to the Magellan Straits, that decade.[6]

Chilean expansion did not stop at these maritime positions in the south. It spilled east over the Andes, into Argentine Patagonia. Argentines, whose nation remained in disarray, objected to this. But Chileans ignored them. When a Chilean colonization agent described his country's geography to European immigrants, he told them that it encompassed both "cisandine" and "transandine" lands. He also referred to Chile's *acción civilizadora*—its civilizing mission—when explaining its long-term intentions there.[7]

As the nineteenth century wore on, Chileans contemplated the surviving Mapuches with less patience. Some advised treating them quite harshly. For example, one newspaper's editors disdained them as "savages…this stupid race…odious and prejudicial guests in Chile," and called for "prompt and extreme measures" to deal with them. The Indian wars that followed were remarkably similar to the ones Americans and Argentines waged at roughly the same time, leading to the forcible removal of Indians from their lands and their subsequent impoverishment in each case.[8]

Meanwhile, Chilean mining operations pushed north into the Atacama, into Bolivian territory, and indeed all the way into Tarapacá, a southern Peruvian province where Chileans had invested about 20 million pesos and imported over 10,000 miners. Chileans, Bolivians, and Peruvians had only recognized this area's importance after they discovered large deposits of *guano*—mountains of bird droppings that had accumulated for centuries—there. Americans and Europeans prized it as high-grade fertilizer, which they also used to fabricate explosives. This created additional conflicts and gave yet more momentum to Chilean expansion.[9]

Thus, it was in this atmosphere that Chileans negotiated an agreement with Bolivia. This agreement fixed the two nations' border at the 24th parallel. Santiago and La Paz would jointly administer and tax the *guano* exported, and—vaguely—"the minerals extracted," from the territory between the 23rd and 25th parallels thereafter. Although Chileans and Bolivians agreed that La Paz would operate a customs office at Mejillones, Santiago's agents would also be there, ensuring that Chilean imports and exports passed through duty, and hassle, free. Bolivians still regarded this area as falling within a peripheral wasteland, so they did not object to what amounted to shared sovereignty on their coast. This soon changed.[10]

Chilean prospector José Díaz discovered the Caracoles silver mine in this region in 1870. Caracoles yielded approximately 1000 metric tons of silver over the next decade. Bolivians came to fear that Chileans were becoming too comfortable and were exploiting too many resources in this territory, and they moved, belatedly, to reassert sovereignty there. They argued that the existing treaty limited Chilean mining to *guano*.

Chileans, intending to consolidate what was rapidly becoming their de facto colony, claimed that it included *any* minerals from there. And so this area became an international flashpoint in the 1870s.[11]

Santiago and La Paz attempted to resolve this by revising their agreement. They reaffirmed that the Chilean-Bolivian border remained at the 24th parallel. But Chileans renounced their claims to condominium between the 23rd and 25th parallels in exchange for Bolivians' pledging to share *guano* revenues and not to raise taxes on Chileans' exporting whatever other minerals they extracted for the next twenty-five years. Acquiescing to the cooperative international relations and then appearing in the transatlantic and inter-American communities, the two governments agreed to submit any new dispute that might arise to arbitration.[12]

But the underlying issues—which nation or nations would control these territories and export these minerals?—remained unresolved, and all three governments prepared to settle them through war. Peruvians and Bolivians had already signed a secret pact against further Chilean expansion, while the Chilean navy bought two state-of-the-art warships from Britain. Then, Bolivia's Gen. Hilarión Daza (1876–1879), determined to restore Bolivian sovereignty in the Atacama, seized power in La Paz.[13]

From Flashpoint to War

Daza's unilateralism, particularly his harassing the *Compañía de Salitres y Ferrocarril de Antofagasta*, a Chilean corporation that specialized in nitrate mining and railroad transportation to ports within the disputed region, triggered the War of the Pacific (1879–1883). In December 1878, Daza raised the company's taxes, instructing it to pay this higher rate retroactively. Chilean President Aníbal Pinto (1876–1881) argued that this violated the two countries' agreement. He asked Daza to submit the issue to arbitration. The general nationalized the company's assets in response. The president dispatched Chilean warships and ground forces to occupy the territory that February. Daza declared war against Chile the next month. Pinto in turn demanded that the

Peruvian government abrogate its pact with Bolivia—it had been an open secret. Lima refused, and Santiago declared war against both in April 1879.[14]

Chileans promptly won this war. They stated their terms during an American-sponsored conference aboard USS *Lackawanna* off Arica in October 1880: Peruvians and Bolivians must acknowledge guilt for the war. The Peruvian government must pay the Chilean government 20 million pesos in reparations and recognize Chilean administrative rights in Tacna and Arica until it had paid this in full. Peru must cede all of Tarapacá to Chile. Bolivia must give up its coastline.[15]

These terms shocked Peruvians and Bolivians, who rejected them. Chileans occupied Lima and continued to prosecute the war. The Peruvian government withdrew from the capital and then launched an insurgency.

Meanwhile, President Domingo Santa María (1881–1886) and his Argentine counterpart agreed that the Andes, "running from the highest summits that divide the waters and passing between the slopes that fall to one side or the other," would mark the Chilean-Argentine border to the 52nd parallel, just north of the straits, which they neutralized, that July. They drew a straight line from Cabo del Espíritu Santo to the Beagle Channel, stipulating that Chilean territory fell to the west of this line, Argentine to the east. Chile would possess "all islands south of the channel to Cape Horn and all to the west of Tierra del Fuego." They would appoint a joint team of experts to mark this border and submit any disputes that might arise to arbitration.[16]

Following this, Chileans negotiated a separate peace with Peru. In the Treaty of Ancón, Lima ceded Tarapacá to Santiago. Chileans would administer Peru's Tacna and Arica provinces for ten years after the treaty's ratification. When this expired, they would jointly supervise a plebiscite, asking residents to decide their future. Chileans would occupy Lima and Las Islas de Lobos until Peruvians ratified the treaty. Peruvians would cede fifty percent of the islands' *guano* revenues to Chileans and pay them 300,000 pesos each month to offset their costs.[17]

This war was primarily about control over resource-rich territories in the Atacama, but it also helped to construct Chilean identity, particularly Chilean exceptionalism—and even a sense of greatness. Chilean elites proudly believed that they had created a model republic that championed the rights of peoples while characterizing their country as the England of South America. As a Chilean senator, dispatched on a confidential mission to the US, would reassure President Franklin Roosevelt (1933–1945) during the early years of the Second World War, "Mr. President, the Pacific Ocean, up to Panama, is ours."[18]

The War of the Pacific and the Inter-American System

Chilean expansion and southern South America's integration into the modern capitalist system were not merely expressions of social and economic processes relating to the possession of *guano*, silver, and other extractive commodities in the Atacama. They were also about politics and diplomacy, particularly legal and commercial cooperation, within the inter-American system, which represented only part of the still nascent international community in the late nineteenth century. All of this happened within the context of a much larger, multifaceted industrial-era global transformation. And Chileans remained actively involved in it.

The *Lackawanna* conference reconfirmed the US and others' growing preference for negotiation and persuasion over older patterns of coercion and force in international relations. Latin American internationalists such as Simón Bolívar had long contributed to this. Bolívar had invited representatives from Mexico, Guatemala, Colombia, Argentina, Chile, and Brazil to Panama in 1826, "to serve as advisors in moments of great conflict, as facilitators of communication in the face of common dangers, as faithful interpreters in public negotiations in difficult times, and lastly as mediators of our differences."[19]

Latin Americans' territorial conflicts, border issues, and the minerals at stake tended to prevent them from working together back then. But Bello and other Spanish-American jurists continued arguing the merits of such a system in the decades that followed. "A congress of plenipotentiaries," he wrote, "does the same thing that ten or twelve men do who have contemplated businesses in which their interests conflict: they sign a contract to prevent, as far as prudence reaches, occasions for dispute...and, with anticipation, to establish rules for settling them in what appears the fairest manner."[20]

Latin Americans continued these conversations during the War of the Pacific, when the Colombian government proposed a regional arbitration agreement, "with the aim of eliminating international wars forever from the American Continent," just as American negotiators were hosting Peruvian, Bolivian, and Chilean representatives aboard *Lackawanna*. However, the moment was still not right. And these efforts failed, too.[21]

Following this, the Garfield administration (1881) attempted to revitalize the endeavor. Secretary of State James Blaine, fearing European intervention in the war, proposed that the US host an inter-American conference in Washington, DC. He hoped to mediate the conflict while also discussing regional cooperation, particularly with respect to trade. He encountered resistance, however, and President James Garfield's assassination led to his resignation before he could overcome it.[22]

President Chester Arthur (1881–1885) and Secretary of State Frederick Frelinghuysen indefinitely postponed this conference upon assuming office. In their estimation, "[the] peaceful condition of the South American Republics, which was contemplated as essential to a profitable and harmonious assembling of the Congress, does not exist." Frelinghuysen still offered to mediate the war through "the consistent policy of equal and unprejudiced friendship towards [the] three sovereign republican states." But these efforts went nowhere.[23]

These endeavors went nowhere partly because they had alarmed Santiago. Chileans were not ready for cooperative international relations where their newly acquired territories were exposed and at risk. Indeed, they viewed the US' efforts as unsolicited meddling between victors and vanquished, and Chilean-American relations deteriorated.[24]

What became a downward trend reached its nadir during Chile's civil war in 1891. The Chilean Congress and Capt. Jorge Montt formed the *Junta Revolucionaria de Iquique* and revolted against President José Balmaceda (1886–1891) that January. Montt's *junta* sailed north and secured the mines there, which now included many valuable nitrate fields around Iquique, as its base of operations. Balmaceda remained in Santiago and retained most of the army's loyalty in a war that pitted Congress, Montt, and the navy against the president and the army.[25]

As Ambassador Patrick Egan reported, this dispute represented an executive-legislative power struggle over the specific balance the Chilean government should strike between presidentialism and parliamentarianism. Egan highlighted "the contention on the part of the President for a popular representative status similar to that occupied by the President of the United States, with the additional power to appoint and remove his ministers at pleasure, which right is given him under the constitution, while the opposition battles for a strictly parliamentary system and the removal of ministers whenever they cease to have the support of a majority in Congress." The *junta* won the war. Adm. Montt returned to Santiago as interim president. Balmaceda's suicide marked the end of the autocratic republic that September.[26]

The *junta* formed a provisional government while persecuting the late president's surviving supporters. It intended to execute some of them. Many had sought asylum in the American embassy and onboard USS *Baltimore* in Valparaíso, both of which the government subjected to blatant surveillance.[27]

This tension exploded after Chileans clashed with around 120 US sailors on liberty from *Baltimore* that October. One American died from gunshot wounds, five suffered injuries, and one died from these injuries later. More than 30 went to jail. Since this involved a US-flagged warship, it brought Washington and Santiago into conflict.[28]

The provisional government's grievances were clear. The Harrison administration (1889–1893) and Egan had sympathized with the Balmaceda government and refused to recognize the *junta* or sell arms to it during the war. Then, *Baltimore* had sheltered some of the surviving *balmacedistas* and transported them to Peru, where many of them were living in exile. Thus, the administration interpreted the incident as retaliatory, and Secretary of State Blaine, now reinstated, pressed Montt to submit the matter to arbitration. According to the Department of State, "our sailors were unarmed and gave no provocation…the assaults upon them were by armed men, greatly superior in numbers, and as we must conclude, animated in their bloody work by hostility to these men as sailors of the United States." Further, "the public police, or some of them, took part in the attack."[29]

The provisional government's foreign minister, Manuel Matta, dismissed this as "a fight between some drunken sailors" and waved off

Harrison and Blaine's position as "erroneous and deliberately incorrect." Meanwhile, Chileans formally elected Montt to the presidency, reestablishing constitutional government that December. The Montt administration (1891–1896) withdrew surveillance from the American embassy in an effort to reduce tension. It also consented to the remaining refugees' leaving the country. But the *Baltimore* affair remained unresolved and Matta's words still hung in the air.[30]

Blaine responded the following month. Chileans had attacked "the uniform of the U.S. Navy, having its origin and motive in a feeling of hostility to this Government, and not in any act of the sailors." Further, "the public authorities…flagrantly failed their duty to protect our men, and…some of the police and of the Chilean soldiers and sailors were themselves guilty of unprovoked assaults upon our sailors before and after arrest." "No self-respecting government," he continued, "can consent that persons in its service, whether civil or military, shall be beaten and killed in a foreign territory in resentment of acts done by or imputed to their government without exacting reparation." The US would therefore "terminate diplomatic relations with the Government of Chile" unless it offered "a suitable apology" and "some adequate reparation."[31]

Montt's new foreign minister, Luis Pereira, expressed his government's regret seventy-two hours later. Pereira suggested that the US Supreme Court arbitrate the matter. The American and Chilean governments resumed normal relations and Santiago eventually paid reparations to the families of the dead. This notwithstanding, US-Chilean relations remained cool into the 1920s. This outcome did show, however, that cooperative international relations rather than coercion and force were gradually, if painfully for some, taking hold in the inter-American system and that Chileans were helping to bring it to life.[32]

The Chilean Communist Party

All of this also set into motion new conflicts within Chile. These conflicts fostered the political, social, and economic problems that led to regime change in the 1890s and 1920s. Congress's victory over Balmaceda in 1891, the revised interpretation of Chile's political system that the winners imposed in its aftermath, and the increased pace of mining operations, industrialization, and globalization that followed, cultivated a Chilean labor movement whose militancy shocked the conservative establishment. The Soviet Union (USSR) and the international communist movement also appeared, explicitly and violently challenging the growing liberal international order. The Chilean Communist Party (PCCh), aligned with Moscow's Third Communist International (Comintern), arose in this environment, provoking the reactionary violence in Chile that culminated in the Ibáñez dictatorship in the late 1920s.

Much of this started in Chile's northern mining communities, where Chilean and British investors were jointly exploiting the Atacama's nitrate fields. The Chilean government had inherited public ownership of these works after seizing them during the war—Lima had nationalized them in 1875. Public ownership, however, remained anathema to Chilean conservatives' *laissez-faire* philosophy at the time, and Congress privatized the fields in 1881. Both Chilean and British investors quickly bought them. Chilean presidents remained content to tax their exports. This was just as the Chilean government wanted it; it was not imposed by foreign countries or financial institutions. As Santa María explained, "Let the gringos work the nitrate freely. I shall be waiting for them at the door."[33]

These attitudes also accounted for American investment in Chilean copper—whose mines were also in the Atacama—at the turn of the century. Chilean miners had exhausted the copper deposits most easily accessible to human labor by the 1880s. Since they lacked the expertise and equipment to dig deeper, production declined over the next twenty years. Then, American entrepreneur William Braden, founder of the Braden Copper Company, introduced the capital, managerial know-how, and technology that enabled Chilean copper to survive and even thrive thereafter.

These mines remained the Chilean government's primary source of income. They enabled Santiago to spend on public employment and other programs. These funds, which had not existed before the War of the Pacific, contributed to the civil war of 1891, as Balmaceda and Congress clashed, in part, over how the government should use this money. Balmaceda favored investment in the public sector and the development of infrastructure while Congress preferred small government and a strictly free-market approach.

Congress carried the argument when it won the war. Legislators—mostly landowners with aristocratic pretentions—dominated national politics during Chile's so-called parliamentary era, from the 1890s until it collapsed in the 1920s. They jealously controlled the government's budget and constantly removed cabinet members via interpellation, a procedure they had learned while observing politics in Europe. But they merely created "a shallow, grossly inefficient copy of the British parliamentary system," according to historian Frederick Nunn and other informed observers.[34]

Parliamentary-era politicians constantly maneuvered for position in a fluid environment of rapidly shifting alliances and coalitions, backroom deals in the *Club de la Unión*, and rampant vote buying on the street. They ignored the social conflicts that were engulfing the nation—indeed, they seemed to focus on an earlier, preindustrial era while remaining oblivious to them. As President Ramón Barros (1910–1915), perhaps best known for the sandwich that still bears his name, put it, "There are two kinds of problems: those that solve themselves, and those that have no solution."[35]

Thus, the presidency remained immobilized as an institution of government during these years. Presidents could not have engaged these problems even if they had been inclined to. By historian Frederick Pike's count, about 120 ministers of interior, the chief cabinet officer, came and went while countless other officials passed through the revolving door of government.[36]

Meanwhile, expanding mining activities and the industrialization and urbanization that had followed the War of the Pacific produced Chile's working class, which emerged in the northern mining communities, where nitrate companies required larger, more specialized labor to carry out their operations. Coal mining also brought Chilean entrepreneurs such as Matías Cousiño, Jorge Rojas, and Federico Schwager, and still more miners to Coronel and Lota in the south. Chileans also improved ports and built trains. This too required labor. Chilean cities, from Iquique to Concepción, boomed. This growth required yet more labor to construct and service new buildings, horse-drawn trolleys, and streets with electric lighting.[37]

Chileans did not import immigrant labor from Europe and East Asia as Americans did. They recruited peasants and Indians from the central valley and southern regions. Most of these workers found low-wage and unpredictable employment in the mines, their identity as an emerging working class, and their political voices as well. Wealthy and middle-class Chileans employed others in the informal domestic-services sector, mostly as housekeepers and babysitters. The rest, the majority, remained tied to the nation's quasi-feudal *haciendas* as peasants. Some of these peasants drifted from *hacienda* to *hacienda* for seasonal work.

Nitrate miners served a particularly unstable export market that often left them laid off or worse. They lived in poor housing, had no insurance or retirement, and remained subject to company scrip, company stores, and company bars. Their earliest leaders demanded nothing more ambitious than that management might cover the scorching pits that processed nitrate ores. Some had fallen into them and burned to death. Others were so badly disfigured that they could never work again. They could not have returned to the *haciendas*, either, as landowners did not want anyone who had had even passing contact with mining and the labor movement on their property. So, they struggled for subsistence, often resorting to begging, in what remained of their lives.[38]

Landowners' fears derived from their knowledge of the Chilean labor movement, which had arisen in Iquique and within other northern mining communities. It had begun as a collection of loosely networked, mutual-aid groups. Workers, although initially responding to the immediate problems they faced, soon came into contact with the anarchist, socialist, and Marxist literature that had been crossing the Atlantic since as early as the 1850s. PCCh historian Hernán Ramírez counted Henri de Saint-Simon, Pierre-Joseph Proudhon, and Karl Marx among the authors whose works were popular in Chilean bookstores that decade. This literature helped the movement develop its political worldviews and vocabulary, which in turn helped workers make sense of their situation.[39]

European socialists started arriving in Chile in the late nineteenth century, too. Ramírez recounted how "many...had been militants in workers' organizations and adhered to socialist doctrines. So, for example, some 300 French nationals arrived in Punta Arenas in the 1870s.

They had been exiled from their country for their participation in the Paris Commune." Chilean authorities distributed these immigrants throughout the nation. The Chilean labor movement embraced these transatlantic connections with the international labor movement and matured in the years that followed. Thus, the movement's leaders and many of its rank and file members gradually came to believe that their problems derived from an exploitative political-economic system that was oppressing workers all over the world, and not merely from their own troubles in the northern mining communities.[40]

This movement doubled at the turn of the century. According to Ramírez, it increased from approximately 150,000 in 1890 to 300,000 in 1910. It was increasingly confrontational. Political scientist Brian Loveman counted 10 strikes involving nearly 5000 workers in 1911. This rose to 105 strikes with some 50,000 by 1920.[41]

Marxist-inspired calls to action began appearing in the movement's press in the 1890s. Such calls led to suppression. The worst case on record occurred in Iquique in December 1907. Miners and sympathetic workers had gathered there to protest the inflationary hardships they were experiencing as prices rose and the peso's value decreased while their wages remained the same. They demanded pay raises, the introduction of new businesses that would compete with company services inside their towns and camps, and iron bars to cover the pits. Around 1000 had started marching that January in what coalesced into a larger strike by December. They pledged to maintain the shutdown until their employers met their demands.[42]

Somewhere between 15,000 and 23,000, strikers had arrived in Iquique by 21 December. Minister of Interior Rafael Sotomayor declared a state of siege, dispatched warships to seize the port, and instructed workers to leave the city. Some complied with this order. Others defied it, seeking refuge with their families in a local schoolhouse. Gen. Roberto Silva's soldiers fired upon them, killing about 200 and wounding some 300. Another 90 died from their wounds later.[43]

The PCCh's founders first appeared in the northern mining communities at about this time. They filled a vacuum in an increasingly diverse Chilean political spectrum. Conservatives represented Chileans' centralized, authoritarian tendencies as manifested in the revised, post-civil war constitutional order. Liberals wanted to further reform this constitution to create a more decentralized, explicitly secular system. But these two parties, representing Chile's conservative establishment, remained socially and economically indistinct apart from these issues. The Radical Party, representing the emerging middle class and featuring even more pronounced anticlerical and liberal-democratic interests, had broken away from Liberals in the 1860s. The Democratic Party represented artisans and some skilled workers. Its members had splintered from Radicals in 1887.

One of these Democrats, Luis Recabarren, led a small, class-conscious faction that joined the Second International in 1908. Recabarren convened approximately 20 miners and shoemakers in Iquique on 6 June 1912. He asked them to break from the Democratic Party because it did not advocate the kind of social change he believed necessary. He proposed they create the Socialist Workers' Party (POS), which would unify and educate laborers under one banner while working to abolish private property. This motion passed 15–5, and several sections arose from the Atacama to the Magellan Straits. Recabarren was an indefatigable internationalist. He created the Chilean Labor Federation (FOCH) in 1916 and helped to organize what would become the Argentine Communist Party as well.[44]

Recabarren and his colleagues closely followed the First World War. When Vladimir Lenin's Bolsheviks seized power in November 1917 and then formed the Comintern, "to unite the efforts of all truly revolutionary parties of the world's proletariat, thus facilitating and hastening the victory of the communistic revolution throughout the world," Recabarren proposed that the POS join it. The party assembled in Valparaíso in 1920, where it reinvented itself as "an authentic communist party, integrated in the international communist movement." It changed its name to the PCCh and purged "reformers and counterrevolutionaries"—that is, anarchists, noncommunist socialists, and anyone whose political sympathies remained closer to the Second International than the Comintern—from its ranks.[45]

The PCCh's leadership forwarded these resolutions to its various sections throughout the country for comment in 1921. These sections followed the reasoning that appeared in one Antofagasta newspaper that March: "There is no middle ground…There are only two paths to follow: Either we go with our Russian brothers and social revolution or not…Those who go against the Russian proletariat necessarily stand with capitalist society, with our oppressors." The party reconvened for its first congress in Rancagua in January 1922. There, it proclaimed that it "constitutes the Chilean Section of the Communist International, accepts its thesis and fights for its cause, the cause of the proletariat." M.A. Komin-Alexandrovski, the Comintern's representative in Buenos Aires, reported favorably on the PCCh and its counterparts in Brazil, Uruguay, and Argentina that month, urging Moscow to take the region seriously.[46]

Recabarren travelled to the USSR in December 1922. He reported on Chilean conditions and the PCCh's organization and strength and requested support. He found that although Moscow was interested in Latin America, it could not send any money to Chile because it was concentrating its resources in Germany. The Kremlin advised him to make contacts with neighboring communists. Meanwhile, the Comintern trained Recabarren in subversion and tradecraft.[47]

The Soviet Union announced its strategy in southern South America in 1924. "In those Latin American countries where sections of our party exist, these sections' oral and written propaganda should demonstrate the advance of imperialism…The Argentine, Uruguayan, and Chilean parties should denounce all manifestations of imperialism in neighboring countries such as Bolivia, Peru, Paraguay, and even Ecuador and Colombia, to influence worker and peasant opinion there." This should unite the region behind Moscow in world affairs. The Comintern created its South American Bureau, headquartered in Buenos Aires, to oversee this in February 1925.[48]

Chilean Communists accepted this and later advice from Moscow by their own choice and they did so quite zealously. The Kremlin regarded the PCCh very favorably in turn, cultivating what historian Olga Ulianova characterized as "a privileged relationship." As historian María Soledad Gomez understood, too, this partly accounted for the party's changing structure, strategies, and tactics for the remainder of the twentieth century.[49]

To the Ibáñez Dictatorship

Chilean anticommunism arose in response to the labor movement, its militancy, and Chilean Communists' internationalism. Although Chilean anticommunists remained well connected within the inter-American and transatlantic communities, their movement remained an indigenous one, led by Chilean elites—primarily landowners, mine owners, and other businessmen—and the Chilean army's Prussian-trained professional officer corps. They were not puppets, and no one from Washington, London, Paris, or Berlin pulled their strings.

The Chilean government invested some of its earnings from nitrate and copper exports in military modernization in the late nineteenth and early twentieth centuries. This created a new class of officers with their own sense of identity and purpose. These officers perceived themselves as the nation's truest guardians and last line of defense, and they became openly anti-Soviet by the 1920s. They altered the nature of the conflict between the conservative establishment and labor movement, leading to military dictatorship and a new constitution.

This partly reflected German influences. Chileans contracted Capt. Emil Körner to command a Prussian military mission to Chile in the mid-1880s. Körner established the *Academia de Guerra* (the War College) in September 1886. The War College offered a two- to three-year course that trained select, early career officers in military professionalism. These courses included seminars in Western military history and geography, war games and tactics, weapons and ballistics, fortifications, and physics and inorganic chemistry. Cavalry and infantry officers learned world history and German while engineers and artillerymen studied higher mathematics. Those who remained for a third year specialized in Chilean military history, with attention to the country's territorial and border disputes and an introduction to command and staff planning. They also completed some coursework in international law.[50]

As historian Enrique Brahm García explained, no other foreign influence—not British, French, or American—would imprint the Chilean army as profoundly as Körner's mission. This went beyond the technical training, uniforms, and arms the Prussians offered. It fostered an elite identity and distinctly antipolitical outlook that taught Chilean officers, like their German counterparts at the time, to see themselves as the fatherland's ultimate protectors, not only against foreign, but also domestic threats, including civilian politicians, whom they viewed as irredeemably corrupt. While Peruvians, Argentines, and Brazilians contracted European missions, too, "Nowhere," in Loveman's estimation, "did European military missions more thoroughly penetrate a Latin American army than Chile, and nowhere did a supposedly apolitical professional army become more imbued with doctrine that made its officers contemptuous of civilian politics and politicians."[51]

These officers became the parliamentary regime's strikebreakers in the northern mining communities. This further politicized them and alienated them from the ruling class and the government. They soon began deliberating their nation's problems. Politicians' paralysis, selfishness, and pettiness, mixed with the country's growing instability—which many officers feared was empowering Bolshevism—contributed a sense of urgency. These officers' discontent became manifest in several minor conspiracies against the government in the early 1920s.[52]

It was in this environment that Arturo Alessandri (1920–1924, 1925, and 1932–1938) won the presidency. He challenged the parliamentary regime, promising to strengthen the executive branch, and, among other things, to pass labor legislation and other reforms. He came from outside the establishment and he approached politics through direct appeals to the masses. He commanded large popular demonstrations and had the old regime on the run. But he encountered an obstructionist, business-as-usual Congress after his inauguration. Even senators and deputies from his own coalition failed to back him. Some even opposed him.[53]

Four years into this, in September 1924, 20–50 army officers attended Senate hearings on congressional salaries. They were exasperated by congressmen's ignoring the nation's social problems while they granted themselves raises. The officers' presence represented its own message. They made a show of applauding those lawmakers who spoke against the salary bill for those who had not received that message.

Senators demanded the minister of war instruct these officers to leave when they appeared in the gallery the next day. The minister ran into unexpected insubordination when he ordered a captain to record the names of all present, and the captain retorted that he was not a stenographer. The minister fell back on persuasion, the officers eventually agreeing to retire to the *Club Militar*, literally rattling their sabers on the way out.[54]

When the army's high command, which consisted of an older generation that remained connected to landowners through kinship ties, declined to discipline the younger officers lest it lose control of them, it only emboldened them. These younger officers formed the *Junta Militar y Naval*, rallying around Maj. Carlos Ibáñez, a cavalryman who emerged as their spokesman on Friday, 5 September. On that day, Ibáñez demanded that Congress reject the salary proposal, enact the labor code that Alessandri had been trying to pass, put forward an income-tax law, and improve army pay and benefits. Alessandri received Ibáñez in *La Moneda*, the presidential palace, and forwarded his demands to Congress. Lawmakers submitted within hours. But it was not over.[55]

Ibáñez next instructed Alessandri to dismiss the minister of war and two other cabinet ministers. The president declined, ordering the major to disband the *junta*. He refused, creating a constitutional crisis. The three ministers resigned on their own to save Alessandri further embarrassment. But Ibáñez remained committed to intervention even after this, the *junta* being in no mood to suffer civilian politicians anymore.

Alessandri, sensing this hostility, dissolved Congress. The president feared that he was in personal danger. He and his family sought asylum in the American embassy very late on Tuesday evening, 8 September. He was moving into exile in Rome.

Ambassador William Collier accompanied Alessandri as far as Mendoza, reporting that the president had offered his resignation twice before the *junta* finally granted him six months' leave. Alessandri resigned a third time in Buenos Aires, explaining that "he believes it to be inconsistent with his self-respect and dignity to remain in office when he is not permitted by the military junta to perform the duties of his office." He informed the press that "there is no constitutional government in Chile." Two days later, on Friday, 11 September, a military government assumed power. It was short-lived; Ibáñez overthrew it four months later.[56]

Ibáñez's *junta* and the armed services' senior officers formed an Army-Navy administration, led by a general, an admiral, and a professional foreign service officer—and with Ibáñez as minister of war—days after this coup, in January 1925. They acknowledged that Alessandri remained president, invited him to return, and started drafting a new constitution. They believed that time was running out. The labor movement remained agitated and the PCCh was advocating revolution. As Collier reported, "Country is seething with social unrest."[57]

Those writing the constitution completed their work while Chileans approved it that August. It became effective the following month, in time for congressional elections. This new constitution strengthened the presidency, formally separated church and state, and created the liberal-democratic order that governed Chile to 1973. Meanwhile, Ibáñez refused to leave the cabinet. He planned to remain in office until the new system functioned not only on paper, but in practice. This renewed the tension in what became a bitter rivalry between Alessandri and Ibáñez—and it led to the president's resigning yet again in October 1925.

Following this, Emiliano Figueroa (1925–1927) was elected president. Both he and Congress returned to parliamentary-era habits, much to Ibáñez's continuing dismay. Ibáñez assumed the office of minister of interior in February 1927. From this position, he removed judges, replacing them with those committed to the new constitutional order. An increasingly powerless Figueroa resigned, leaving Ibáñez, now acting president, in sole control. Ibáñez formalized his presidency through a special election that May. So began his dictatorship (1927–1931).[58]

Ibáñez intended to rid Chile of politicians and corruption once and for all. Many fell within his sights. But he systematically targeted the PCCh and, behind it, the Soviet Union, as he had signaled he would do months before—and as his counterparts were doing in Brazil, Uruguay, and Argentina. He intended to settle accounts with Chilean Communists while breaking "the red ties of Moscow."[59]

Thus, Ibáñez outlawed the PCCh in 1927. He sent 89 Chilean Communists to detention on Más Afuera. They remained defiant. Their first act upon arrival was to form the party's Más Afuera section. Others fled the country; some were murdered. Those who remained denounced Ibáñez's "national-fascist government," "evidently an agent of Yankee imperialism," as Ibáñez nearly destroyed the PCCh through decapitation and sustained suppression over the next two years.[60]

Ibáñez directed an activist government between 1927 and 1931, investing nearly a billion pesos in Chile's infrastructure. His dictatorship was the first of several administrations to attempt to stimulate local manufacturing and industrial development to cope with Chile's political, social, and economic problems. He also created the Chilean air force, transformed the *Carabinero* Regiment into the *Carabineros de Chile*, one of Latin America's most professional police forces, and enacted Chile's labor code, among many other accomplishments. This required heavy spending. He borrowed from foreign banks—primarily British, Swiss, and American—to sustain it. The Chilean government owed £62 million to these banks by 1930.

Ibáñez, like his predecessors, relied on mining revenues to support this. But Chilean nitrate production had slowed since the First World War, when German chemists created synthetic nitrates to compensate for Germany's inability to import these and other Chilean products through Britain's blockade. Chilean nitrate production never recovered. The Great Depression destroyed what was left. As nitrate and other exports collapsed, and as foreign loans fell from $682 million in 1930 to $22 million in 1932, the Ibáñez dictatorship met its end.[61]

Ibáñez could neither maintain spending nor service the debt by the end of 1930. So he cut spending, suspended repayments, and raised import taxes to compensate. This austerity program led to his laying off large numbers of public employees and reducing the salaries of those who remained. This failed to halt the depression's calamitous effects. Massive public disapproval, including a wave of strikes, forced him to resign on 26 July 1931. He fled to Buenos Aires and a provisional government appeared, announcing it would hold elections soon. After another year of mutinies, coups, and instability, a calmer Alessandri returned to the presidency, initiating the five decades of relatively peaceful multiparty democracy that followed.[62]

Conclusion

Chilean expansion drove the construction of the Chilean nation and its institutions, its political parties and labor movement, and Chile and southern South America's integration into the modern capitalist system. The processes that propelled much of this derived from Chilean investment in and reliance on mining operations and Chileans' need to control the territories in which they occurred, which led to the War of the Pacific, the subsequent civil war, and the country's worsening political and social problems. Thus, mining helped to unleash the forces that created modern Chile and then swept it into the turbulent twentieth century, where these processes would continue to play out through the end of the Cold War, in 1991. Although British, American, and other foreign financial institutions participated in this, and even though European military missions and the Soviet Union's Comintern influenced part of it, Chileans remained the ones who decided their own history. Indeed, they helped to make inter-American and Atlantic history as well.[63]

The processes and outcomes surrounding this history, that is, Chileans' struggles to gain control over territories and commodities like *guano*, nitrates, and copper, had more to do with Chileans' forceful impositions, violence, and counter-violence—sometimes against Peru, Bolivia, or Argentina; more often against other Chileans, particularly miners and the rest of the working class—than reasoned debate and the achievement of anything resembling a balanced consensus, either nationally or internationally, at least not initially. But by the time the dust settled in the early 1930s, Chile had risen as a liberal nation aligned with others in Latin America, the US, and Europe and taken its place as an integral part of the modern capitalist system. This was something they did, not something that happened to them.

Even Alessandri and Ibáñez, who would oppose each other to the end of their lives, marched in step with this. As Ambassador Juan Fernández elaborated, Alessandri, far from the Bolshevik some of his contemporaries feared he might be, was interested in "a policy based on international law and hemispheric cooperation" in the early 1920s. He saw the US as an emerging leader and chose to nurture close relations with it to facilitate this. He found an easygoing, friendly, and businesslike relationship with President Warren Harding (1921–1923) and his successors. They sent Spanish-speaking ambassadors who charmed Santiago while improving US-Chilean relations for the first time since the *Baltimore* affair. "Mutual economic and trade interests," Fernández concluded, "did the rest." Following this, in 1929, Ibáñez, the Peruvian government, and President Herbert Hoover (1929–1933) finally resolved the Tacna-Arica dispute through arbitration.[64]

These results would become more pronounced as Chileans entered the United Nations (UN), helped charter the Organization of American States (OAS), and then persuaded the UN to headquarter CEPAL (*Comisión Económica para América Latina*), which encouraged further regional economic cooperation, in Santiago in the late 1940s. The Chilean left challenged this, particularly in the late 1940s and early 1970s, but failed to reverse it. The dice had already been cast.

Notes

1. For dependency theory, Fernando Cardoso and Enzo Faletto, *Dependency and Development in Latin America* [1971] (Berkley and Los Angeles: University of California Press, 1979); Eduardo Galeano, *Open Veins of Latin America: Five Centuries of the Pillage of a Continent* [1971], 25th Anniversary ed. (New York: Monthly Review Press, 1997); and Andre Gunder Frank, *Capitalism and Underdevelopment in Latin America: Historical Studies of Chile and Brazil* (New York: Monthly Review Press, 1967). For the world-system, Immanuel Wallerstein, *The Modern World-System*, 3 vols. [1974–1989] (Berkeley and Los Angeles: University of California Press, 2011).
2. For another argument for taking Latin American agency seriously when interpreting global histories of the modern capitalist system, Steve Stern and Immanuel Wallerstein's exchange, "Feudalism, Capitalism, and the World-System in the Perspective of Latin America and the Caribbean," *American Historical Review* 93 (1988): 829–97.
3. For the autocratic republic and subsequent Chilean history, Simon Collier and William Sater, *A History of Chile, 1808–2002* [1996], 2nd ed. (Cambridge: Cambridge University Press, 2004); Brian Loveman, *Chile: The Legacy of Hispanic Capitalism* [1979], 3rd ed. (New York: Oxford University Press, 2001).
4. For the Peruvian-Bolivian confederation, Frederick Nunn, *The Military in Chilean History: Essays on Civil-Military Relations, 1810–1973* (Albuquerque: University of New Mexico Press, 1976), 46–50; Robert Burr, *By Reason or Force: Chile and the Balancing of Power in South America,*

1830–1905 [1965] (Berkeley and Los Angeles: University of California Press, 1974), 12–57.

5. Biblioteca Nacional de Chile, "Trabajadores y empresarios en la industria del carbón: Lota y Coronel (1854–1995)," n.d., http://www.memoriachilena.cl; Collier and Sater, *History of Chile*, 73–103; Loveman, *Chile*, 119–44; and Burr, *By Reason or Force*, 107–16.
6. Burr, *By Reason or Force*, 72.
7. Vicente Pérez, *Ensayo sobre Chile* [1857] (Santiago de Chile: Ediciones de la Universidad de Chile, 1986), 47.
8. Loveman, *Chile*, 135.
9. Burr, *By Reason or Force*, 131–32.
10. "Tratado de límites entre Chile y Bolivia," 10 August 1866. A. Bascuñan, *Recopilación de tratados y convenciones celebrados entre la República de Chile y las potencias extranjeras, edición autorizada por el supremo gobierno y revisada por el Ministerio de Relaciones Exteriores II: 1863–1893* (Santiago de Chile: Imprenta Cervantes, 1894), 22–28. Also see Jorge Basadre, *Chile, Perú y Bolivia independientes* (Barcelona and Buenos Aires: Salvat Editores, 1948), 454.
11. Biblioteca Nacional de Chile, "Mineral de Caracoles," n.d., http://www.memoriachilena.cl; Collier and Sater, *History of Chile*, 77.
12. "Tratado de límites entre Chile y Bolivia," 6 August 1874. Bascuñan, *Recopilación de tratados y convenciones*, 101–7. Also see Basadre, *Chile, Perú y Bolivia independientes*, 457–58. For cooperative international relations, Daniel Gorman, *International Cooperation in the Early Twentieth Century* (London: Bloomsbury, 2017); Frank Ninkovich, *The Global Republic: America's Inadvertent Rise to World Power* (Chicago: University of Chicago Press, 2014); and Elizabeth Cobbs Hoffman, *American Umpire* (Cambridge: Harvard University Press, 2013).
13. Juan Fernández, *Chile y Perú: Historia de sus relaciones diplomáticas entre 1879–1929* (Santiago de Chile: RIL editores: Asociación de Funcionarios Diplomáticos de Carrera del Ministerio de Relaciones Exteriores, 2004), 22; Burr, *By Reason or Force*, 124; and Basadre, *Chile, Perú y Bolivia independientes*, 455–56.
14. Fernández, *Chile y Perú*, 17–30; Collier and Sater, *History of Chile*, 125–31; Burr, *By Reason or Force*, 117–39; and Basadre, *Chile, Perú y Bolivia independientes*, 458.
15. Fernández, *Chile y Perú*, 41–45; Burr, *By Reason or Force*, 152–53.
16. "Tratado de límites chileno-argentino," 23 July 1881. Bascuñan, *Recopilación de tratados y convenciones*, 120–25.

17. "Chile-Peru tratado de amistad," 20 October 1883. Bascuñan, *Recopilación de tratados y convenciones*, 158–66. Also see Basadre, *Chile, Perú y Bolivia independientes*, 497–98.
18. Marta Cruz-Coke, *Eduardo Cruz-Coke: Testimonios* (Santiago de Chile: Fundación Procultura, 2015), 291. For Chileans' sense of greatness, Alejandro San Francisco, "'La excepción honrosa de paz y estabilidad, de orden y libertad': La autoimagen política de Chile en el siglo XIX," in *Nación y nacionalismo en Chile* Vol. 1: *Siglo XIX*, ed. Gabriel Cid and Alejandro San Francisco (Santiago de Chile: Ediciones Centro de Estudios Bicentenari, 2009), 55–84; and Burr, *By Reason or Force*, 33–72.
19. Simón Bolívar, "Invitation to the Governments of Colombia, Mexico, Río de la Plata, Chile, and Guatemala to Hold a Congress in Panama [7 December 1824]." David Bushnell, ed., Frederick Fornoff, trans., *El Libertador: Writings of Simón Bolívar* (New York: Oxford University Press, 2003), 159.
20. Andrés Bello, "An American Congress," *El Araucano*, November 1844. Robert Burr and Roland Hussey, eds., *Documents on Inter-American Cooperation I: 1810–1881* (Philadelphia: University of Philadelphia Press, 1955), 87.
21. Eustancio Santa María to Governments of Spanish America, 11 October 1880. Burr and Hussey, *Documents on Inter-American Cooperation*, 168–70.
22. James Blaine to Diplomatic Representatives of the United States in the Capitals of Latin America, 29 November 1881. James Scott, ed., *The International Conferences of American States, 1889–1928* (New York: Oxford University Press, 1931), 447–48.
23. Frederick Frelinghuysen to Diplomatic Representatives of the United States in the Capitals of Latin America, 9 August 1882. Scott, *International Conferences of American States, 1889–1928*, 449. Frelinghuysen to Cornelius Logan, 30 July 1883. Department of State, *Papers Relating to the Foreign Relations of the United States, Transmitted to Congress, with the Annual Message of the President, 4 December 1883* (Washington, DC: Government Printing Office, 1884), 118.
24. Fernández, *Chile y Perú*, 51–112; Frederick Pike, *Chile and the United States, 1880–1962: The Emergence of Chile's Social Crisis and the Challenge to United States Diplomacy* (Notre Dame: University of Notre Dame Press, 1963), 47–62.

25. For reports of the civil war's outbreak, Patrick Egan to Blaine, 12 January 1891; Egan to Blaine, 12 January 1891; and Egan to Blaine, 17 January 1891. United States Department of State, *The Executive Documents of the House of Representatives for the First Session of the Fifty-Second Congress, 1891–1892* (Washington, DC: Government Printing Office, 1892), 91–93. See Balmaceda's explanation, attached to Egan to Blaine, 19 January 1891. Ibid., 94–104. Many historians tend to concur with Egan's assessment that the war represented an executive-legislative power struggle while others, primarily Marxists and *dependistas,* tend to interpret it as evidence of capitalist penetration and imperialism. See Alejandro San Francisco, *La guerra civil de 1891*, 2 vols. (Santiago de Chile: Ediciones Centro de Estudios Bicentenario, 2016); Harold Blakemore, *British Nitrates and Chilean Politics, 1886–1896: Balmaceda and North* (London: Athlone Press for the Institute of Latin American Studies, 1974); and Hernán Ramírez, *Balmaceda y la contrarrevolución de 1891* (Santiago de Chile: Editorial Universitaria, 1958).
26. Egan to Blaine, 12 January 1891. For Balmaceda's suicide, see Egan to Blaine, 21 September 1891. Department of State, *Executive Documents for Fifty-Second Congress, 1891–1892*, 165–66.
27. For example, Egan to Blaine, 7 September 1891; Egan to Blaine, 24 September 1891; Egan to Blaine, 29 September 1891; Egan to Blaine, 30 September 1891. Ibid., 161–62, 66, 168–71.
28. Egan to Blaine, 18 October 1891; Egan to Blaine, 19 October 1891, which includes the *Baltimore's* commanding officer's protests to Chilean authorities; and William McCreery to Blaine, 8 November 1891. Ibid., 194–95, and 220–21.
29. William Wharton to Egan, 23 October 1891. Ibid., 196–97. See the *Baltimore's* reports and Egan and the *junta's* foreign minister's exchange enclosed in Egan to Blaine, 28 October 1891. Ibid., 204–10.
30. See the *junta's* foreign minister's response in Egan to Blaine, 3 November 1891. Ibid., 211–17; Manuel Matta to Pedro Montt, 11 December 1891, read in the Chilean Senate, published in Chilean newspapers, and distributed to the American press in Washington the following day, enclosed in Egan to Blaine, 12 December 1891. Ibid., 267–69; and Egan to Blaine, 12 January 1892. Ibid., 285.
31. Blaine to Egan, 21 January 1892. Ibid., 307–8.
32. See Egan to Blaine, 25 January 1892. Ibid., 309–12; and Blaine's correspondence with the Chilean ambassador in Washington on this subject. Ibid., 347–52.

33. Collier and Sater, *History of Chile*, 144.
34. Frederick Nunn, *Chilean Politics, 1920–1931: The Honorable Mission of the Armed Forces* (Albuquerque: University of New Mexico Press, 1970), 10.
35. Biblioteca Nacional de Chile, "Ramón Barros Luco (1835–1919)," n.d., http://www.memoriachilena.cl.
36. Pike, *Chile and the United States*, 86.
37. For coal mining, Biblioteca Nacional de Chile, "Trabajadores y empresarios en la industria del carbón: Lota y Coronel (1854–1995)"; Jody Pavilack, *Mining for the Nation: The Politics of Chile's Coal Communities from the Popular Front to the Cold War* (University Park: Pennsylvania State University Press, 2011), 29–66.
38. For labor conditions in the late nineteenth and early twentieth centuries, Loveman, *Chile*, 119–44, 162–95; Carmelo Furci, *The Chilean Communist Party and the Road to Socialism* (London: Zed, 1984), 8–27; Pike, *Chile and the United States*, 103–11; and Hernán Ramírez, *Origen y formación del Partido Comunista de Chile* (Santiago de Chile: Editora Austral, 1965), 19–62.
39. Ramírez, *Origen y formación del Partido Comunista*, 26–28.
40. Ibid., 28.
41. Loveman, *Chile*, Table 7.2, 171; Ramírez, *Origen y formación del Partido Comunista*, 35.
42. For example, *El Obrero*, 29 April 1893. Ramírez, *Origen y formación del Partido Comunista*, 37–38.
43. See Biblioteca Nacional de Chile, "Masacrede la Escuela Santa María de Iquique," n.d., http://www.memoriachilena.cl; Alberto Edwards and Eduardo Frei, *Historia de los partidos politicos chilenos* (Santiago de Chile: Editorial del Pacifico, 1949), 153–55.
44. Julio Faúndez, *Marxism and Democracy in Chile: From 1932 to the Fall of Allende* (New Haven: Yale University Press, 1988), 20–23; Furci, *Chilean Communist Party*, 24–27; and Ramírez, *Origen y formación del Partido Comunista*, 45–46, 51–62.
45. Leon Trotsky, "Manifesto of the Communist International to the Proletarians of the World," March 1919; Robert Daniels, ed., *A Documentary History of Communism and the World: From Revolution to Collapse* (Hanover: University Press of New England, 1994), 25; and Ramírez, *Origen y formación del Partido Comunista*, 123–27.
46. M.A. Komin-Alexandrovski to Comintern, 18 January 1922. Olga Ulianova and Alfredo Riquelme Segovia, eds., *Chile en los archivos*

soviéticos, 1922–1991 I: Komintern y Chile, 1922–1931 (Santiago de Chile: Dirección de Bibliotecas, Archivos y Museos/LOM Ediciones, 2005), 111–12; *El Socialista*, Antofagasta, 21 March 1921; Ramírez, *Origen y formación del Partido Comunista*, 126; and PCCh, "Declaración de principios," First Party Congress in Rancagua, January 1922. Ibid., 134–35.

47. Luis Emilio Recabarren, "Chile 1922," presented to Profintern, Moscow, 1922; Ulianova and Segovia, *Chile en los archivos soviéticos: Komintern y Chile*, 116–22; and Profintern to Recabarren, 20 November 1923. Ibid., 123–25.
48. Comintern to communist parties in Mexico, Brazil, Uruguay, Argentina, and Chile, September 1924. Ibid., 125–26; Comintern to communist parties in South America (Argentina, Brazil, Chile, Uruguay, Bolivia, Peru, Paraguay, and Colombia), 18 February 1925. Ibid., 130–31.
49. Olga Ulianova, "La Unidad Popular y el golpe military en Chile: percepciones y análisis soviéticos," *Estudios Públicos* 79 (2000), 88; María Soledad Gómez, "Factores nacionales e internacionales de la política interna del partido communista de Chile (1922–1952)," in *El partido comunista en Chile: Estudio multidisciplinario*, ed. Augusto Varas, Compilador (Santiago de Chile: Centro de Estudios Sociales/FLACSO, 1988), 65–139.
50. Domingo Santa María and Carlos Antúnez, "Fundación de la Academia de Guerra," 9 September 1886; Alejandro San Francisco, ed., *La Academia de Guerra del Ejército de Chile, 1886–2006: Ciento veinte años de historia* (Santiago de Chile: Ediciones Centro de Estudios Bicentenario, 2006), 211–19.
51. Enrique Brahm García, "La impronta prusiana de la Acadamia de Guerra del Ejército (1885–1914)," in *Academia de Guerra*, ed. San Francisco, 3–25; Brian Loveman, *For la Patria: Politics and the Armed Forces in Latin America* (Wilmington: Scholarly Resources, 1999), 81.
52. Nunn, *Military in Chilean History*, 119–27; Nunn, *Chilean Politics*, 10–12, 17–18, and 50–52.
53. Nunn, *Chilean Politics*, 19–27; Edwards and Frei, *Historia de los partidos politicos chilenos*, 183–91.
54. Nunn, *Chilean Politics*, 55–56; Edwards and Frei, *Historia de los partidos politicos chilenos*, 192–93.
55. Nunn, *Chilean Politics*, 47–66.
56. William Collier to Department of State, 9 September 1924; and 10 September 1924. Department of State, *Foreign Relations of the United*

States 1924 I (Washington, DC: Government Printing Office, 1939), 357, 358–59; Charles Evan Hughes to Collier, 13 September 1924. Ibid., 359.

57. Collier to Department of State, 27 January 1925. Department of State, *Foreign Relations of the United States 1925 I* (Washington, DC: Government Printing Office, 1940), 585–86; Collier to Department of State, 12 February 1925. Ibid., 586.
58. Ibáñez ran unopposed and won 98% of the vote in 1927. Ricardo Cruz-Coke, *Historia electoral de Chile, 1925–1973* (Santiago de Chile: Editorial Juridica de Chile, 1984), 94–97. Chile has no vice president. The minister of interior becomes vice president and acting president in the event the president leaves the country, becomes incapacitated, gets impeached, or dies.
59. Carlos Ibáñez, Declaration, 9 February 1927. Nunn, *Chilean Politics*, 183–84. Most southern South American nations severed relations with the Soviet Union in the late 1920s and 1930s and then reestablished them during and immediately after the Second World War.
60. Unlisted author, "Informe de los camaradas comunistas que estuvieron en la Isla Más Afuera," December 1928. Ulianova and Riquelme, *Chile en los archivos soviéticos: Komintern y Chile*, 377–79; South American Bureau to PCCh's Santiago Committee and all members of the PCCh, August 1929. Ibid., 405–9; and Provisional Central Committee of the PCCh to South American Bureau, "Informe al Secretariado Sudamericano de la Internacional Comunista," 15 November 1929. Ibid., 416–35.
61. Faúndez, *Marxism and Democracy*, 14–16.
62. For the fall of the Ibáñez dictatorship, Collier and Sater, *History of Chile*, 214–21; Loveman, *Chile*, 183–88; Nunn, *Chilean Politics*, 117–59; William Culbertson to Department of State, 26 July 1931. Department of State, *Foreign Relations of the United States 1931 I* (Washington, DC: Government Printing Office, 1946), 905; and Culbertson to Department of State, 27 July 1931. Ibid., 907.
63. For a fuller discussion of this larger pattern, James Lockhart, *Chile, the CIA and the Cold War: A Transatlantic Perspective* (Edinburgh: Edinburgh University Press, 2019); and Odd Arne Westad, *The Cold War: A World History* (New York: Basic Books, 2017).
64. Fernández, *Chile y Perú*, 355, 358; Department of State, Bureau of Intelligence and Research, Office of the Geographer, "International Boundary Study No. 65: Chile-Peru Boundary," 28 February 1966, http://www.law.fsu.edu.

Bibliography

Basadre, Jorge. *Chile, Perú y Bolivia independientes*. Barcelona and Buenos Aires: Salvat Editores, 1948.

Bascuñan, A. *Recopilación de tratados y convenciones celebrados entre la República de Chile y las potencias extranjeras, edición autorizada por el supremo gobierno y revisada por el Ministerio de Relaciones Exteriores II: 1863–1893*. Santiago de Chile: Imprenta Cervantes, 1894.

Biblioteca Nacional de Chile. "Masacre de la Escuela Santa María de Iquique," n.d., http://www.memoriachilena.cl.

———. "Mineral de Caracoles," n.d., http://www.memoriachilena.cl.

———. "Ramón Barros Luco (1835–1919)," n.d., http://www.memoriachilena.cl.

———. "Trabajadores y empresarios en la industria del carbon: Lota y Coronel (1854–1995)," n.d., http://www.memoriachilena.cl.

Blakemore, Harold. *British Nitrates and Chilean Politics, 1886–1896: Balmaceda and North*. London: Athlone Press for the Institute of Latin American Studies, 1974.

Bravo, Bernardino. *De Portales a Pinochet: Gobierno y régimen de gobierno en Chile*. Santiago de Chile: Editorial Jurídica de Chile and Editorial Andrés Bello, 1985.

Burr, Robert. *By Reason or Force: Chile and the Balancing of Power in South America, 1830–1905* [1965]. Berkeley and Los Angeles: University of California Press, 1974.

Burr, Robert, and Roland Hussey, eds. *Documents on Inter-American Cooperation I: 1810–1881*. Philadelphia: University of Philadelphia Press, 1955.

Bushnell, David, ed. *El Libertador: Writings of Simón Bolívar*. New York: Oxford University Press, 2003.

Cardoso, Fernando, and Enzo Faletto. *Dependency and Development in Latin America* [1971]. Berkley and Los Angeles: University of California Press, 1979.

Cid, Gabriel, and Alejandro San Francisco, eds. *Nación y nacionalismo en Chile* Vol. 1: *Siglo XIX*. Santiago de Chile: Ediciones Centro de Estudios Bicentenari, 2009.

Cobbs Hoffman, Elizabeth. *American Umpire*. Cambridge: Harvard University Press, 2013.

Collier, Simon, and William Sater. *A History of Chile, 1808–2002* [1996]. 2nd ed. Cambridge: Cambridge University Press, 2004.
Cruz-Coke, Marta. *Eduardo Cruz-Coke: Testimonios*. Santiago de Chile: Fundación Procultura, 2015.
Cruz-Coke, Ricardo. *Historia electoral de Chile, 1925–1973*. Santiago de Chile: Editorial Juridica de Chile, 1984.
Daniels, Robert, ed. *A Documentary History of Communism and the World: From Revolution to Collapse*. Hanover: University Press of New England, 1994.
Department of State. *Foreign Relations of the United States* (FRUS). Washington, DC: Government Printing Office, 1861–present.
Edwards, Alberto. *La fronda aristocrática: Historia política de Chile* [1928]. Santiago de Chile: Imprenta Nacional, 1945.
Edwards, Alberto, and Eduardo Frei. *Historia de los partidos politicos chilenos*. Santiago de Chile: Editorial del Pacifico, 1949.
Faúndez, Julio. *Marxism and Democracy in Chile: From 1932 to the Fall of Allende*. New Haven: Yale University Press, 1988.
Fernández, Juan. *Chile y Perú: Historia de sus relaciones diplomáticas entre 1879–1929*. Santiago de Chile: RIL editores: Asociación de Funcionarios Diplomáticos de Carrera del Ministerio de Relaciones Exteriores, 2004.
Frank, Andre Gunder. *Capitalism and Underdevelopment in Latin America: Historical Studies of Chile and Brazil*. New York: Monthly Review Press, 1967.
Furci, Carmelo. *The Chilean Communist Party and the Road to Socialism*. London: Zed, 1984.
Galeano, Eduardo. *Open Veins of Latin America: Five Centuries of the Pillage of a Continent* [1971]. 25th Anniversary ed. New York: Monthly Review Press, 1997.
Gorman, Daniel. *International Cooperation in the Early Twentieth Century*. London: Bloomsbury, 2017.
Lockhart, James. *Chile, the CIA and the Cold War: A Transatlantic Perspective*. Edinburgh: Edinburgh University Press, 2019.
Loveman, Brian. *Chile: The Legacy of Hispanic Capitalism* [1979]. 3rd ed. New York: Oxford University Press, 2001.
———. *For la Patria: Politics and the Armed Forces in Latin America*. Wilmington: Scholarly Resources, 1999.
Ninkovich, Frank. *The Global Republic: America's Inadvertent Rise to World Power*. Chicago: University of Chicago Press, 2014.

Nunn, Frederick. *Chilean Politics, 1920–1931: The Honorable Mission of the Armed Forces*. Albuquerque: University of New Mexico Press, 1970.

———. *The Military in Chilean History: Essays on Civil-Military Relations, 1810–1973*. Albuquerque: University of New Mexico Press, 1976.

Pavilack, Jody. *Mining for the Nation: The Politics of Chile's Coal Communities from the Popular Front to the Cold War*. University Park: Pennsylvania State University Press, 2011.

Pérez, Vicente. *Ensayo sobre Chile* [1857]. Santiago de Chile: Ediciones de la Universidad de Chile, 1986.

Pike, Frederick. *Chile and the United States, 1880–1962: The Emergence of Chile's Social Crisis and the Challenge to United States Diplomacy*. Notre Dame: University of Notre Dame Press, 1963.

Ramírez, Hernán. *Balmaceda y la contrarrevolución de 1891*. Santiago de Chile: Editorial Universitaria, 1958.

———. *Origen y formación del Partido Comunista de Chile*. Santiago de Chile: Editora Austral, 1965.

San Francisco, Alejandro, ed. *La Academia de Guerra del Ejército de Chile, 1886–2006: Ciento veinte años de historia*. Santiago de Chile: Ediciones Centro de Estudios Bicentenario, 2006.

———. *La guerra civil de 1891*, 2 vols. Santiago de Chile: Ediciones Centro de Estudios Bicentenario, 2016.

Scott, James ed. *The International Conferences of American States, 1889–1928*. New York: Oxford University Press, 1931.

Stern, Steve, and Immanuel Wallerstein. "Feudalism, Capitalism, and the World-System in the Perspective of Latin America and the Caribbean." *American Historical Review* 93 (1988): 829–97.

Ulianova, Olga. "La Unidad Popular y el golpe military en Chile: percepciones y análisis soviéticos." *Estudios Públicos* 79 (2000): 83–171.

Ulianova, Olga, and Alfredo Riquelme Segovia, eds. *Chile en los archivos soviéticos, 1922–1991 I: Komintern y Chile, 1922–1931*. Santiago de Chile: Dirección de Bibliotecas, Archivos y Museos and LOM Ediciones, 2005.

Varas, Augusto, Compilador. *El partido comunista en Chile: Estudio multidisciplinario*. Santiago de Chile: Centro de Estudios Sociales and FLACSO, 1988.

Wallerstein, Immanuel. *The Modern World-System*, 3 vols. [1974–1989]. Berkeley and Los Angeles: University of California Press, 2011.

Westad, Odd Arne. *The Cold War: A World History*. New York: Basic Books, 2017.

8

Red Fever: Natural Resource Companies and the Global Copper Mining Frontier 1890–1939

Robrecht Declercq

Introduction: Copper Frontiers and International Business

Few developments have more profoundly marked the modern world as the light and energy powered by electrification. The large-scale application of electrification became possible after 1890 with the breakthrough of electro-technical industries, the rapid expansion of public utilities based on electricity and the electrification of transport systems like tram- and subways.[1] Copper was the central material of electricity due to its high conductivity. Electrification therefore unleashed new and unseen attempts to exploit new sources of copper across the globe, an undertaking that could easily be described as a period of red fever. Indeed, world production in copper quintupled over the course of 18 years, from 302,000 tons in 1890 to 1,579,000 tons in 1918. Global production expanded unabated after

R. Declercq (✉)
Postdoctoral Researcher—Research Foundation Flanders (FWO), Ghent University, Ghent, Belgium
e-mail: robrecht.declercq@ugent.be

S. Joseph (ed.), *Commodity Frontiers and Global Capitalist Expansion*, Palgrave Studies in Economic History, https://doi.org/10.1007/978-3-030-15322-9_8

World War I, reaching 2,305,000 tons in 1940.[2] Previously, copper production was limited to a few countries, primarily the USA. Copper production after 1890 expanded globally, by contrast, incorporating new copper mines in the African copper belt (Katanga in Belgian Congo and Northern Rhodesia) and South and Central America (in Chile, Mexico and Peru). By the end of the 1920s, Belgian Congo produced 5.7% of the world copper production, and Chile 14.6%. Northern Rhodesia set off somewhat later, but claimed a global market share of 9.4% on average between 1930 and 1939.[3] This chapter is devoted to this period of red fever and the new global commodity frontiers of copper that were incorporated during it. In particular, it focuses on the business actors that ultimately made possible the increased availability of this precious red metal: the natural resource companies. Natural resource companies are companies that primarily invested in the exploitation of natural resources, both renewable and non-renewable. In spite of industry-specific variations, natural resource companies rank as principal drivers of economic globalization and usually attained significant economies of scale.[4]

The period of red fever was far from an isolated phenomenon. In the decades after 1870, the world economy went through an unprecedented process of transformation involving spectacular growth levels, increased global interconnectivity and productivity.[5] Frontier expansion or "exploiting or converting new sources of resources for production processes" became a central activity underlying this transformation.[6] The quest to find new (natural) resources continued unabated after World War I. Processes like electrification, next to other inventions and industrial demands, triggered a spectacular increase in the exploitation of natural resources, foremost subsoil minerals and energy resources. The natural resource companies were arguably critical in this period of exploiting the global resource frontier. As Barbier wrote: "by 1950, industrial development and rapid growth had become dependent on expanding knowledge, expertise and industries to exploit global frontiers".[7] Resource extraction was the principal form of international business in this period, consuming up to 60% of all FDI on the eve of World War II.[8]

However, historical research exhibits a remarkable deficit in understanding the role of the natural resource company in connection with this intensified effort of frontier expansion between 1870 and 1950. In extension, this also applies to the expansion of new copper frontiers. Three major reasons can be held accountable for this scholarly deficit. Firstly, scholarship on global and multinational business, more generally, has largely prioritized examining the internationalization of industrial production.[9] Secondly, a demand-driven perspective on industrial capitalism remains popular in forwarding the success of the natural resource company at that time.[10] Thirdly, while the role of business as an integrative force of economic globalization is generally acknowledged, it is still often neglected precisely "how" businesses integrated new contexts and areas into the world economy.[11] In addition, Dejung and Petersson recently argued that border-crossing business activities are typically studied "without being very specific about either the social, cultural and political environments in which these enterprises operated".[12]

Especially, the last deficit has caused a major lacuna in terms of business-economic history in connection with exploiting the global resource frontier after 1870. Indeed, business investments in frontiers were about much more than simply extracting resources. Many of the new global resource frontiers were situated in remote and less accessible areas, largely untouched by capitalist intrusion. In setting up processes of frontier expansion, companies had to organize, first and foremost, the availability and access to labour, land, resources (food and energy) in, secondly, often "hostile" social (labour unrest, crime) and natural environments that were difficult to control.[13] What seems to be striking, given this particular nature of resource frontier expansion, is that current scholarship on international business does not appropriately question "how" private enterprises operated under these unstable conditions. Surprisingly little is known, in other words, on the plans and methods of natural resource companies to allow for complex frontier investments. Much insight into frontier activities remains strongly compartmentalized or fragmentally narrated in individual corporate histories. What is forwarded from a more general perspective, in addition, remains quite fragmentary or catch-all in nature in accounting for the many challenges and risks. Geoffrey Jones, for instance, stressed the importance of "entrepreneurial perceptions" of FDI in natural resources and that locational factors were far more critical, without however extrapolating upon the frontier-like nature of this critical factor.[14] More recent accounts like Fitzgerald remain somehow catch-all in nature, referring to a whole range of "particular capabilities in managerial (…), technology, finance or access to trade networks and consumer markets".[15] He thereby acknowledged that international business literature structurally underplays risks like weak legal protection, civil unrest and violence, and macro-economic instability, risks which are particularly applicable to investments in natural resource frontiers.

This chapter explores the activities of natural resource companies as critical actors in commodifying the new copper frontiers that marked the period of red fever after 1890. It takes seriously the claim that modern natural resource companies, in order to organize the extraction of copper on a massive and industrial scale, needed to do much more than organize the extraction of this red metal, but also needed to build up expertise and ownership domains far beyond the scope of mining, like organizing the input of energy resources, provision of supplies, and controlling the unstable social and natural landscapes of the new commodity frontiers in copper.[16] Thus far, specific scholarship on the copper mining business has stressed the fact that new and more complex mining and metallurgical techniques triggered the increase in scale of copper businesses.[17] A central assumption of this paper is that such explanations are not entirely satisfying and remain incomplete, as the growth of large-scale companies was also a result of the specific local risks and complexity that companies encountered in expanding the frontiers of copper. The contradiction of setting up new large-scale and more complex operations in a new set of more remote commodity frontiers to provide a world in dire need of copper for power and light has largely been underestimated. As I will demonstrate in this chapter, it required companies to acquire expertise and practices that went beyond mere geological and mining technology issues. The first part describes the new commodity frontiers of copper that marked the period of red fever, and the rise of the modern large-scale natural resource company and how it came to dominate the global copper mining industry. The second part then offers a commodity frontier perspective on the way in which the business practices of the natural resource companies were shaped. It focuses on how companies responded to the most critical shortages and problems in commodity frontiers. In putting such responses into practice, copper mining companies transformed into the organizational machinery that were able to satisfy the booming demands for copper during the early twentieth century.

The Coming of the Copper Giants

The Expansion Zones of Copper (1850–1940)

Before the big expansion triggered by electrification, copper mining occurred in but a few countries only, foremost in the USA, Chile and Australia, and generally on a limited scale.[18] The needs for copper were first satisfied by the USA, where some of the main new commodity frontiers were situated. Gradual expansion of copper mining made the USA the single largest producer, as it produced roughly 56% of the world's primary output in copper by 1900 as compared to 17% in 1880.[19] Copper mining in the USA in the second half of the nineteenth century was not a settled pasture, but already a story of rapidly shifting domestic commodity frontiers. The initial swell in US copper mining largely overlapped the development of copper deposits in the northern parts of Michigan, at the Keweenaw Peninsula bordering Lake Superior. Around 1880, Michigan copper mining reached its height and accounted for 84% of the US output.[20] The need for copper soon pushed investors and miners much deeper in the American frontiers. The first new sites of development were situated in Montana, with principal mining activities taking place in the heights surrounding Butte, which soon received its epithet the "richest hill on earth". Montana swiftly replaced the Michigan mines as the largest producer, in 1890, when the share of Michigan had fallen to 38% whereas the new mining frontier of Montana accounted for 42%. But also the leading role of Montana was short-lived, and copper mining then spread out to the south-west of the USA, with new copper mining activity in Arizona and Utah that was developed at the turn of the century.[21] Next to the south-west, copper mining was also developed in Alaska.

From Arizona, American interests quickly spilled over in the adjacent province Sonora in Mexico, foremost around Moctezuma and Nacozari. The Moctezuma mine accounted after 1909 for 20% of Mexican copper production with an annual output of 13,000 tons.[22] While American frontiers dominated the story of red fever in the beginning, copper mining increasingly took more global proportions. In the second half of the nineteenth century, Japan invested heavily in mineral and metal mining to support its endeavours in modernizing and industrializing the economy. In 1913, there were 66 copper mines in Japan, most of them small. The largest of them were the Ashio, Hitachi, Besshi, Kosaka and Osarizawa.[23]

A pivotal year of red fever was 1906 when other large copper mining areas outside the USA were opened up, foremost in Belgian Congo and Chile. European exploration that led to the "discovery" of Katangese Copperbelt started in the 1890s, while indications of copper presence in the form of objects traversed the region well before these expeditions.[24] In 1906, the first mine, the "Star of the Congo" mine was in the process of being opened up. The second pivotal development in 1906 was the prospection of new copper deposits in El Teniente, Chile, by William Braden, which marked the beginning of a new rush on copper mining in Chile. In 1913, next to the El Teniente mine, work started on the Chuquicamata properties in the Atacama Desert, and after World War I on the Potrerillos mine in northern Chile. The Chuquicamata property held the largest reserves in copper ore throughout the globe. Together with El Teniente, both mines become the two largest copper mines of Chile in the twentieth century.

The Katanga mines were part of the central African Copperbelt, composed of large underground copper deposits that took no notion of the colonial borders drawn between Belgian Congo and Northern Rhodesia (Zambia). But copper mining in the latter area was developed significantly later, only by the end of the 1920s. Prospectors encountered more difficulties in exploring mining opportunities in the British part of the Copperbelt, in contrast to the smaller-scaled ore veins that were more easily found on the surface in Katanga.[25] In addition, the British South Africa Company (BSAC), the chartered company which held the mineral and administrative rights on the territory, did little to develop the territories and chiefly saw Northern Rhodesia as a valuable labour reserve for mines in Katanga and Southern Rhodesia, rather than a future mining hub on its own.[26] Only after 1923, when the BSAC deferred its administrative rights to the Colonial Office, mining concessions were granted to prospectors and mining corporations and the first mines were prepared for operation by the late 1920s. In the 1930s, the Northern Rhodesian mines further added to the swell in global copper production.

Drivers of Growth

By the beginning of the twentieth century, copper mining had expanded significantly in a geographical sense. The increased demand for copper spawned new production areas, especially when the pace of American expansion could no longer satisfy both global and domestic demands, and thereby formed the object of new investments in South America, as well as copper mining became a major colonial mining frontier in the heartlands of central Africa. In order to understand how commodity frontier expansion shaped corporate development in this period, the main objective of this chapter, we need to take a look at some of the more general developments that took place in copper mining and that made possible the rapid expansion. In terms of techniques and methods, some fundamental changes took place that enabled commodity frontier expansion, but which had also ramifications for business practices and the mining industry.

In order to understand these changes, let us first take a look at the geology of copper. It is not possible to extract copper from the earth as a pure metal, as it always forms a percentage of a certain geological substance and is attached to a parent rock. Copper is extracted from three source types or geological ore bodies: massive sulphide, stratabound and porphyry deposits. Massive sulphide, found in veins and sedimentary rocks, carries as a rule, the highest grade of the red metal, whereas porphyry deposits (mainly underground) typically exhibit the lowest grades in copper. Stratabound ore types are situated somewhere in the middle in the spectrum of copper concentration. Until around 1900, copper was mainly extracted from these high-grader deposits, being relatively straightforward to mine and process. It was long believed in the nineteenth century that it was uneconomical to develop the mining of porphyry ore bodies, as the additional refining works to separate copper from the parent rock required significant (technology) investments. The growing demand for copper, however, left miners and engineers with no choice but to reconsider this. Experimental techniques that allowed to mine and process the lower-graded ores were spearheaded by mining companies in North America, especially in Utah.[27] The mining engineer Daniel Jackling hypothesized that lower-graded copper deposits could be profitably mined by combining the latest metallurgical processing techniques in combination with the new techniques of what is generally called "non-selective mining". In terms of new mining techniques, it involved the seemingly simple yet impactful technological innovations such as the use of fully revolving shovels, explosives and open-pit mining. This imposed a transition from selective mining, which drew upon the dexterity of the individual miner to extract the most valuable pieces of the metal, towards non-selective mining, which implied the complete removal of the soil. Non-selective mining was combined with new innovations in metallurgy as to extract the copper from its parent rock, like new types of concentrating mills and smelting plants, but also flotation plants which allowed to separate copper from the parent rock through chemical treatment.[28] Jackling put his theories into practice in the Bingham mine near Salt Lake City, in the beginning years of the twentieth century, and quickly set a new benchmark in global mining copper. Upon a visit in 1910, business magnate John D. Rockefeller Jr. saw the great steam shovels at work in the Bingham pit and called it "the greatest industrial sight in the whole world".[29] The open pit and the smokestacks of copper metallurgy infrastructure on-site became the strikingly industrial image of what could be called a new generation in copper frontiers.

The combination of both new mining techniques and metallurgy allowed mining companies to work these new deposits, but it also required a much larger amount of investments in equipment and facilities, hence a larger scale of operations, that cannot be compared to the first-generation mines of purer copper veins of before 1900.

Another geological logic, furthermore, added to the rising costs of operating the lower-graded copper mines. As a rule, the size of the copper deposits is negatively correlated to the purity of copper. In other words, porphyry deposits, leaving aside a few exceptions, are much larger in size than the higher-graded copper veins. In the field of resource appraisal, this law is referred to the law of Lasky, stating that the available metal (generally) increases as grade decreases. So the new copper deposits not only required the implementation of new processing techniques, but they were also of a different order in scale. Schmitz has pointed to this geological factor as the main factor in scale increase in the copper mining industry.[30] The shift to what was called a second generation of copper mining, with new techniques but also larger economies of scale, opened the door for a few giants to dominate copper production. Only a few American corporations like Anaconda, Kennecott (owned by the Guggenheims), Calumet and Hecla and Phelps Dodge possessed the means to implement the new techniques and processing methods on a larger scale.

It was these companies that grew larger as they invested in the development of second-generation copper mining. Daniel Jackling, lacking the financial resources to put his theory into practice, managed to convince one of the Guggenheim's mining engineers, Alfred Chester Beatty, of this powerful combination experimented in Utah, and secured their investments.[31] The cooperation with Jackling strengthened the Guggenheim's appetite to further invest in new copper deposits. The Kennecott corporation was the vehicle of the Guggenheims that acquired and invested in new copper mines in Utah, Alaska and the El Teniente mine of Chile.[32] Next to the Guggenheims, Anaconda became one of the large American trusts of the early twentieth century, based on its successful operations on the large copper deposits in Montana, Butte and later in Chile. Phelps Dodge also rapidly applied non-selective mining techniques in Bisbee, Arizona. Instead of building shafts, it blew up the nearby Sacramento Hill, as to start open-pit mining and the collection of its lower-graded copper ores. Some of the larger companies, however, emerged while working on the higher-graded copper deposits. Typically, richer copper veins coexisted with the larger low-grade copper deposits underneath, so existing mining companies could shift their operations. Once Calumet and Hecla, the company that had a virtual monopoly in Michigan started to exhaust the richest veins and focused on the more difficult ores, the scale and depth of its operations dramatically widened. By the end of the nineteenth century, most of its mines were now operating 600 metre underground, which made costs higher in terms of building and maintaining shafts. Calumet and Hecla became a larger company and acquired more mines to keep operations profitable.[33]

A result from scale increase was that larger mining corporations also started to integrate forwards, as it became more profitable to process (smelting and refining) the larger quantities of copper by themselves and to be less dependent on other firms. Processing was often developed nearby the mine, as the larger volumes of low-graded copper ores were costly to transport. Previously, such activities were typically developed elsewhere, far away from the mining areas. Swansea held a leading position in copper smelting until the mid-nineteenth century, while later new American mines served copper smelters on America's east coast. By World War I, however, most mining companies owned their own smelting and refining infrastructure and thus combined mining and industrial processing. The new commodity frontiers of copper quickly became heavily industrialized frontiers. The Anaconda Copper Company constructed a large smelter in Anaconda in 1902, the Washoe Reduction Works in Anaconda (Montana) as to process the copper ores mined in Butte.[34] In 1918, a new smokestack of 178.3 metres towered over the town, which still ranks as the highest masonry work in the world. Phelps Dodge also built a large smelter in Dawson, Arizona, which served the Bisbee mines and those in Sonora, just across the Mexican border. In 1901, for the purpose of controlling metallurgical processing connected to their mining operations, the Guggenheims took over the American Smelting and Refining company (ASARCO), which was used to process the ores produced by the Bingham open-pit mine. To support the experiments of Jackling, the Garfield smelter plant near Salt Lake City was built. When opened in 1906, it was the largest copper smelter in the USA.[35] The ASARCO expertise in processing copper ores was an advantage to the Guggenheims in taking over other mines in South America and Alaska. After World War I, the copper giants even raised their game by further integrating forwards, by producing copper end products, like brass and wires. After World War II, the 4 largest US copper enterprises, Anaconda, ASARCO, Kennecott and Phelps Dodge, produced 90% of all primary copper in the USA but also processed 65% of all copper they produced.[36]

The transition towards second-generation mining and the scale increase that went along with it also enabled American firms to assume a leading role in copper mining abroad, especially South America. In Chile, copper extraction was far from a new phenomenon as the mining of richer copper veins was an integral part of the colonial economy and early independence. In fact, during the early nineteenth century, Chile was one of the leading producers in the world. However, Chilean copper mining remained stuck in low-capital intensive mining of the higher-grade veins, which granted it a relatively stable position on the world market around 1850. But the Chilean mining industry was ill-prepared to shift to the "second generation copper mining" from a technological and organizational point of view, and the underlying lower-graded deposits were left untouched.[37] Contrary, the large Chilean reserves growingly attracted the attention of the American giants. The high investments in mining equipment and metallurgical facilities could not be carried out by the smaller Chilean mining businesses, and at the same time, Chilean politicians set the door-wide open for the moneyed and experienced American copper corporations. The discrepancy in technological-financial capacity between American and Chilean entrepreneurs was of course exacerbated by the support and protectionism of the USA towards its domestic copper industry on the one hand, and the inability of the Chilean government to set out a similar policy towards copper mining and smelting business in its own national boundaries on the other.[38]

American corporate invasion in Chilean copper got under steam at the beginning of the twentieth century. The Guggenheims in particular took an interest in Chilean copper, by supporting William Braden's copper prospection at El Teniente. As a former employee of ASARCO, William Braden had his connections to the Guggenheim family. Later, the Guggenheims turned their eye on Chuquicamata. Chuquicamata was a typical example of the transition in copper mining, as its richest veins (generally between 10 and 15% in copper) had been mined already, while its enormously large reserves—the mine is still operative—of lower-graded ores underneath were left untouched. The influx of American capital and technology enabled a new life of the mine, incomparable to previous activities.[39] In 1908, the Guggenheims placed the other large Chilean mine, the El Teniente mine, under the Kennecott company (a holding company under the control of the Guggenheims). The Chuquicamata mine was sold for the phenomenal price of 22 million dollars in 1923 to the Anaconda company as the Guggenheim family gambled on the nitrate mining business in Chile. In 1927, Anaconda further strengthened its position in Chile by opening the Potrerillos mine in the Andes. As a result, American corporate interests represented 87% of Chile's copper output, and production shot up from 41,000 tons in 1912 to 200,000 tons in 1926.[40]

But also outside the Americas, large-scale mining and big business became the name of the game. The African Copperbelt largely consisted of stratabound deposits, in contrast to porphyry deposits in South America, and was thus generally higher-graded than the latter. Yet the larger stratabound mines of Katanga also required new technology implementation, in terms of mining and processing, similar in kind as in the USA and Chile. In addition, the Katangese copper consisted of oxide ores which required extra investments in terms of research and development, as most of the existing techniques had been designed for sulphide ores.[41] In 1906, Belgian administrators and investors established a company with the abilities to further explore and exploit the many copper deposits of Katanga. The new company was called the Union Minière du Haut Katanga (UMHK). Also here, however, American influence loomed large. It soon became apparent that Belgian managers and miners, of which there were but a handful on the terrain, lacked the necessary expertise to operate a modern large-scale copper mining enterprise. The management therefore heavily drew, especially in its beginning years, on foreign expertise, on the one hand white miners and engineers originating from the South African Rand, but especially American consultants and engineers with experience in the latest copper mining techniques on the other.[42] Americans, British and South African employees held top positions in the company.

The first operational director in Katanga, Preston K. Horner, was a consulting engineer from the USA.[43] US mineworkers were of utmost importance to introduce those non-selective mining techniques critical to second-generation mining, like "operators on large steam shovels and equipment unfamiliar in Africa".[44] Next to the importance of American staff, the Guggenheims did make an attempt to acquire a direct stake in the copper mines of Belgian Congo. In 1913, Daniel Guggenheim, who had already gained a substantial stake in the Congolese diamond mining company Forminière, offered a deal whereby the UMHK would acquire a stake in the Chuquicamata property probably in exchange for a foot in the door in Katanga. Jean Jadot, the UMHK president, however, turned the offer down.[45] Only from the 1920s onwards, and once operations were more firmly on track, the input of Belgian capital and staff became gradually much stronger, and the number of foreign staff was likewise reduced.[46] By 1924, UMHK, the largest colonial enterprise of Belgian Congo by far, had joined the ranks of the American giants as largest copper producers in the world—it produced 91,000 tons of copper per year.

American interests also gave a strong impetus to mining development in Northern Rhodesia and the formation of its mining corporations. The American mining engineer Alfred Chester Beatty ranked as one of the most ardent believers in the potential of Rhodesian copper mines. Beatty was an essential figure of second-generation copper mining, as a former consulting engineer for the Guggenheims deeply involved in the development of porphyry mining in Utah between 1900 and 1904. In 1914, he had established his London-based mining company called the "Selection Trust". With British investors and mining companies responding rather lukewarm to his ideas, Beatty reached an agreement with the American Metal Company.[47] The various concessions acquired by Beatty and the American Metal Company were consolidated in the Rhodesian Selection Trust and Beatty's company set forth to develop the first Northern Rhodesian mines with the Roan Antelope (Luanshya) mine as its centrepiece. The Rhodesian Selection Trust formed an integral part of Beatty's Selection Trust. From the point of view of British colonialism, the strong American influence was, however, considered a threat. A counter-movement of South African–British mining interests was set up to prevent an American mining monopoly in North Rhodesia. A key figure of this counter-movement was Ernest Oppenheimer, director of the Anglo-American Corporation, who endeavoured to keep colonial mining operations in British hands. Also, the Rio Tinto company, operating copper mines in Spain, formed part of this British reaction.[48] Both large mining ventures floated a new company, the Rhokana Corporation which kept the remaining mines (Rhokana and Nchanga) out of American hands. As such, American and British business interests clearly divided Northern Rhodesian copper mining by the early 1930s and could both rely on sufficient means and expertise in order to develop copper mining in Northern Rhodesia as a large-scale project. By the end of 1935, both mining corporations in Northern Rhodesia already accounted for about 14% of the world's copper production.[49]

Mining Corporations and the Commodity Frontier

Risks and Complexity

Corporate growth in the copper mining industry has largely been accounted for in terms of geology and its technological and organizational implications. Scholars like Schmitz have rightly pointed to geological factors that required companies to create economies of scale to bring production costs at an acceptable level. Given the large-scale investments in the second-generation copper mines, furthermore, the mining concerns were also growingly integrating forwards in smelting and refining as to exert control over the production chain and keep prices and consumption for their products somewhat predictable.[50] However, this section reminds us of the statement made in the introduction that such an explanation remains quite narrow to understand corporate development in the copper mining business during the period of red fever. In my view, the rise of the modern mining companies also needs to be more clearly connected to processes of frontier expansion, especially in the abilities of the firm to deal with the risks and complexity in preparing commodity frontiers for production. Copper mining was developed in typical commodity frontier locations that marked global expansion after 1850, in areas with little or no pre-existing infrastructure, unwelcoming climates, and landscapes and environmental conditions that were difficult to control. A quick overview of the most important new mines makes this clear. The new mines of Chile were surely not the most straightforward locations to set up large-scale mining activities, with the Chuquicamata mine deep in the Atacama Desert, as were the Potrerillos and El Teniente high in the Andes Mountains. Also, sparsely populated and difficult to access were the mines in Katanga. Shaky frontier conditions were of course also essential to the American experience, with copper mining being set up under icy conditions in Alaska, or the frontier territory of the American south-west. Arizona, one of the chief locations of low-grade mining, became an official state only in 1912. Uncertain locational circumstances made it extremely difficult for most of the mining companies to set up mining activities, with all the on-site processing capacity that was being required, and the larger amounts of energy, resources and labour that went along with it.

It is this connection that made large-scale copper mining in a desolate setting a notoriously risky and often dizzyingly expensive investment. Illustrative is that a few companies, named above, were exposed to enormous financial risks. The Guggenheims invested a staggering 50 million dollars just in trying to get the El Teniente in the Andes towards the required levels of mass production. The difficult construction of infrastructure and industrial equipment on high altitude coupled with the high costs made this project initially look very unpromising, and it was publicly derided in investment circles.[51] In addition, the Great War, which interfered with the development of new commodity frontiers in copper, surely gave a rise to the demands for metals, but it also badly affected the further development of new copper mines. Cokes were three times as expensive to ship to El Teniente than before the war.[52] Such risks could be carried by a powerful family enterprise like the Guggenheims, which made sufficient earnings elsewhere to compensate for the high development costs in new mining property. In 1918, for instance, the Guggenheims earned a staggering $142 million dollars on their Utah operations.[53] In Katanga, the UMHK struggled to get the mines at a profitable level, already before the war, faced with the absence of infrastructure and shortage of labour. A couple of years after this very difficult start, the UMHK management discussed shutting down operations completely as a serious option.[54] In Northern Rhodesia, the high prices of the 1920s stimulated copper mining, but the economic depression thwarted further development. In the 1930s, mines like Mufulira and Nchanga were temporarily closed, whereas the Roan Antelope and Nkana reduced productive capacity by 50%.[55] The financial riskiness also applied to operations in Alaska. Here, copper mining ventures were set up by the Guggenheims with the support of the Morgan family, in the vehicle called the Alaska Syndicate. The syndicate poured $30 million in Alaska for the development of coal and copper mines. But the return on investment remained low. The Bonanza mine made an operating profit, but not sufficiently high enough to account for the high investments made. Scholarship on the Guggenheims and Morgans made the sobering claim that profits of the Syndicate were rather made by "smart manoeuvring of stock" than by its operations on the ground.[56] The Alaska mines did not survive the troubled 1930s.

Transportation and Input Substitution

Companies had to make significant investments to meet the demands of second-generation copper mining, in terms of new mining and metallurgy, but also had to solve complex frontier-related problems. First and foremost, new copper frontiers required large-scale investments in terms of (transportation) infrastructure, without which they could not operate efficiently. In the beginning years of the UMHK, Katanga could not be reached by train, and Broken Hill in Northern Rhodesia, which was connected to the ports of South Africa, served as the last stop on the line. From Broken Hill, a tedious 214 kilometres had to be covered by porters on foot to the Star of the Congo mine near Lubumbashi, the company's first copper mine in operation.[57] Next to carriers, the UMHK later made use of tractor vehicles, the so-called loco-mobiles. Before the arrival of the train in Bisbee, Arizona, a similar steam-powered tractor was used by Phelps Dodge to replace the mules used to carry equipment and supplies. The efficiency gains of these clumsy vehicles were but narrow, as the wheels got stuck easily in the terrain especially under wet conditions.[58] Since the future of the UMHK depended upon a link to the outside world, better sooner than later, the development of the Katanga railroad was given absolute priority by the colonial administration.[59] In October 1910, the branch line between Broken Hill and Elizabethville was finally completed, which then finally allowed the UMHK to ship in the material to build a smelting plant near the mine. But transport infrastructure remained incomplete, in the eyes of the management as well as the colonial administration, since the Katanga mines were unconnected to the domestic Congolese interior and depended on foreign railway freighters. Only in 1928, this issue was resolved, when the line between Bukama and Port Francqui was completed and connected Katanga to the Congolese mainland.[60] The development of the Northern Rhodesian Copperbelt went significantly swifter, precisely because of this pre-existing railway infrastructure.

The construction of transportation infrastructure presented an even more gargantuan task in the copper mines of Alaska. The largest part of the expenditure made by the Syndicate flowed to the construction of a 315-km railroad from Cordova, south of Valdez where the original depot was planned, to the Kennecott mine at the Wrangell Mountains.[61] One of the main challenges included crossing the Kuskulana River canyon, where builders had to build a bridge over a deep river valley. Because of its heavy expenses, the bridge was soon dubbed as the "million dollar bridge". But building bridges and railways seemed not enough. In 1907, the Syndicate took over the Alaska Steamship Company, Alaska's largest steam shipping company, as to ensure (and control) the maritime connection with the American west coast.[62] Through the overarching holding company, the Guggenheims acquired not only mining concessions and land but also transportation infrastructure and companies.

Copper mining investments in remote areas thus easily spilled over in transportation investments and ownership. The same was true for Phelps Dodge in Arizona, in order to organize transportation to and from the mines in Arizona and, later, the new concessions in Mexico. The company had a long history of disputes with the Southern Pacific Railway Company over freight rates and the construction of necessary branch lines, for instance between the mine Bisbee and the smelter in Douglas. The mining company therefore set up a railway company, the El Paso and Southwestern Railway company, on its own account in 1888. This subsidiary company later built the transborder connection towards the Phelps Dodge mining concessions in Sonora, Mexico, connecting Nacozari to the smelting plant at Douglas. By integrating the Arizona and Mexico copper frontiers, the mining company gained the status as second largest industrial railway operator in the USA after United States Steel.[63] In Montana, the smaller "Butte, Anaconda and Pacific Railway Company" was established by the Anaconda company as a rail operator that carried the ores from Butte to the Smelter in Anaconda. Similar transportation investments were made as to reach the mines in the Andes and Atacama Desert in Chile. Only El Teniente could profit from pre-existing railroads, as they only had connected Rancagua to the mine via a narrow gauge line in 1911.[64]

Underlying the often very heavy investments for transportation infrastructure was not only the obvious need to transport copper away from the frontier, but also to provide the necessary inputs for the mining camps, like food, but also energy resources to keep the innovative machinery and processing plants of second-generation mining up and running. Going back to the case of Phelps Dodge, transportation investments were also strongly related to the acquisition of coal mines in New Mexico, from which the copper mines were provided with coal, a critical energy resource.[65] Both the concentrators in Bisbee and the smelting in Douglas needed large amounts of coal to run on, and the railway company could be used to ship in coal next to shipping out copper. Anaconda also provided its installations with coal from its own mines, from smaller mining settlements in Washoe, Sand Coulee (both Montana) and Diamondville (Wyoming).[66] As such, the activities of the copper companies in providing energy to the copper installations, and related transport investments, in turn gave a further impetus to secondary frontier development in the wider vicinity. The majority of Anaconda coal flowed to the mines and smelter in Montana, whereas excess production was sold on the market. The diversification into other activities as transportation and procuring energy resources stemmed from both a desire to bypass unruly suppliers and transporters, but also simply because of the absence thereof.

The acute shortage of energy and resources was thereby one of the strongest risks in frontier expansion. This was clear in the case of Katanga, where cokes were initially imported from Europe to operate the smelter in Lubumbashi, which heavily pressured on operating costs. Next to importing cokes, the Union Minière du Haut Katanga consumed alarming amounts of the surrounding forest, as firewood for the boilers as well as locomotives, which increased worries about deforestation.[67] Desperate to find cheap energy, the UMHK also looked for coal sources in the surrounding hinterland. An employee was sent to the Wankie colliery in Southern Rhodesia, who established to the relief of the management that it could be used for cokes.[68] Later, the UMHK developed its own coal mine in Katanga, Luena. For the exploitation of the coal mine, a new company was set up by the UMHK and the Katanga railway operator BCK, the Charbonnages de la Luena S.A. The company rose production from 30,000 tons in its first year to 120,000 tons in 1930. In Japan, the larger copper mines could also no longer be sustained by input from its immediate surroundings. The Fujita and Co company that owned the Kosaka mine, the largest Japanese copper producer at the turn of the century, had found a way to process the copper ores in 1900 by building a modern smelter. Access to fuel was the main challenge, and the mine depended upon wood and charcoal transported in with horses. Only in 1904, a railway line was completed.[69]

In the absence of nearby coal and wood in the barren Atacama Desert, the Chuquicamata mine relied on energy input organized far away from the mine. The Guggenheims installed a power plant in the port town of Tocopilla on the Pacific Coast in 1913 that ran on fuel oil, from where electricity was wired to the mine. Electricity was critical for the further development of the gigantic Chuquicamata mine, as the Guggenheims had built an electrolysis refining plant, a new technique which made use of electricity to further separate copper from other impurities. The case of Chuquicamata illustrates that the isolated copper mines were essential not only in providing the metals needed for global electrification, but that they quickly turned into electricity enclaves themselves in spite of their remoteness.[70] Like with other energy sources, mining companies were thereby the main providers of electricity in the area. In 1930, the UMHK switched to hydro-electrical energy sources. The first hydro-electrical power plant was built on the waterfall of Mwadingusha. For this reason, it set up a subsidiary company Société Générale des Forces Hydro-Electriques du Katanga (Sogéfor), in order to develop hydro-electrical power generation.[71] The electrification had an unintended side effect of temporarily closing the now obsolete coal mine in Luena, until World War II. In America too, mining companies were pioneers in providing electricity to the region. The Anaconda company electrified its branch railway line between Butte and Anaconda in 1912.[72]

Next to providing energy, mining companies also shifted away from their core business as to host chemical industries in providing their processing plants on-site. Anaconda produced its own sulphuric acids for its flotation and smelting on-site. The chemical industry was primarily oriented on the mining business, but not exclusively. With its excess capacity, the company produced agricultural fertilizer. The sulphuric acid was used to treat the phosphate rocks mined in Idaho, and to a product called Treble-Super-Phosphate phosphate.[73] Since 1922, Anaconda produced 1200 tons of this fertilizer, which was primarily marketed in the Midwestern states and on the Pacific coast.[74] The UMHK finished its own flotation plant in 1929. In order to provide the necessary chemicals, yet another daughter company "Sogechim" was established that was also supported by Belgium's newest chemical industry conglomerate "Union Chimique Belge". In creating the chemicals needed, Sogechim made use of colonial resources to the fullest, as a basic component in the flotation process adapted to the Katangese ores was based on palm oil acid.[75] The substitution of resources, energy and resources that were needed to develop the copper mines leads to a significant increase in scale of the companies, in terms of branching out in affiliated activities. Frontier expansion thus meant not only scale increase, and vertical integration, but also diversification like the organization of related activities in terms of transportation and organizing the substitution of needed inputs.

"Benevolent" Frontier Capitalists?

Another challenge that affected virtually every new commodity frontier of copper was the shortage of labour. All copper corporations created mine camps virtually in the middle of nowhere and had to attract (and maintain) labour to the vicinity of the mine. In the mountains of Chile, the Kennecott Copper Corporation attracted Chilean migrants, mainly from the countryside, but had enormous difficulties in keeping the workers there on a long-term basis.[76] For the UMHK in Katanga, labour recruitment posed a severe problem, especially in the formative years. Between 1906 and 1911, the company had troubles in finding its 600 indigenous workers. Once it streamlined its labour recruitment with the help of the colonial administration, the number of workers shot up dramatically. In 1919, the company employed 12,000 workers and 10 years later 17,200. Initially, many of the workers were attracted from distant territories, like Rhodesia. Later, the UMHK preferred Congolese workers.

The shortage of labour can only be understood while understanding the complexity of frontier expansion set out above. Labour was in high demand, not only for developing mining, but also for the construction of much of the above-mentioned infrastructure and railroads, all of them involving at least equally labour-intensive processes. As such making copper mines operational as well as the necessary broader infrastructural development of the frontier strangled one another. The UMHK, to open the mines, and the railroad constructor BCK, to make transportation of copper possible, both hindered each other by fishing in the same pond. This problem of labour competition between companies in Katanga was partially solved by establishing a common labour recruitment office, the Bourse du Travail du Katanga in 1910, which was modelled to the South African labour recruitment office Witwatersrand Native Labour Association (WNLA). Another challenge in Katanga was that labourers often successfully resisted selling their labour in the mines, by profiting from the very process of frontier expansion in other ways. African farmers in particular profited from the growing needs of the mining camps by moving into agriculture.[77] The Syndicate faced a similar problem of competition within Alaska's tiny labour market, where the railway project drained the labour needed in the mines.[78] The vast emptiness of Alaska of 1907 housed only 76,000 inhabitants.[79] In less remote frontiers, in Nacozari Mexico, for instance, Phelps Dodge also lost its workers to other mining and railroad camps and to other employers distributed over the whole south-western USA.[80]

Next to labour shortages, mining frontiers formed the bitter stage of countless strikes and, often, outright class wars. The Guggenheims were confronted with a serious uprising in 1912 in Bingham, the epicentre of modern copper mining, when labourers armed with mining explosives and rifles fought out a small war with the state militia.[81] In 1919, Kennecott reported that the El Teniente mine had to stop production for nearly two weeks in November, and a few days later another strike caused damage to company property and further curtailed production.[82] Like in Utah, the 1919 strikes were put down only with the help of local forces. The repertoire in dealing with unrest existed primarily in violence and repression. Anaconda created blacklists for the mines in Chuquicamata (after 1923) and in Montana as to prevent the hiring of labour militants and activists.[83] The copper mining industry remained the sight of some of the most dramatic class struggles in American history. The Western Federation of Mining organized a strike in the Michigan copper mines, which lasted from July 1913 to April 1914. In a packed gathering of the union in December 1913, 62 were killed due to panic originating from a false fire alarm.[84] A most notorious strike incident occurred in 1917 at the Bisbee mines of Phelps Dodge. This large-scale strike resulted in the deportation of 1100 strikers in cattle cars over 320 km to New Mexico.[85] The company orchestrated the deportation with the willing help of local authorities. But copper strikes were not limited to America. In 1919, the white workforce of the UMHK decided to strike, demanding a pay increase.[86] It took a longer while for African workers in the Copperbelt to organize, but the black workforce also struck en masse: two times in Northern Rhodesia in 1935 and 1940, and a large strike occurred in 1941 in Katanga. These strikes were resolved by the point of the gun. Before these big strikes, the principal strategy of black miners to resist coerced mining work was "desertion".

It soon became apparent to the mining companies that the problem of labour shortage and unrest in the copper frontier could not be held in check by repression and violence alone. Especially after World War I, company paternalism began to take the upper hand and growingly surfaced in terms of organizing the social landscape. In 1918, the President of Phelps Dodge realized that improving conditions in the mining camps, particularly in Mexico, was needed to prevent workers from running away.[87] Instead of the organically grown and chaotic Bisbee with all its "vices" for labourers, Phelps Dodge preferred to build orderly and modern mining villages to support new operations. This was exemplified by the entire new mining city that was built in Tyrone, New Mexico, between 1915 and 1918. Phelps Dodge hired the renowned New York architect Bertram Goodhue to construct the village. The new model mining city quickly became a ghost town, however, as mining activities lasted only 5 years, and was lost on the falling copper prices in 1921.[88] In the 1920s, similarly, the UMHK created better living conditions in the mining compounds in order to stabilize the workforce, by investing in health infrastructure, education, housing conditions and education.[89] In 1928, the company offered workers longer-term contracts, allowed them to marry and settle permanently in mining villages. Mining camps in Katanga had an ephemeral character, as the straw huts were annually destroyed as to counter the infection by kimputu ticks. They were gradually replaced by permanent brick houses. The new housing policy was overseen by a small team of doctors hired by the UMHK to develop housing that could improve hygienic conditions. Despite the nationalization, the company still looked for expertise and practices across the border. The permanent brick houses used by the UMHK were modelled on housing types used in the mining compounds of the Rand.[90]

The company policy of the Guggenheims vis-à-vis mining camps similarly took a volt-face turn around the same time. In 1915, Daniel Guggenheim adopted a new set of labour policies inspired by the concept of welfare capitalism, aware of the damaging nature of strikes and particularly the affiliated violence. To this end, the Guggenheims followed new recommendations made by the former US Commissioner of Labor, Charles P. Neill, whom they had hired, and who set out a new course of "welfare capitalism".[91] Guggenheim's interpretation of welfare capitalism involved pension and health plans, but also accident prevention strategies. It went along with the creation of a brand-new welfare department in the Guggenheim headquarters. The notion of welfare capitalism was also extended to the South American operations. Harry Guggenheim described in 1920 in great detail to his colleagues of the mining industry the activities of the welfare department in creating mining cities in South America, and how the company organized housing, water supply, sewage and schooling. While ideas of such company paternalism had gained currency elsewhere, it was precisely frontier conditions that had triggered the adoption of such policies, as Harry Guggenheim asserted "on the account of their isolation, and the magnitude of the operations centralized at one point, [the mining companies] have lent themselves to the development of welfare work similar to that practiced in some of the large progressive industrial works but unusual in mining camps".[92] Putting the principles of "welfare capitalism" in practice added to the rising costs and magnitude of operations. The Guggenheims invested 2 million dollars in the El Teniente, which were used for: "housing, healing, educating and amusing a total population of some 10,000 souls".[93] The strategies of welfare and paternalism in controlling the social landscape were a visible expression of the fact that new forms and practices of expertise were required to stabilize and build out the new commodity frontiers during the period of red fever. Together with the rising costs induced in non-selective mining and metallurgy, the frontier-related challenges marked the growth and business practices of the modern copper mining industry.

Conclusion

The aim of this chapter was to present an overview of the global copper mining frontiers that were opened up from the late nineteenth century onwards, as demand for copper skyrocketed due to global electrification and the growing needs for the red metal by the new industries of the second industrial revolution. The aim of the chapter in particular was to explore the copper mining business, its business practices and how the period of red fever was formative to the development of the modern natural resource company. The natural resource company was arguably a critical actor in opening new sources of resources across the globe, yet its activities are not sufficiently brought into connection with the process of commodity frontier expansion.

The swelling demand for copper triggered an enormous wave of expansion, unleashing a large number of new commodity frontiers in copper in the USA, Alaska, South America and Central Africa into the world economy. Industrializing countries like Japan also frantically looked to exploit domestic sources of copper. This period of red fever, which took full force after 1890, was not only marked by a geographical shift in copper mining, but it also involved what we have called a second generation of copper mining of deeper and lower-graded copper deposits. With the richer copper veins—the low hanging fruit—increasingly exploited, miners and engineers turned their attention to copper deposits deeper beneath the soil that consisted of lower-graded ore types, breaking the long-held spell of the impossibility to mine such lower-grade ore bodies. In order to overcome this fundamental bottleneck, new innovations were put into practice. The principal innovation was the simple but effective coupling of non-selective mining techniques, which involved the destruction of the landscape by new techniques like open-pit mining, next to new metallurgical methods in smelting, refining (flotation and electrolysis), which gave the new commodity frontiers a distinctively industrial character. This opening of a Pandora's box allowed mining companies to find and exploit new copper mines across the world. The combination has also been seen as the main driver behind business growth in the copper mining industry. The opening up of low-graded copper mines indeed required enormous investments in machinery, facilities and technology ownership. In addition, lower-graded deposits were often of a far larger substance, which necessitated larger economies of scale. From the more complex and larger mining operations, a few large copper mining companies emerged that took over the smaller ones and came to dominate the copper mining scene. In addition, mining companies growingly integrated forwards in the supply chain, assuming control over end-markets and demand for the red metal in which they had invested so much.

The second-generation copper mining techniques in combination with corporate growth were indeed the driving force behind the expansion of the global copper frontier. However, in this chapter, it was also argued that such a narrative has too easily overlooked the complex nature of commodity frontier expansion in the period of red fever. Not only were new mines consistently larger, but they were also mostly situated in desolate and sparsely populated areas, lacking necessary basic infrastructure, energy resources and labour needed to set up this new type of mining system that needed the mining of larger quantities of ores and drew on industrial processing techniques. The expansion of red fever was not simply a matter of financing new technologies and scale increase, but also one of organizing and managing distant and complex commodity frontiers. Remoteness in itself was one of the most important cost factors, determining to a very large extent the riskiness of an investment project. The period of red fever indeed consisted of a few extreme cases in terms of remoteness like Alaska, Chuquicamata and Katanga. We have established that the necessary business capacities of frontier expansion should therefore, without downplaying its importance, not be narrowed down to mining engineering, geology science and technology. What companies needed to do was the build-up of knowledge, expertise and managerial/organizational qualities that enabled firms to control the political, economic and social risks involved in mining and frontier development.

This "frontier factor" gave an additional impetus to the formation of the modern copper mining industry and accounts for much of the business practices. In order to turn the commodity frontier into a modern, efficient and industrially organized mining hub, the chapter has explored how natural resource companies organized the input of labour, energy and resources, and how such efforts affected the practices and development of natural resource companies themselves. Transforming commodity frontiers implicated that firms had to move into a number of activities with which they held previously little experience and they set up affiliated businesses or integrated new activities within their own company structure. First of all, copper companies became large-scale organizers of transportation infrastructure by branching out into transportation companies. The organization of transportation to and from the copper mines was of critical importance, and the absence thereof, cast a large shadow on the prospect of new ventures.

The majority of the investments in the case of Alaska and Katanga flowed to the development of the railroads. However, the priority given to transport infrastructure and all things related created unintended side effects. It added to the problem of labour shortages, as the mines had to compete with other commodity frontier developers (often owned by the same overarching company) over the scarce labour that was present. This problem of competition affected virtually every commodity frontier in the beginning.

Next to transportation, secondly, the input of resources and energy was another major concern and also triggered diversification. The copper mines of the second generation needed enormous amounts of energy, and due to its criticality, natural resource companies acquired ownership in energy sources as well. In Montana, Arizona and Katanga, companies ran coal mines by themselves and integrated the provision of coal in the transportation network they controlled. The requirements for second-generation copper mining also made mining hubs into hot spots of electrification. Input substitution was, thirdly, also a factor that determined the business practice. Businesses tried to limit the input of resources and provisions to a minimum by producing supplies needed for copper refining on-site. Once energy resources were fully covered by electrification, the process of input substitution continued to play a large role in improving existing processes. A remarkable development was the formation of chemical industries in the copper frontier, which further added to the "industrial sight" of the copper mining areas.

Once this industrial sight of the copper frontier became more apparent, the management of labour changed accordingly. In the first phase of frontier development, the copper giants had large difficulties in finding and maintaining labour, due to its scarcity and competition. Labour unrest and uprising was chiefly checked by violence and coercion. During World War I, when the second generation of copper mining was fully underway, most natural resource companies changed their attitude towards labour significantly. The Great War was of course an era that witnessed new compromises between capital and labour, but mining companies were also growingly aware that the need to stabilize the commodity frontier in particular required a new course of action. In addition, whereas a first phase needed intensive but unskilled forces to build infrastructure, skilled labour became a vital part of the more complex copper mining industry, as an increasing amount of production stages were done on-site, like smelting and refining. This may in large part account for a move towards more benevolent and paternalistic behaviour that centred on the notion of "welfare capitalism". The modern copper mining company came to organize virtually every aspect of mining life, from housing, schooling and sewage to entertainment. This further attests to the fact that natural resource companies attracted expertise other than mining and engineering, such as in architecture, medicine and social policy. It made their presence and influence all pervasive. This expertise, too, was essential to the company's strategies in controlling the copper frontier during red fever.

Notes

1. William J. Hausman, Peter Hertner, and Mira Wilkins, *Global Electrification: Multinational Enterprise and International Finance in the History of Light and Power, 1878–2007* (Cambridge: Cambridge University Press, 2011).
2. Charles K. Hyde, *Copper for America: The United States Copper Industry from Colonial Times to the 1990s* (Tucson: University of Arizona Press, 1998), 66.
3. Christopher Schmitz, "The Changing Structure of the World Copper Market, 1870–1939," *Journal of European Economic History* 2, no. 26 (1997): 301.
4. Geoffrey Jones, *Multinationals and Global Capitalism: From the Nineteenth to the Twenty-First Century* (Oxford and New York: Oxford University Press, 2005), 45.
5. Steven C. Topik and Allen Wells, "Warenketten in einer globalen Wirtschaft," in *1870–1945: Weltmärkte und Weltkriege*, ed. Emily S. Rosenberg (München: Beck, 2012), 590.
6. Edward Barbier, *Scarcity and Frontiers: How Economies Have Developed Through Natural Resource Exploitation* (Cambridge, UK and New York: Cambridge University Press, 2011), 7.
7. Barbier, 552.

8. John H. Dunning and Sarianna M. Lundan, *Multinational Enterprises and the Global Economy* (Cheltenham: Edward Elgar, 2008), 69.
9. Youssef Cassis, "Big Business," in *The Oxford Handbook of Business History*, ed. Johathan Zeitlin and Jones Geoffrey (Oxford: Oxford University Press, 2008), 174; Robert Fitzgerald, *Rise of the Global Company: Multinationals and the Making of the Modern World* (Cambridge University Press, 2016), 9.
10. Dunning and Lundan, *Multinational Enterprises and the Global Economy*, 69.
11. Robrecht Declercq, *World Market Transformation: Inside the German Fur Capital Leipzig 1870–1939* (New York: Routledge, 2017).
12. Christof Dejung and Niels P. Petersson, "Introduction: Power, Institutions, and Global Markets-Actors, Mechanisms and Foundations of Worldwide Economic Integration, 1850–1930," in *The Foundations of Worldwide Economic Integration: Power, Institutions, and Global Markets, 1850–1930*, ed. Christof Dejung and Niels P. Petersson (Cambridge: Cambridge University Press, 2013), 2.
13. Jason W. Moore, "Sugar and the Expansion of the Early Modern World-Economy: Commodity Frontiers, Ecological Transformation, and Industrialization," *Review (Fernand Braudel Center)* 23, no. 3 (January 1, 2000): 409–33; Jürgen Osterhammel, *Die Verwandlung der Welt: eine Geschichte des 19. Jahrhunderts* (München: Beck, 2009); and Topik and Wells, "Warenketten in einer globalen Wirtschaft."
14. Jones, *Multinationals and Global Capitalism*, 52.
15. Fitzgerald, *Rise of the Global Company*, 25.
16. Corey Ross, *Ecology and Power in the Age of Empire: Europe and the Transformation of the Tropical World* (Oxford: Oxford University Press, 2017), 264.
17. Christopher Schmitz, "The Rise of Big Business in the World Copper Industry 1870–1930," *Economic History Review* 3, no. 29 (1986): 392–410.
18. Jonathan Leitner, "Red Metal in the Age of Capital: The Political Ecology of Copper in the Nineteenth-Century World-Economy," *Review (Fernand Braudel Center)* 3, no. 24 (2001): 373–437.
19. Hyde, *Copper for America*, 110.
20. William Bryam Gates, *Michigan Copper and Boston Dollars: An Economic History of the Michigan Copper Mining Industry* (Cambridge, MA: Harvard University Press, 1951), 230; Noam Maggor, *Brahmin Capitalism: Frontiers of Wealth and Populism in America's First Gilded Age*, 2017.

21. Christopher Schmitz, "The World Copper Industry: Geology, Mining Techniques and Corporate Growth, 1870–1939," *The Journal of European Economic History* 1, no. 29 (2000): 87.
22. Hyde, *Copper for America*, 168.
23. Patricia Sippel, "Technology and Change in Japan's Modern Copper Mining Industry," in *Institutional and Technological Change in Japan's Economy: Past and Present*, ed. Janet Hunter and Cornelia Storz (London: Routledge, 2012), 21.
24. Timo Särkkä, "The Lure of Katanga Copper: Tanganyika Concessions Limited and the Anatomy of Mining and Mine Exploration 1899–1906," *South African Historical Journal* 68, no. 3 (July 2, 2016): 7, https://doi.org/10.1080/02582473.2016.1153707.
25. Tomas Frederiksen, "Seeing the Copperbelt: Science, Mining and Colonial Power in Northern Rhodesia," Global Production Networks, Labour and Development, *Geoforum* 44, no. Supplement C (January 1, 2013): 271, https://doi.org/10.1016/j.geoforum.2012.08.007; Francis L. Coleman, *The Northern Rhodesia Copperbelt, 1899–1962 Technological Development Up to the End of the Central African Federation* (Manchester: Manchester University Press and A.M. Kelley, 1971), 59.
26. Andrew D. Roberts, *A History of Zambia* (London: Heinemann, 1981), 176–77.
27. Thomas Miller Klubock, "Class, Community, and Gender in the Chilean Copper Mines: The El Teniente Miners and Working-Class Politics, 1904–1951" (1993), 24; Schmitz, "The World Copper Industry: Geology, Mining Techniques and Corporate Growth, 1870–1939," 87.
28. Timothy J. LeCain, *Mass Destruction: The Men and Giant Mines That Wired America and Scarred the Planet* (New Brunswick, NJ: Rutgers University Press, 2009), 154.
29. John H. Davis, *The Guggenheims: An American Epic* (New York: S.P.I. Books, 1994), 115. The Rockefellers owned the oil giant "Standard Oil" but were also behind Anaconda. The Guggenheims had however been first to support the Bingham mines.
30. Schmitz, "The Rise of Big Business in the World Copper Industry 1870–1930," 398–99.

31. John Phillips, "Alfred Chester Beatty: Mining Engineer, Financier and Entrepreneur 1898–1950," in *Mining Tycoons in the Age of Empire, 1870–1945: Entrepreneurship, High Finance, Politics and Territorial Expansion*, ed. Raymond E. Dumett (Farnham, England: Ashgate, 2009), 220.
32. Charles Hawley, *A Kennecott Story* (Salt Lake City: University of Utah Press, 2014).
33. Maggor, *Brahmin Capitalism*, 44; Gates, *Michigan Copper and Boston Dollars: An Economic History of the Michigan Copper Mining Industry*, 89.
34. Patrick F. Morris, *Anaconda, Montana: Copper Smelting Boom Town on the Western Frontier* (Swann Publishing, 1997), 182.
35. Irwin Unger and Debi Unger, *The Guggenheims: A Family History* (Pymble, NSW: HarperCollins e-books, 2006), 88, http://search.ebscohost.com/login.aspx?direct=true&scope=site&db=nlebk&db=nlabk&AN=184961.
36. Alfred Dupont Chandler, *The Visible Hand: The Managerial Revolution in American Business* (Cambridge, MA: The Belknap Press of Harvard University Press, 1997), 441.
37. William W. Culver and Cornel J. Reinhart, "Capitalist Dreams: Chile's Response to Nineteenth-Century World Copper Competition," *Comparative Studies in Society and History* 31, no. 4 (1989): 722–44; Enrique Fernández-Domingo, *Le négoce français au Chili: 1880–1929*, Histoire (Rennes: Presses universitaires de Rennes, 2015), http://books.openedition.org/pur/25227.
38. Culver and Reinhart, "Capitalist Dreams," 132; *Tracing the Veins*, 87, accessed July 4, 2018, https://www.ucpress.edu/book/9780520211377/tracing-the-veins.
39. Theodore H. Moran, *Multinational Corporations and the Politics of Dependence: Copper in Chile* (Princeton, NJ: Princeton University Press, 1977), 23.
40. Thomas F. O'Brien, "'Rich Beyond the Dreams of Avarice': The Guggenheims in Chile," *The Business History Review* 63, no. 1 (1989): 131.
41. Frans Buelens, *Congo, 1885–1960: een financieel-economische geschiedenis* (Berchem: EPO, 2007), 195.
42. Dirk Waterschoot, *Union Minière du Haut Katanga: ontstaan en arbeidsbeleid tot 1960* (Brussel: GRESEA, 1985), 6. Following on earlier agreements made in 1901 with the Katangese authorities, the Tanganyika Concessions Ltd retained a controlling interest in the UMHK of 44%. Robert Williams, the president of Tanganyika Concessions, acted as the vice-president of the Union Minière board.

43. René Brion and Jean-Louis Moreau, *Van mijnbouw tot Mars: de ontstaansgeschiedenis van Umicore* (Tielt: Lannoo, 2006), 111.
44. Charles Perrings, *Black Mineworkers in Central Africa: Industrial Strategies and the Evolution of an African Proletariat in the Copperbelt 1911–41* (London: Heinemann, 1979), 50.
45. Brion and Moreau, *Van mijnbouw tot Mars*, 82.
46. Jan Frederik Abbeloos, "Connections, Connections, Connections! Making Sense of the Relationship Between National Economic Development and Natural Resource Dependence on the Atlantic Copper Market During the Long Twentieth Century," in *Andre Gunder Frank and Global Development: Visions, Remembrances, and Explorations*, ed. Patrick Manning and Gills Barry (London: Routledge, 2010), 115; Perrings, *Black Mineworkers in Central Africa*, 43.
47. Simon Ball, "The German Octopus: The British Metal Corporation and the Next War, 1914–1939," *Enterprise & Society* 5, no. 3 (2004): 464.
48. Coleman, *The Northern Rhodesia Copperbelt, 1899–1962: Technological Development Up to the End of the Central African Federation*, 71.
49. Charles Harvey, *The Rio Tinto Company: An Economic History of a Leading International Mining Concern, 1873–1954* (Penzance: Alison Hodge, 1981), 247.
50. Schmitz, "The Rise of Big Business in the World Copper Industry 1870–1930," 403–4.
51. Klubock, "Class, Community, and Gender in the Chilean Copper Mines," 28–29.
52. ARA2, Umicore nr. 1041, Kennecott Copper Corporation, Second Annual Report 1916, f. 25.
53. Unger and Unger, *The Guggenheims*, 89. Of this amount, 92 millions was paid out in dividends, whereas the rest was kept for the much needed working capital.
54. Buelens, *Congo, 1885–1960*, 197.
55. L. Butler, *Copper Empire: Mining and the Colonial State in Northern Rhodesia c.1930–64* (New York: Palgrave Macmillan, 2007), 19.
56. Vincent Phillip Carosso and Rose C. Carosso, *The Morgans: Private International Bankers, 1854–1913* (Cambridge, MA: Harvard University Press, 1987), 463; Hawley, *A Kennecott Story*, 7.
57. *Compagnie Du Chemin de Fer Du Bas-Congo Au Katanga. Inauguration de La Ligne Port Francqui-Bukama*, 1928; Harvey, *The Rio Tinto Company*, 25.

58. Samuel Truett, *Fugitive Landscapes: The Forgotten History of the U.S.-Mexico Borderlands* (New Haven, CT and London: Yale University Press, 2008), 34.
59. Buelens, *Congo, 1885–1960*, 347.
60. Simon Katzenellenbogen, *Railways and the Copper Mines of Katanga* (Oxford: Clarendon Press, 1973).
61. Hawley, *A Kennecott Story*, 7–8.
62. Melody Webb Grauman, "Kennecott: Alaskan Origins of a Copper Empire, 1900–1938," *The Western Historical Quarterly* 9, no. 2 (1978): 210.
63. Carlos A. Schwantes, *Vision & Enterprise: Exploring the History of Phelps Dodge Corporation* (Tucson: University of Arizona Press; Phoenix, AZ: Phelps Dodge Corporation, 2000), 99–102.
64. Hawley, *A Kennecott Story*, 107.
65. F.E. Richter, "The Copper-Mining Industry in the United States, 1845–1925," *The Quarterly Journal of Economics* 41, no. 2 (February 1, 1927): 700.
66. ARA2, Umicore Archives, nr. 1018, Anaconda Annual Report 1914, p. 10.
67. Ross, *Ecology and Power in the Age of Empire*, 192.
68. Edgar Van der Straeten, "Edgar Sengier," *Biographie Belge d'Outre-Mer* VII-A (1997): 430.
69. Sippel, "Technology and Change in Japan's Modern Copper Mining Industry," 22.
70. Hausman, Hertner, and Wilkins, *Global Electrification*, 146.
71. *Union minière du Haut Katanga, 1906–1956* (Bruxelles: L. Cuypers, 1956), 150.
72. Charles Vincent Mutschler, *Wired for Success: The Butte, Anaconda & Pacific Railway, 1892–1985* (Washington State University Press, 2002).
73. ARA 2, Umicore Archives, nr. 1018, Anaconda Annual Report 1921.
74. Gerald Francis Loughlin, *Contributions to Economic Geology (Short Papers and Preliminary Reports), 1927: Part I.—Metals and Nonmetals Except Fuels* (U.S. Government Printing Office, 1928), 164.
75. R. du Trieu de Terdonck, E. Weberg, and L. Theys, *Union Minière du Haut-Katanga, 1906–1956: évolution des techniques et des activités sociales*, 1957, 110.
76. Klubock, "Class, Community, and Gender in the Chilean Copper Mines," 39.
77. Perrings, *Black Mineworkers in Central Africa*, 19.
78. ARA 2, Umicore, nr. 1041, Kennecott Annual Report 1917.

79. Unger and Unger, *The Guggenheims*, 104.
80. Truett, *Fugitive Landscapes*, 179.
81. Davis, *The Guggenheims*, 116.
82. ARA 2, Umicore nr. 1041, Kennecott Annual Report 1919, p. 26.
83. *Tracing the Veins*, 35.
84. C. Harry Benedict, *Red Metal: The Calumet and Hecla Story* (Ann Arbor: University of Michigan Press, 1952), 232.
85. Katherine Benton-Cohen, *Borderline Americans: Racial Division and Labor War in the Arizona Borderlands* (Cambridge, MA: Harvard University Press, 2011). See Chapter 7 for a full account of the Bisbee deportation in 1917.
86. Perrings, *Black Mineworkers in Central Africa*, 51.
87. Truett, *Fugitive Landscapes*, 179.
88. Schwantes, *Vision & Enterprise*, 123. The Tyrone mine was finally put in practice in 1969.
89. Dácil Juif and Ewout Frankema, "From Coercion to Compensation: Institutional Responses to Labour Scarcity in the Central African Copperbelt," *Journal of Institutional Economics* 14, no. 2 (April 2018): 313–43.
90. ARA2, UMHK, eerste overdracht, nr. 350? La main d'oeuvre Indigène de L'UMHK. Questionnaire de la commission de MOI. Juin 1928.
91. Thomas F. O'Brien, "Copper Kings of the Americas—The Guggenheim Brothers," in *Mining Tycoons in the Age of Empire, 1870–1945: Entrepreneurship, High Finance, Politics and Territorial Expansion*, ed. Raymond E. Dumett (Farnham, England: Ashgate, 2009), 200.
92. Harry F. Guggenheim, "Building Mining Cities in South America," *Mining and Engineering Journal* 110, no. 5 (1920): 204–10.
93. ARA 2, Umicore, nr. 1041, Braden Copper Company, Second Annual Report 1916, 27.

Bibliography

Abbeloos, Jan Frederik. "Connections, Connections, Connections! Making Sense of the Relationship Between National Economic Development and Natural Resource Dependence on the Atlantic Copper Market During the Long Twentieth Century." In *Andre Gunder Frank and Global Development: Visions, Remembrances, and Explorations*, edited by Patrick Manning and Gills Barry, 175–95. London: Routledge, 2010.

Ball, Simon. "The German Octopus: The British Metal Corporation and the Next War, 1914–1939." *Enterprise & Society* 5, no. 3 (2004): 451–89.

Barbier, Edward. *Scarcity and Frontiers: How Economies Have Developed Through Natural Resource Exploitation*. Cambridge, UK and New York: Cambridge University Press, 2011.

Benedict, C. Harry. *Red Metal: The Calumet and Hecla Story*. Ann Arbor: University of Michigan Press, 1952.

Benton-Cohen, Katherine. *Borderline Americans: Racial Division and Labor War in the Arizona Borderlands*. Cambridge, MA: Harvard University Press, 2011.

Brion, René, and Jean-Louis Moreau. *Van mijnbouw tot Mars: de ontstaansgeschiedenis van Umicore*. Tielt: Lannoo, 2006.

Buelens, Frans. *Congo, 1885–1960: een financieel-economische geschiedenis*. Berchem: EPO, 2007.

Butler, L. *Copper Empire: Mining and the Colonial State in Northern Rhodesia c.1930–64*. New York: Palgrave Macmillan, 2007.

Carosso, Vincent Phillip, and Rose C. Carosso. *The Morgans: Private International Bankers, 1854–1913*. Cambridge, MA: Harvard University Press, 1987.

Cassis, Youssef. "Big Business." In *The Oxford Handbook of Business History*, edited by Johathan Zeitlin and Jones Geoffrey, 171–94. Oxford: Oxford University Press, 2008.

Chandler, Alfred Dupont. *The Visible Hand: The Managerial Revolution in American Business*. Cambridge, MA: The Belknap Press of Harvard University Press, 1997.

Coleman, Francis L. *The Northern Rhodesia Copperbelt, 1899–1962 Technological Development Up to the End of the Central African Federation*. Manchester: Manchester University Press and A.M. Kelley, 1971.

Compagnie Du Chemin de Fer Du Bas-Congo Au Katanga. Inauguration de La Ligne Port Francqui-Bukama, 1928.

Culver, William W., and Cornel J. Reinhart. "Capitalist Dreams: Chile's Response to Nineteenth-Century World Copper Competition." *Comparative Studies in Society and History* 31, no. 4 (1989): 722–44.

Davis, John H. *The Guggenheims: An American Epic*. New York: S.P.I. Books, 1994.

Declercq, Robrecht. *World Market Transformation: Inside the German Fur Capital Leipzig 1870–1939*. New York: Routledge, 2017.

Dejung, Christof, and Niels P. Petersson. "Introduction: Power, Institutions, and Global Markets-Actors, Mechanisms and Foundations of Worldwide Economic Integration, 1850–1930." In *The Foundations of Worldwide Economic Integration: Power, Institutions, and Global Markets, 1850–1930*, edited by Christof Dejung and Niels P. Petersson, 1–21. Cambridge: Cambridge University Press, 2013.

Dunning, John H., and Sarianna M. Lundan. *Multinational Enterprises and the Global Economy*. Cheltenham: Edward Elgar, 2008.

Fernández-Domingo, Enrique. *Le négoce français au Chili: 1880–1929*. Histoire. Rennes: Presses universitaires de Rennes, 2015. http://books.openedition.org/pur/25227.

Fitzgerald, Robert. *Rise of the Global Company: Multinationals and the Making of the Modern World*. Cambridge: Cambridge University Press, 2016.

Frederiksen, Tomas. "Seeing the Copperbelt: Science, Mining and Colonial Power in Northern Rhodesia." Global Production Networks, Labour and Development, *Geoforum* 44, no. Supplement C (January 1, 2013): 271–81. https://doi.org/10.1016/j.geoforum.2012.08.007.

Gates, William Bryam. *Michigan Copper and Boston Dollars: An Economic History of the Michigan Copper Mining Industry*. Cambridge, MA: Harvard University Press, 1951.

Grauman, Melody Webb. "Kennecott: Alaskan Origins of a Copper Empire, 1900–1938." *The Western Historical Quarterly* 9, no. 2 (1978): 197.

Harvey, Charles. *The Rio Tinto Company: An Economic History of a Leading International Mining Concern, 1873–1954*. Penzance: Alison Hodge, 1981.

Hausman, William J., Peter Hertner, and Mira Wilkins. *Global Electrification: Multinational Enterprise and International Finance in the History of Light and Power, 1878–2007*. Cambridge: Cambridge University Press, 2011.

Hawley, Charles. *A Kennecott Story*. Salt Lake City: University of Utah Press, 2014.

Hyde, Charles K. *Copper for America: The United States Copper Industry from Colonial Times to the 1990s*. Tucson: University of Arizona Press, 1998.

Jones, Geoffrey. *Multinationals and Global Capitalism: From the Nineteenth to the Twenty-First Century*. Oxford and New York: Oxford University Press, 2005.

Juif, Dácil, and Ewout Frankema. "From Coercion to Compensation: Institutional Responses to Labour Scarcity in the Central African Copperbelt." *Journal of Institutional Economics* 14, no. 2 (April 2018): 313–43.

Katzenellenbogen, Simon. *Railways and the Copper Mines of Katanga*. Oxford: Clarendon Press, 1973.

Klubock, Thomas Miller. *Class, Community, and Gender in the Chilean Copper Mines: The El Teniente Miners and Working-Class Politics, 1904–1951*, 1993.

LeCain, Timothy J. *Mass Destruction: The Men and Giant Mines That Wired America and Scarred the Planet*. New Brunswick, NJ: Rutgers University Press, 2009.

Leitner, Jonathan. "Red Metal in the Age of Capital: The Political Ecology of Copper in the Nineteenth-Century World-Economy." *Review (Fernand Braudel Center)* 3, no. 24 (2001): 373–437.

Loughlin, Gerald Francis. *Contributions to Economic Geology (Short Papers and Preliminary Reports), 1927: Part I.—Metals and Nonmetals Except Fuels*. Washington, DC: U.S. Government Printing Office, 1928.

Maggor, Noam. *Brahmin Capitalism: Frontiers of Wealth and Populism in America's First Gilded Age*. Cambridge, MA: Harvard University Press, 2017.

Moore, Jason W. "Sugar and the Expansion of the Early Modern World-Economy: Commodity Frontiers, Ecological Transformation, and Industrialization." *Review (Fernand Braudel Center)* 23, no. 3 (January 1, 2000): 409–33.

Moran, Theodore H. *Multinational Corporations and the Politics of Dependence: Copper in Chile*. Princeton, NJ: Princeton University Press, 1977.

Morris, Patrick F. *Anaconda, Montana: Copper Smelting Boom Town on the Western Frontier*. Bethesda, MD: Swann Publishing, 1997.

Mutschler, Charles Vincent. *Wired for Success: The Butte, Anaconda & Pacific Railway, 1892–1985*. Pullman, WA: Washington State University Press, 2002.

O'Brien, Thomas F. "'Rich Beyond the Dreams of Avarice': The Guggenheims in Chile." *The Business History Review* 63, no. 1 (1989): 122–59.

———. "Copper Kings of the Americas—The Guggenheim Brothers." In *Mining Tycoons in the Age of Empire, 1870–1945: Entrepreneurship, High Finance, Politics and Territorial Expansion*, edited by Raymond E. Dumett, 195–215. Farnham, England: Ashgate, 2009.

Osterhammel, Jürgen. *Die Verwandlung der Welt: eine Geschichte des 19. Jahrhunderts*. München: Beck, 2009.

Perrings, Charles. *Black Mineworkers in Central Africa: Industrial Strategies and the Evolution of an African Proletariat in the Copperbelt 1911–41*. London: Heinemann, 1979.

Phillips, John. "Alfred Chester Beatty: Mining Engineer, Financier and Entrepreneur 1898–1950." In *Mining Tycoons in the Age of Empire, 1870–1945: Entrepreneurship, High Finance, Politics and Territorial Expansion*, edited by Raymond E. Dumett, 215–39. Farnham, England: Ashgate, 2009.

Richter, F.E. "The Copper-Mining Industry in the United States, 1845–1925." *The Quarterly Journal of Economics* 41, no. 2 (February 1, 1927): 236–91. https://doi.org/10.2307/1883502.

Roberts, Andrew D. *A History of Zambia*. London: Heinemann, 1981.

Ross, Corey. *Ecology and Power in the Age of Empire: Europe and the Transformation of the Tropical World*. Oxford: Oxford University Press, 2017.

Särkkä, Timo. "The Lure of Katanga Copper: Tanganyika Concessions Limited and the Anatomy of Mining and Mine Exploration 1899–1906." *South African Historical Journal* 68, no. 3 (July 2, 2016): 318–41.

Schmitz, Christopher. "The Rise of Big Business in the World Copper Industry 1870–1930." *Economic History Review* 3, no. 29 (1986): 392–410.

———. "The Changing Structure of the World Copper Market, 1870–1939." *Journal of European Economic History* 2, no. 26 (1997): 295–330.

———. "The World Copper Industry: Geology, Mining Techniques and Corporate Growth, 1870–1939." *The Journal of European Economic History* 1, no. 29 (2000): 77–105.

Schwantes, Carlos A. *Vision & Enterprise: Exploring the History of Phelps Dodge Corporation*. Tucson: University of Arizona Press, 2000.

Sippel, Patricia. "Technology and Change in Japan's Modern Copper Mining Industry." In *Institutional and Technological Change in Japan's Economy: Past and Present*, edited by Janet Hunter and Cornelia Storz, 10–27. London: Routledge, 2012.

Topik, Steven C., and Allen Wells. "Warenketten in einer globalen Wirtschaft." In *1870–1945: Weltmärkte und Weltkriege*, edited by Emily S. Rosenberg, 589–815. München: Beck, 2012.

Tracing the Veins. Accessed July 4, 2018. https://www.ucpress.edu/book/9780520211377/tracing-the-veins.

du Trieu de Terdonck, R., E. Weberg, and L. Theys. *Union Minière du Haut-Katanga, 1906–1956: évolution des techniques et des activités sociales*, 1957.

Truett, Samuel. *Fugitive Landscapes: The Forgotten History of the U.S.-Mexico Borderlands*. New Haven, CT and London: Yale University Press, 2008.

Unger, Irwin, and Debi Unger. *The Guggenheims: A Family History*. Pymble, NSW: HarperCollins e-books, 2006.

Union minière du Haut Katanga, 1906–1956. Bruxelles: L. Cuypers, 1956.

Van der Straeten, Edgar. "Edgar Sengier." *Biographie Belge d'Outre-Mer* VII-A (1997): 429–37.

Waterschoot, Dirk. *Union Minière du Haut Katanga: ontstaan en arbeidsbeleid tot 1960.* Brussel: GRESEA, 1985.

9

A Toxic Development: Pollution and Change in an Amazonian Oil Frontier

Deborah Delgado Pugley

Introduction

The Amazon Basin covers roughly 40% of South America, an area of about 7,500,000 square km^2. The Marañon and the Ucayali River are two of its main tributaries. They raise in the Andes Mountains at the west of South America. Economic cycles based on natural resource extraction (be it rubber, oil, gold, cocaine or cocoa) have unraveled in these basins since European occupation. Acting as frontiers that provided new resources, these basins embodied novel connections between natural resources and institutional orders.

As Rasmussen and Lund[1] claim, frontiers can be understood as transitional, liminal spaces in which existing regimes of resource control are suspended. Throughout different historical periods, the Amazon has been approached as a "resource frontier," or commodity frontier,[2] where entrepreneurs, missionaries and armies were able to disengage natural

D. Delgado Pugley (✉)
Pontificia Universidad Católica del Perú, Lima, Peru
e-mail: deborah.delgado@pucp.pe

S. Joseph (ed.), *Commodity Frontiers and Global Capitalist Expansion*,
Palgrave Studies in Economic History, https://doi.org/10.1007/978-3-030-15322-9_9

elements of its previous ecologies, making them the natural resources that bureaucrats or generals could offer as raw material for corporate economies.[3]

Revenue from extraction has not been significantly reinvested in the Western Amazon Basin, despite the considerable amount of resources exploited there. None of the historical cycles that involved the basin has effectively promoted its sustainable development. Towns and cities have grown, and access to basic services has improved in urbanized areas, but local populations continue to suffer drawbacks of extractive industries, such as pollution, deforestation and displacement. As Jason Moore argues, environmental degradation played a key role in compelling geographical expansion (Moore 2011).

A new *boom* of natural resources (2000–2014) led to a more ambitious expansion of extractive activities in indigenous territories in scale and impact. Tension fostered around land tenure and resource access, as traditional occupants relocated, having seen their territories transformed by frontier economies tolerated or supported by national governments. Particular forms of political action emerged during this period. Clashes implicating informal entrepreneurs, indigenous peoples, environmentalists, farmers and extractive corporations continued after the boom. These are often described in the literature as "conflicts between endogenous versus exogenous models," or between "conservationists versus developers". I argue that this classification of "actors in conflict" lacks ethnographic ground. It does not capture the contradictory process of interaction that has constructed shared meaning among social actors in resource frontiers. As many researchers have pointed out, the coexistence and interaction between oil companies, conservation initiatives, indigenous peoples and local elites have created a particular common ground that can be extremely paradoxical.[4] But more importantly, to keep a typology of actors that sets two clear camps in conflict fails to show what is at stake for local actors when the conditions of extractive frontiers change by commodities' boom or bust, by heavy pollution and profound degradation of the ecosystem.

Projects of environmental governance have been introduced progressively in places of active and long-standing resource extraction in the form of protected areas, environmental monitoring, climate change mitigation mechanisms and "green investment" in water management and energy.[5] I argue here that the deepening of social inequality and limited access to traditional sources of livelihood are evidence of the limitations of environmental governance and policy efforts in the region. In fact, the lack of law reinforcement and dichotomic classifications of peoples and territories exposed to an extractive frontier are not helping to mainstream environmental policies and build the foundation for local environmental governance.

To elaborate this argument, this chapter will be structured as follows: the section "Not That New: Oil in the Western Amazon (1970–2016)" will focus on the history of this commodity frontier during the twentieth century. The chapter then goes on to explore the effects of oil frontiers on the management of environmental disasters. Finally, the last section delves deeper into the case of a Kukama community, Cuninico, on the Marañon River, analyzing the effects of oil spills on gender relations, access to livelihoods and local indigenous politics. This section is based on fieldwork conducted during three field-visits, two of them done during May and October 2016 and one in February 2017. I end by drawing some conclusions about the interaction between commodity frontiers and the introduction of environmental governance in the Western Amazon.

Not That New: Oil in the Western Amazon (1970–2016)

The Western Amazon is the richest part of the Basin in oil. Ecuador and Peru share most of its reserves. The northern Amazon region of Peru has been a site of oil extraction since the 1920s, but it was only in the 1970s, during the first stage of a revolutionary military government (1968–1975), that its exploitation took on important dimensions. This was a result of the exploration by the public company Petroperú of Trompeteros in 1971 (in the then province of Loreto, on the Corrientes basin). The enthusiasm awakened by this discovery of oil soon increased further, when Occidental Petroleum Co. (Oxy) found other deposits in the area. This sparked an exploratory boom that led 14 companies to operate in the region in 1974.

International and domestic factors favored this process. In 1970, the military government approved a new oil law to stimulate exploration, particularly in the Amazon region. Because it was considered a strategic area in geopolitical terms (and to avoid the emergence of a foreign quasi-monopoly like the one that the International Petroleum Co. had in the Brea and Pariñas zones), the government involved the new State Company, PetroPerú, allocating it several exploration lots. Meanwhile, the military government applied the so-called Modelo Perú contract to foreign companies. Under these contracts, the State declared itself the owner of the reserves and the extracted production, and the companies, which assumed the investments and risks, delivered up to 50% of the crude oil in exchange for tax exemption.[6] Soon after, companies also obtained exemption benefits on tariffs over capital goods imports during a limited period. More than the conditions offered, however, what initially attracted some big oil companies to make risky investments in the Amazon was the consolidation of OPEC, the Organization of Petroleum Exporting Countries, which advocated for control of the oil market and increased oil prices (so non-member countries had to secure new reserves in other parts of the world).

Regarding infrastructure, what made extraction in Loreto feasible was the construction of the Norperuano Oil Pipeline and its northern spur, to which other sections were later added. The pipeline, very important in its scale, was financed with a Japanese loan taken by the Peruvian state, which turned out to have a very high cost.[7]

The euphoria deflated quickly. Smaller companies did not achieve the same success as the first two. It became clear that the characteristics of Peru's heavy crude did not justify high operating costs. For this reason, most investors left the area between 1975 and 1976. Extraction stabilized and continued, particularly concentrated near the border with Ecuador. Peruvian Amazon oil production peaked in 1979 at about 129,000 barrels/day. There has been a steady decline in oil extraction ever since.[8]

Even after the 1970s rush, the oil economy had social and economic prominence in the region. It has been a major driver shaping the political administration of the land. Hydrocarbon Law 26221, enacted in 1993 during the authoritarian regime of Alberto Fujimori, clearly established the right of the State over subsurface resources which facilitate new mining and hydrocarbon concessions. The State therefore retained the power to allow companies to establish oil facilities, roads, drill sites and pipelines on indigenous lands, even when those lands were titled.

High oil prices from 2003 to 2008 were one of the causes of a second oil exploration boom in the Western Amazon.[9] The speed of concession granting can be attributed to increasing energy needs expected in South America, financial markets speculation and amplified corruption, as significant increase on extraction did not follow once the lots were in the hands of oil companies. It is important to keep in mind that this second boom of investment occurred after a history of almost 40 years of continued extraction activity. From 2006 to 2010, most of the Peruvian Amazon was partitioned into concessions allocated to oil and gas companies by national authorities. Never before had such a large area of the Amazon been granted for private extractive concessions. Probable and possible reserves, from lesser to greater uncertainty, in the Peruvian Amazon, jumped by 255 million barrels in 2006 to nearly 465 million barrels.[10]

After this second wave of oil enthusiasm, in August 2015, Pluspetrol abandoned one of the largest oil lots in Peru, the Block 1AB (subsequently renamed 192), without remedying the serious environmental impacts resulting from 45 years of drilling. At the same time, Petroperú, the state-owned oil company, remained responsible for the oil pipeline in times when the industry's activity had dramatically decreased. In this context, the indigenous peoples who inhabit polluted lands and waters still rallied against the responsible enterprises. They did not have enough power to achieve adequate reparation, remediation and compensation measures, and the future living conditions of the affected people and forest remained uncertain.

The Transformation of Place: Drilling Sites and Oil Pipelines in Western Amazonia

The deep impact of oil extraction and transportation in the Western Amazon is due to several factors, some of them being the engagement of local population (including indigenous peoples) as cheap labor, public institutional dependency on a single commodity as a source of revenue and environmental transformations driven by the oil industry.

Pipeline transportation is a high-cost, high-labor and technology-intensive investment. In fact, the massive use of labor in the phases of exploration and construction of the pipeline and drilling sites deeply transformed Loreto's forests. During the pipeline construction, it was common to find only women for long periods in the hamlets and in the communities surrounding the oil zones. Food became scarce in the province and prices rose. The situation reached its climax in the late 1970s, when this unusual demographic pressure aggravated the situation. Later, when oil companies started to leave, having failed to find light oil, there was a massive exodus of the rural population to cities. Iquitos city[11] was the most concerned.

At the same time, the subnational government structure also changed. In 1976, following the discovery of oil fields, strong pressure from regional political movements arose in Loreto. After tenacious negotiations and threats of separatism, the central government decided to give 10% of the value of oil production to Loreto. This transfer became known as the "*canon petrolero*." In Spanish, "canon" means a tax related to a specific activity; further, in Peru "canon" has come to mean a rule for the devolution of revenues collected by the national government to subnational governments.[12]

The allocation of "canon" to Loreto and the absence of other big investments have made the regional government dependent on resources from oil activities. A lack of a proactive attitude by authorities toward the monitoring and regulation of the industry accompanied this process. This is reflected in the lack of proposals from the regional government to improve the conditions in which companies operate. Meanwhile, districts such as Trompeteros, Tigre, Andoas and Urarinas, where most of the oil is produced (47% of the wells are there located), or Morona, where intense exploration activity is carried out, receive very small amounts of the total canon.[13]

These areas were not of particular importance for the National System of Support for Social Mobilization (SINAMOS) or the Peruvian Institute of Indigenous Affairs[14] when a wave of land titling was in place back in the 1970s. Few Amazonian indigenous peoples obtained land titles, and most of those who did receive official titles had recognized small areas thought to be adequate for their settlement. The situation has not changed much in terms of land rights recognition, as Loreto is still one of the regions of the Peruvian Amazon with the lowest rates of land titling to indigenous peoples.[15]

The Current Face of "Development": Environmental Pollution and Paperwork

In 2014, an oil spill in the Marañon Basin caused significant biological and water deterioration, affecting the well-being of local people.[16] In 2016, the leakage of about 3000 barrels of oil occurred in three points, close to this same river.[17] Far from being isolated cases, several other spills followed until the present.

As research on biology and medical science shows, oil spills have high potential to negatively impact freshwater aquatic ecosystems and can severely affect biodiversity and, by consequence, human beings. Oil affects aquatic invertebrate and vertebrate fauna both directly, by toxicity, and indirectly, by decreasing oxygen diffusion.[18] The 2014 oil spill in the Marañon River killed a massive amount of fish immediately. This probably affected other organisms, since fish are common prey for caimans, birds and mammals. Community and food web structures may remain disrupted for years as a result of spills. Disturbances like these, therefore, can compromise water resources and services, including drinking water and fisheries.[19]

The State and Environmental Disasters: Official Reports, no Meaningful Action

Usually, state actions after oil spills have focused solely on monitoring and assessment of the situation in the area. Ecosystem remediation, medical care and compensation have not been part of the actions taken by the state. As this section will show, there are a series of examples of this behavior repeatedly through the history of the sector, although regulation has evolved and improved.

Historically, Peru's central state has issued several official reports on the state of health and pollution in Loreto. Since 1980, state agencies have delivered reports describing the ravages caused by the contamination. In 1984, the National Office for the Evaluation of Natural Resources (ONERN) noted that the lot where OXY operated was "one of the most damaged critical environmental zones in the country."[20] In 1988, Roberto Pezo, director of research at the Peruvian Amazon Research Institute, presented the conclusions of the analysis of the waters of the Tigre River, noting that the concentrations of lead and chlorides were "a hundred times higher than the normal concentration" [which] indicates that these waters are not suitable for human consumption."[21] After an oil spill in 2006, both the Ministries of Production and Health reported that the concentration of heavy metals in both fish and humans was above the limits set by the World Health Organization.[22]

The unexpected inconsistency is what comes next: Once reports and official assessments are issued by public authorities, no public agency has the power to follow up with concrete actions. These reports often are simply filed and ignored or forgotten until deadlines for action expire. For example, of the one hundred companies that figure among the more than one thousand reports in the archive of the Agency for Environmental Assessment and Control (OEFA) in which deadlines for action have expired, 54.2% correspond to 17 companies. The majority share commercial interests and figure among the most fined by OEFA. For example, the two operators of the Argentine group, Pluspetrol, appear among the most sanctioned for environmental infractions between 2007 and 2014 with more than 22 million dollars. While Pluspetrol Perú Corporation has 136 prescribed reports, its twin, Pluspetrol Norte, has another 13 reports. The latter company operated in Loreto in lot 8 and 192 (ex 1AB), where indigenous communities denounce the impact on the environment and their health.[23]

The design of reports can also be problematic, particularly when dealing with health issues. Sample design for health evaluations is often controversial. For example, in the oil spill case analyzed by O'Callaghan-Gordo et al.,[24] the sampling conducted by regional authorities and Pluspetrol were a form of "unruly engagement," as the authors put it. Two different institutions handled the environmental samples taken after the oil spill: DIRESA-Loreto (the regional branch of the National Directorate for Health, DIGESA, ascribed to the Ministry of Health) and IIAP (Research Institute of the Peruvian Amazon, ascribed to the Ministry of the Environment, but considered autonomous). The institutions' findings concerning the level of contamination contradicted each other on major points. DIRESA's reports indicated no presence of hydrocarbons in the Marañón River. They found only a very small concentration of another type of hydrocarbon that does not disturb the river's sanitary quality.[25] DIRESA concluded that by 60 days after the incident, the water recovered its usual quality.[26] In complete contrast, IIAP's independent report indicated high levels of contamination. As was announced by IIAP's report, to the present, the negative effects of the spill on the health of the local population can be observed.

Living with Pollution: The Cuninico Case

> *We have found a big fish; it was very alive, but well decayed, of the ribs well rotten.*
>
> *All the bones were exposed... and that is my concern.*
>
> *I tell my children that that is the way we are going to die, maybe, with all that oil.*
>
> *It will happen to us like it happen to that animal, because it was an animal that was in the water, living, but it was well rotten. After that we found another fish with a big head, very skinny, in its bones, but alive, it was living there, on the oil.*[27]

In June 2014, a spill of about 2300 barrels of crude from the Norperuano Oil Pipeline severely affected a small river bordering the indigenous community of Cuninico. The spill occurred in the canal built to contain the pipeline. Much of the pipeline was underwater in the canal, which is connected to the Cuninico River by several streams. There is strong evidence that this had a damaging impact on the community's livelihoods, health and psychological state, which was reported to a wider audience by Amnesty International. Ultimately, the community opened a legal case.[28]

The spill has resulted in a loss of natural resources, decreased access to land and a reduction to land-based livelihoods. Nutrition has seriously worsened. The most outstanding aspect is the shortage of fisheries and traditional crops, as water and soil are contaminated. Game is also scarce, as animals have migrated to distant places. As a resident of Cuninico puts it:

> *It's not the same, our children do not stop being sick. You cannot say, "Today I will tell my partner to go fishing", because the fish is deformed. The aguaje plant is not tasty, the banana is not anymore either. We are not living a normal life anymore.*[29]

As in several other cases, state agencies, including The Agency for Environmental Assessment and Control OEFA (2014), The National Fisheries Health Agency SENIPES (2014) and the Ministry of Culture (2014),[30] visited Cuninico and reported on the state of the community after the oil spill, pointing out the economic (related to fisheries) and environmental problems. Despite all of these official reports and claims in Court where the Cuninico community has presented its case—supported by human rights lawyers' organizations (Institute of Legal Defense) and the Catholic Church—Petroperú has not acted to remedy the long-lasting effects of the spill.

Disaster-control measures undertaken both by the national petroleum company and the Peruvian state have been insufficient at best. There is no regular access to clean water after the Cuninico River was polluted. As of today, rainwater is stored and used as a replacement for river or stream water. In dry seasons, families are forced to collect water from the Marañon River for drinking and cooking, which is also severely polluted. Most adults and children suffer from headaches, nausea, diarrhea, as well as muscle and bone pain. Freshwater and fish scarcity have brought inflation. Families had to cope with higher prices for food that used to be produced locally (such as fish and bananas) and now must come from further places.

Although surrounded by pollution, local people have perceived a sort of "development" in the community. Despite the high levels of toxicity, the oil spill has changed visions of the future for people living in Cuninico. While health problems related to routine exposure to toxic elements are strongly felt and identified as coming from the oil spill, the cash flow that came with the work of cleaning the Cuninico River and other spill sites has brought improvements in the infrastructure for some households. Houses have been improved, and access to short-term salaries as well as opportunities to start small enterprises dealing with environmental disasters are new conditions that indicate a change in local people's lifestyles and expectations.

The oil frontier has created a deep dependence on cash flow and it has diminished, by its devastating environmental impacts, other sources of livelihood, such as fishing and agriculture. The money is spent fast. Living in a monetarized economy quickly drains the income of local communities and does not replace devastated ecosystem services.

Being a Mother in a Polluted Community

Several articles and policy reports on the impacts of extractive industries around the world affirm that these are differentiated by gender and that women are more likely to be negatively affected by extractive industries than their partners. For example, the World Bank's 2009 guidance volume on gender and the extractive industries states that:

> Men have most access to the benefits, which consist primarily of employment and income, while women and the families they care for are more vulnerable to the risks created by Extractive Industries, which consist of mostly harmful social and environmental impacts.[31]

Several empirical studies demonstrate that extractive industries have differentiated gender impacts, in a variety of ways (Falla 2010; Jenkins 2014; Armah et al. 2016; Behzadi 2019; von der Goltz and Barnwal, in press). Some of the usual factors include varying involvement in decision-making, access to employment, and negative consequences of disruptions on established social patterns. In societies where traditional livelihoods rely upon the surrounding environment, socio-ecological impacts on women can be particularly adverse.[32] Extractive industry-induced environmental changes, including loss of land, decreased water quality and quantity, and increased air pollutants, tend to impact disproportionally upon the well-being of women and children. For example, in many societies, such as indigenous Amazonian ones, it is a woman's responsibility to collect water. When water quality and quantity are affected by operations, it is women's responsibility to find alternative water sources or care for associated health problems in the family.

The proletarianization of men by their work in cleanup activities of spills takes family members far away from their villages, usually to other spill sites. Men leaving the household results in additional work for women who stay in the village. In the case of Cuninico, the extension of the working day for mothers was dramatic. As men come and go to work out of town, women handle household activities without their spouses' and older sons' support. At the same time, as fisheries were extremely affected, fishing has taken place far from the community and the spill. This changes patterns of traditional fishing and has resulted in men being out of the community for longer periods, discouraging family fishing practices that were in place before the spill. All this means that water collection, food gathering, cooking, the health treatment of children exposed to toxins as well as several activities related to local political representation are in women's hands. In this context, women prioritize activities such as agriculture, the raising of farm-animals and sale of handicrafts. A monetarized economy gained ground in food exchange and state-sponsored social programs became key for the nutrition of kids as mothers' capacities to gather food decreased.

The women that we interviewed felt the emotional burden of motherhood. They expressed their deep concern about the lack of clean water and their inability to provide enough food for their children. The situation also presented women with an emotional dilemma: They lacked the means to find a new place to live and felt constantly worried for the safety of their children exposed to pollutants. Children's health is visibly affected by exposure to toxins and is their mothers' primary concern. Women spend more time and money to go to the health center, with the closest operative one being in the town of Maipuco, a couple of hours away from the community.

Overall, the environmental crises resulted in a devaluation of non-monetarized activities, since the productivity of the land and fisheries experienced profound decay. In fact, all work that is not absorbed by a strong and an aggregate market (in this case, the cleanups of the oil industry and other commercial activities related to urban centers) tend to suffer from symbolic and economic devaluation. As a result, several actors affected by the harsh environmental conditions feel intimate resentment after the spill.

Social changes are strongly interlinked with the toxicity of the environment. They foreshadow a future of abnormality and can be understood, as Nixon proposes, as a kind of slow and pervasive violence.[33] Violence is customarily conceived as an event or action that is immediate in time, explosive and spectacular in space and as erupting into instant sensational visibility. Nixon suggests, that we must pay more attention to another kind violence, that is neither spectacular nor instantaneous, but rather incremental and accretive, with calamitous repercussions playing out across a range of temporal scales. It is a violence that occurs gradually, and out of public sight, of delayed destruction that is dispersed across time and space.

The Persisting Question of Indigenous Peoples' Politics in Extractive Frontiers

As oil frontiers have instigated extensive environmental transformation, they have also influenced the way indigenous peoples articulate their political voice and demand for the protection of their collective human rights. Indigenous movements emerged as key political actors in South America during the 1990s.[34] The literature of this period has helped us to understand the reasons for their appearance as well as their diversity. Strong mobilization of indigenous peoples of the Peruvian Amazon Basin had a substantial impact on environmental law and on the national implementation of international legal provisions for indigenous peoples. Indigenous movements are particularly active in oil extraction sites, as the Bagua case has shown.[35] Today, it is necessary to question the effects of extractive industries on indigenous political organizations and communities.

Commodity frontiers produce processes and conditions that situate indigenous actors in complex scalar interactions and trans-local networks. Frontiers of extraction are not simply sites for value extraction, they are also sites for making globalized politics.[36] The politicization of indigenous peoples in extractive sites is a nonlinear multiscale process: Local communities interact with enterprises operating close to them; indigenous peoples organize at the watershed level, at the regional level or by peoples. This kind of multiscale organization helps them negotiate a range of issues with different actors, ranging from cultural recognition, benefit sharing conditions, or reparations when human rights violations occur.

The intricate phenomenon of indigenous peoples' representation in extractive frontiers can be equivocal, as politics do not mean the same thing for different cultural horizons.[37] In this regard, ethnographic studies of new movements of Amazonian peoples and their leadership question the adequacy of concepts such as "identity" and "professionalism," related to the way "identity politics" is usually analyzed, finding them too rigid to adjust to the cases dealt with. Indeed, these notions do not account for the profound fluidity that marks the individual positions of indigenous actors, particularly motivated by a logic of accumulation of experiences and knowledge more than by efforts at specialization or professionalization as politicians.[38]

At least two contemporary trends of local mobilization do not fall within the logic of professional representation in hierarchical political organizations: female leadership and environmental monitoring activities in the affected basins. Indigenous peoples have extensively registered and monitored oil spills in extractive sites. A remarkable program of local monitoring has developed a database of sites damaged by the oil industry across more than 40 years of extraction (part of it can be accessed online at the *Observatorio Petrolero*).[39] Leaders that sustain these efforts do not necessarily enter into federations of collective action.

At the same time, the local leadership of indigenous woman is more influential than it used to be in the new phase that the oil industry is going through. As oil prices go down, and the capacity of the industry to absorb labor is lower, the pollution is felt more strongly by households. Women tend to be more vocal about it, expressing the difficulties they face as mothers.[40] Their leadership do not follow hierarchical models of a federation. They struggle to make their voice escalate but they do gain visible positions at national and international arenas offering an intimate account of the changes in their lives and communities.

Conclusions

This chapter sheds light on the challenges of environmental governance in the context of the long-lasting impact of the oil industry in the Amazon Basin. It documents salient social processes occurring in its Western edge, providing insights on the state of a resource frontier in a moment of industrial decline. It also emphasizes the importance of intimate social changes, particularly related to gender and politics in local communities. Indigenous peoples' integration into the market, especially the labor market, due to the expansion pattern of hydrocarbon concessions in the twentieth century, is one of the most significant changes that has impacted the Western Amazonian environment, altering core socio-environmental dynamics in this important ecosystem. This kind of slow violence should be made visible and in turn addressed by environmental policies. To comprehend the many facets of the changes induced by oil, scholars need to consider gender relations, inequality and space-making. Effective local governance plays a key role in achieving the sustainability-related outcomes at the heart of environmental governance.

Acknowledgements A meaningful part of the fieldwork conducted to write this article was done in the framework of the course "Fieldwork practice for Sociology" during 2016, with the participation of several undergraduate students to whom I extend my gratitude. Sharing their thoughts and ideas was an immense privilege. I would like to thank especially the now graduate sociologists Vania Martinez, Carolina Pin, Aymara Leon, Tania Gomez and Alejandra Barrera. Hernán Maldonado was the teaching assistant and a creative mind in this process. My gratitude goes also to Barbara Fraser, for reading an early version of this article.

Notes

1. Mathias Rasmussen and Christian Lund, "Reconfiguring Frontier Spaces: The Territorialization of Resource Control," *World Development* 101 (2018): 388–99, http://dx.doi.org/10.1016/j.worlddev.2017.01.018.
2. Fernando Santos-Granero and Frederica Barclay, *La Frontera Domesticada: Historia Económica y Social de Loreto 1850–2000* (Lima, Peru: Fondo Editorial PUCP, 2002), 450; David Cleary, "After the Frontier: Problems with Political Economy in the Modern Brazilian Amazon," *Journal of Latin American Studies* 25, no. 2 (1993): 331–49; and Jason W. Moore, "Ecology, Capital, and the Nature of Our Times: Accumulation & Crisis in the Capitalist World-Ecology," *Journal of World-Systems Research* 17, no. 1 (2011): 107–46, https://doi.org/10.5195/jwsr.2011.432.
3. Anna Lowenhaupt Tsing, "Natural Resources and Capitalist Frontiers," *Economic and Political Weekly* 38, no. 48 (2003): 5100–6.
4. Paige West, *Conservation Is Our Government Now: The Politics of Ecology in Papua New Guinea* (NC, USA: Duke University Press, 2006), 352; Peter Larsen, *Post-Frontier Resource Governance: Indigenous Rights, Extraction and Conservation in the Peruvian Amazon* (London, UK: Springer, 2015), 185.
5. Peter Bille Larsen, "Oil Territorialities, Social Life, and Legitimacy in the Peruvian Amazon," *Economic Anthropology* 4, no. 1 (2017): 50, https://doi.org/10.1002/sea2.12072.
6. Frederica Barclay, "¿Qué ha significado el petróleo en la configuración de Loreto como una región?", 2011, accessed September 19, 2018, http://www.actualidadambiental.pe/wp-content/uploads/2011/11/Qu%C3%A9-ha-significado-el-petr%C3%B3leo-en-la-consolidaci%C3%B3n-de-Loreto-como-una-regi%C3%B3n-Frederica-Barclay.pdf.
7. Ibid.
8. Matt Finer and Martí Orta-Martínez, "A Second Hydrocarbon Boom Threatens the Peruvian Amazon: Trends, Projections, and Policy Implications," *Environmental Research Letters* 5, no. 1 (2010): 014012, https://doi.org/10.1088/1748-9326/5/1/014012.
9. Ibid.
10. Martí Orta-Martínez and Matt Finer, "Oil Frontiers and Indigenous Resistance in the Peruvian Amazon," *Ecological Economics* 70, no. 2 (2010): 207–18, https://doi.org/10.1016/j.ecolecon.2010.04.022.

11. Barcalay, "Qué ha significado el petróleo en la configuración de Loreto como una región?" 8.
12. Javier Arellano-Yanguas, "Aggravating the Resource Curse: Decentralisation, Mining and Conflict in Peru," *The Journal of Development Studies* 47, no. 4 (2011): 617–38, https://doi.org/10.1080/00220381003706478.
13. Lily La Torre López, *¡Sólo queremos vivir en paz! : experiencias petroleras en territorios indígenas de la Amazonia peruana* (Copenhague: IWGIA, 1998).
14. Alejandra Zamora and Iliana Monterroso, "Visiones regionales y locales sobre la inseguridad de tenencia en Loreto y Madre de Dios," CIFOR Infobrief no. 198, November 2017, accessed April 15, 2019, http://www.cifor.org/publications/pdf_files/infobrief/6637-infobrief.pdf.
15. Anne Larson, Iliana Monterroso, and Peter Cronkleton, "Titulación colectiva en la Amazonía peruana: Una historia en tres actos," *CIFOR Working Paper Series*, 2018, accessed January 20, 2019, http://www.cifor.org/publications/pdf_files/flyer/6915-flyer.pdf.
16. Barbara Fraser, "Oil in the Forest," *Science* 353, no. 6300 (2016): 641–43; Alejandra Barrera, Tanya Gomez, Aymara Leon, and Carolina Pin, *Impactos del derrame de petróleo del 2014 del oleoducto Norperuano en los modos de vida de la comunidad de Cuninic Loreto* (Lima, Peru: Facultad De Ciencias SocialesEspecialidad De Sociología, PUCP, 2016), accessed January 21, 2019, http://observatoriopetrolero.org/wp-content/uploads/2019/01/ImpactosdeDerramePetroleoEnModosDeVia_Informe2016.pdf.
17. Fraser, "Oil in the Forest."
18. Valter M. Azevedo-Santos, James R. Garcia-Ayala, Philip M. Fearnside, Francisco A. Esteves, Fernando M. Pelicice, William F. Laurance, and Ricardo C. Benine, "Amazon Aquatic Biodiversity Imperiled by Oil Spills," *Biodiversity Conservation* 25, no. 13 (2016): 2831, https://doi.org/10.1007/s10531-016-1192-9.
19. David Lytle and Barbara Perckarsky, "Spatial and Temporal Impacts of a Diesel Fuel Spill on Stream Invertebrates," *Fresh Water Biology* 46, no. 5 (2001): 693–704, https://doi.org/10.1046/j.1365-2427.2001.00695.x.
20. Earth Rights International, Racimos de Ungurahui, and Amazon Watch, "A Legacy of Harm: Occidental Petroleum in Indigenous Territory in the Peruvian Amazon," 1 April 2007, accessed April 18, 2018, https://earthrights.org/wp-content/uploads/publications/A-Legacy-of-Harm.pdf, 17. Originally quoted in: "Oficina Nacional de Evaluación de Recursos Naturales (ONERN) and Corporación

Departamental del Desarrollo de Loreto (CORDELOR), *Inventario y evaluación de los recursos naturales de la microregión Pastaza-Tigre*: departamento de Loreto (Reconocimiento) (Lima, Peru: Oficina Nacional de Evaluación de Recursos Naturales, 1984).

21. Gabriela Flores and Milagros Salazar, "Las huellas del petróleo que intentaron esconder," *Convoca*, 23 July 2015, accessed April 18, 2018, http://convoca.pe/investigacion/las-huellas-del-petroleo-que-intentaron-esconder.
22. Ibid.
23. Ibid.
24. Cristina O'Callaghan-Gordo, Juan A. Flores, Pilar Lizárraga, Tami Okamoto, Diana M. Papoulias, Federica Barclay, Marti Orta-Martinez, Manolis Kogevinas, and John Astete, "Oil Extraction in the Amazon Basin and Exposure to Metals in Indigenous Populations," *Environmental Research* 162 (2018): 226–30, https://doi.org/10.1016/j.envres.2018.01.013.
25. Servindi, "Perú: Controversia entre DIGESA e IIAP sobre impacto del derrame en el río Marañón," accessed April 4, 2018, https://www.servindi.org/actualidad/29134.
26. Ibid.
27. Alejandra Barrera, Tania Gomez, Aymara Leon, and Carolina Pin, *Impactos del derrame de petróleo del 2014 del oleoducto Norperuano en los modos de vida de la comunidad de Cuninic Loreto* (Lima, Peru: Facultad De Ciencias SocialesEspecialidad De Sociología, PUCP, 2016), 45, accessed January 21, 2019, (Rocío, Cuninico, October 2016—35'36") http://observatoriopetrolero.org/wp-content/uploads/2019/01/ImpactosdeDerramePetroleoEnModosDeVia_Informe2016.pdf.
28. Amnesty International, "Estado Tóxico," Lima, 2017, accessed September 13, 2018, http://www.estadotoxico.pe/pdf/InformeEstadoToxicoAIPeru.pdf.
29. Barrera, Gomez, Leon, and Pin, *Impactos del derrame de petróleo del 2014 del oleoducto Norperuano en los modos de vida de la comunidad de Cuninic Loreto*, 31 (Andrea, Cuninico, October 2016, 3:08).
30. See the reports of OEFA, SENIPES, Ministry of Culture: OEFA—Environmental Assessment and Control OEFA, *Report 1306-2014-0EFA/DFSAI/PASMCA*, Ministry of Environment, 2015, accessed September 13, 2018, https://www.oefa.gob.pe/?wpfb_dl=18167; Sanipes "Sanipes informa en abril de 2016 que encontró plomo y cadmio en Chiriaco," accessed June 13, 2014, https://es.scribd.com/

document/330779077/SANIPES; and Ministry of Culture of Peru, *Informe sobre el derrame de petróleo del Oleoducto Nor-Peruano en el río Cuninico*, Loreto. Nro. 153-2014-DGPI-VMI/MC, 2014.
31. Adriana Eftimie, Katherine Heller, and John Strongman, *Gender Dimensions of Extractive Industries, Extractive Industries and Development Series* 8 (Washington, DC: The World Bank, 2009).
32. Ibid.
33. Rob Nixon, *Slow Violence and the Environmentalism of the Poor* (London, UK: Harvard University Press, 2011), 370.
34. Deborah Yashar, *Contesting Citizenship in Latin America: The Rise of Indigenous Movements and the Postliberal Challenge* (Cambridge, UK: Cambridge University Press, 2005).
35. Roger Merino Acuña, "The Politics of Extractive Governance: Indigenous Peoples and Socio-Environmental Conflicts," *The Extractive Industries and Society* 2, no. 1 (2015), 85–92.
36. Saskia Sassen, *Territory, Authority, Rights: From Medieval to Global Assemblages* (NJ, USA: Princeton University Press, 2008).
37. Marisol De la Cadena, *Earth Beings: Ecologies of Practice Across Andean Worlds* (NC, USA: Duke University Press, 2015); Mario Blaser, "Political Ontology: Cultural Studies Without 'Cultures'?" *Cultural Studies* 23, no. 5–6 (2009): 873–96.
38. Silvia Romio, "Entre discurso político y fuerza espiritual: fundación de las organizaciones indígenas awajún y wampis (1977–1979)," *Anthropologica* 32, no. 32 (2014): 139–58.
39. Tami Okamoto and Esben Leifsen, "Oil Spills, Contamination, and Unruly Engagements with Indigenous Peoples in the Peruvian Amazon," in *New Political Spaces in Latin American Natural Resource Governance*, ed. Havard Haarstad (New York: Palgrave Macmillan, 2012), 177–97.
40. Amnesty International, "Estado Tóxico," Lima, 2017, accessed September 13, 2018, http://www.estadotoxico.pe/pdf/InformeEstadoToxicoAIPeru.pdf.

Bibliography

Acuña, Roger Merino. "The Politics of Extractive Governance: Indigenous Peoples and Socio-Environment Conflicts." *The Extractive Industries and Society* 2, no. 1 (2015): 85–92.

Amnesty International. "Estado Tóxico." Lima, 2017. Accessed September 13, 2018. http://www.estadotoxico.pe/pdf/InformeEstadoToxicoAIPeru.pdf.

Arellano-Yanguas, Javier. "Aggravating the Resource Curse: Decentralisation, Mining and Conflict in Peru." *The Journal of Development Studies* 47, no. 4 (2011): 617–38. https://doi.org/10.1080/00220381003706478.

Armah, Frederick Ato, Boamah, Sheila A., Quansah, Reginald, Obiri, Samuel, Luginaah, Isaac. Working conditions of male and female artisanal and small-scale goldminers in Ghana: Examining existing disparities. *The Extractive Industries and Society* 3 (2016): 464–74.

Azevedo-Santos, Valter, James R. Garcia-Ayala, Philip M. Fearnside, Francisco A. Esteves, Fernando M. Pelicice, William F. Laurance, and Ricardo C. Benine. "Amazon Aquatic Biodiversity Imperiled by Oil Spills." *Biodiversity and Conservation* 25, no. 13 (2016): 2831–34. https://doi.org/10.1007/s10531-016-1192-9.

Barclay, Frederica. "¿Qué ha significado el petróleo en la configuración de Loreto como una región?" In *Los pueblos indigenas amazonicos peruanos. En busca del desarrollo sostenido*, edited by C. Soria. Guadalajara: Foro Ecológico del Coloquio Internacional de Derecho Internacional Ambiental, 2002. Accessed September 12, 2018. http://www.actualidad-ambiental.pe/wp-content/uploads/2011/11/Qu%C3%A9-ha-significado-el-petr%C3%B3leo-en-la-consolidaci%C3%B3n-de-Loreto-como-una-regi%C3%B3n-Frederica-Barclay.pdf.

Barrera, Alejandra, Tania Gomez, Aymara Leon, and Carolina Pin. *Impactos del derrame de petróleo del 2014 del oleoducto Norperuano en los modos de vida de la comunidad de Cuninic Loreto.* Lima, Peru: Facultad De Ciencias Sociales Especialidad De Sociología, PUCP, 2016. Accessed January 21, 2019. http://observatoriopetrolero.org/wp-content/uploads/2019/01/ImpactosdeDerramePetroleoEnModosDeVia_Informe2016.pdf.

Behzadi, Negar Elodie. Women miners' exclusion and Muslim masculinities in Tajikistan: A feminist political ecology of honor and shame. *Geoforum* (2019).

Blaser, Mario. "Political Ontology: Cultural Studies Without 'Cultures'?" *Cultural Studies* 23, no. 5–6 (2009): 873–96.

Cane, Isabel, Ashlee Schleger, Saleem Ali, Deanna Kemp, Neil McIntyre, Alex Lechner, Byambajav Dalaibuyan, Nena Bulovic, and Kuntala Lahiri-Dutt. *Responsible Mining in Mongolia: Enhancing Positive Engagement.* Brisbane: Sustainable Minerals Institute, 2015.

Convoca. "Las huellas del petróleo que intentaron esconder." Accessed April 4, 2018. http://convoca.pe/investigacion/las-huellas-del-petroleo-que-intentaron-esconder.

Cleary, David. "After the Frontier: Problems with Political Economy in the Modern Brazilian Amazon." *Journal of Latin American Studies* 25, no. 2 (1993): 331–49. https://doi.org/10.1017/S0022216X00004685.

De la Cadena, Marisol. *Earth Beings: Ecologies of Practice Across Andean Worlds.* Durham, NC, USA: Duke University Press, 2015.

Earth Rights International, Racimos de Ungurahui, and Amazon Watch, "A Legacy of Harm: Occidental Petroleum in Indigenous Territory in the Peruvian Amazon," 1 April 2007, accessed April 18, 2018, https://earthrights.org/wp-content/uploads/publications/A-Legacy-of-Harm.pdf.

Eftimie, Adriana, Katherine Heller, and John Strongman. *Gender Dimensions of Extractive Industries, Extractive Industries and Development Series* 8. Washington, DC: The World Bank, 2009.

Falla, Julia Cuadros. *Impactos de la minería en la vida de hombres y mujeres en el sur andino.* Una mirada desde el género y la interculturalidad. CooperAcción, 2010.

Finer, Matt, and Marti Orta-Martinez. "A Second Hydrocarbon Boom Threatens the Peruvian Amazon: Trends, Projections, and Policy Implications." *Environmental Research Letters* 5, no. 1 (2010): 014012. https://doi.org/10.1088/1748-9326/5/1/014012.

Fraser, Barbara. "Oil in the Forest." *Science* 353, no. 6300 (2016): 641–43.

Gabriela Flores and Milagros Salazar, "Las huellas del petróleo que intentaron esconder," *Convoca*, 23 July 2015, accessed April 18, 2018, http://convoca.pe/investigacion/las-huellas-del-petroleo-que-intentaron-esconder.

Jenkins, Katy. Women, mining and development: An emerging research agenda. *The Extractive Industries and Society* 1 (2014): 329–39.

La Torre, Liliana. *Sólo Queremos Vivir en Paz. Experiencias Petroleras En Territorios Indígenas de la Amazonía Peruana.* Lima, Peru: IWGIA, 1998.

Larsen, Peter Bille. *Post-Frontier Resource Governance: Indigenous Rights, Extraction and Conservation in the Peruvian Amazon.* London, UK: Springer, 2015.

———. "Oil Territorialities, Social Life, and Legitimacy in the Peruvian Amazon," *Economic Anthropology* 4, no. 1 (2017): 50–64. https://doi.org/10.1002/sea2.12072.

Larson, Anna, Iliana Monterroso, and Peter Cronkleton. "Titulación colectiva en la Amazonía peruana: Una historia en tres actos." *CIFOR Working Paper Series* 2018. Accessed January 20, 2019. http://www.cifor.org/publications/pdf_files/flyer/6915-flyer.pdf.

Lytle, David, and Barbara Perckarsky. "Spatial and Temporal Impacts of a Diesel Fuel Spill on Stream Invertebrates." *Fresh Water Biology* 46, no. 5 (2001): 693–704.

Ministry of Culture of Peru. *Informe sobre el derrame de petróleo del Oleoducto Nor-Peruano en el río Cuninico, Loreto. Nro. 153-2014-DGPI-VMI/MC.* Vice Ministry of Intercultural Affairs, 2014.

Moore, Jason W. "Ecology, Capital, and the Nature of Our Times: Accumulation & Crisis in the Capitalist World-Ecology." *Journal of World-Systems Research* 17, no. 1 (2011): 107–46. https://doi.org/10.5195/jwsr.2011.432.

Nixon, Rob. *Slow Violence and the Environmentalism of the Poor*. London, UK: Harvard University Press, 2011.

O'Callaghan-Gordo, Cristina, Juan A. Carlos, Pilar Lizárraga, Tami Okamoto, Diana M. Papoulias, Frederica Barclay, Marti Orta-Martinez, Manolis Kogevinas, and John Astete. "Oil Extraction in the Amazon Basin and Exposure to Metals in Indigenous Populations." *Environmental Research* 162 (2018): 226–30. https://doi.org/10.1016/j.envres.2018.01.013.

OEFA—Environmental Assessment and Control OEFA. *Report 1306-2014-0EFA/DFSAI/PASMCA*. Ministry of Environment, 2015. Accessed September 13, 2018. https://www.oefa.gob.pe/?wpfb_dl=18167.

Oficina Nacional de Evaluación de Recursos Naturales (ONERN) and Corporación Departamental del Desarrollo de Loreto (CORDELOR). *Inventario y evaluación de los recursos naturales de la microregión Pastaza-Tigre*: departamento de Loreto (Reconocimiento). Lima, Peru: Oficina Nacional de Evaluación de Recursos Naturales, 1984.

Okamoto, Tami, and Esben Leifsen. "Oil Spills, Contamination, and Unruly Engagements with Indigenous Peoples in the Peruvian Amazon." In *New Political Spaces in Latin American Natural Resource Governance*, edited by Håvard Haarstad, 177–97. New York: Palgrave Macmillan, 2012.

Orta-Martínez, Marti, and Matt Finer. "Oil Frontiers and Indigenous Resistance in the Peruvian Amazon." *Ecological Economics* 70, no. 2 (2010): 207–18. https://doi.org/10.1016/j.ecolecon.2010.04.022.

Rasmussen, Mattias, and Christopher Lund. "Reconfiguring Frontier Spaces: The Territorialization of Resource Control." *World Development* 101 (2018): 388–99. http://dx.doi.org/10.1016/j.worlddev.2017.01.018.

Romio, Silvia. "Entre discurso político y fuerza espiritual: fundación de las organizaciones indígenas awajún y wampis (1977–1979)." *Anthropologica* 32, no. 32 (2014): 139–58.

Santos-Granero, Fernando, and Frederica Barclay. *La frontera domesticada: historia económica y social de Loreto, 1850–2000*. Lima: Fondo Editorial PUCP, 2002.

Sassen, Saskia. *Territory, Authority, Rights: From Medieval to Global Assemblages.* Princeton, NJ, USA: Princeton University Press, 2008.

Servindi. "Perú: Controversia entre DIGESA e IIAP sobre impacto del derrame en el río Marañón." Accessed April 4, 2018. https://www.servindi.org/actualidad/29134.

The National Fisheries Health Agency. "Senipes informa en abril de 2016 que encontró plomo y cadmio en Chiriaco." Accessed September 13, 2018. https://es.scribd.com/document/330779077/SANIPES.

Tsing, Ana Lowenhaupt. "Natural Resources and Capitalist Frontiers." *Economic and Political Weekly* 38, no. 48 (2003): 5100–6.

Van Cott, Donna Lee. *From Movements to Parties in Latin America: The Evolution of Ethnic Politics.* Cambridge, UK: Cambridge University Press, 2007.

von der Goltz, Jan, Barnwal, Prabhat. (in press). Mines: The local wealth and health effects of mineral mining in developing countries. *Journal of Development Economics*. https://doi.org/10.1016/j.jdeveco.2018.05.005.

West, Paige. *Conservation Is Our Government Now: The Politics of Ecology in Papua New Guinea*. Durham, NC, USA: Duke University Press, 2006.

Yashar, Deborah. *Contesting Citizenship in Latin America: The Rise of Indigenous Movements and the Postliberal Challenge*. Cambridge, UK: Cambridge University Press, 2005.

Zamora, Alejandra, and Iliana Monterroso. "Visiones regionales y locales sobre la inseguridad de tenencia en Loreto y Madre de Dios." *CIFOR* Infobrief no. 198. November 2017. http://www.cifor.org/publications/pdf_files/infobrief/6637-infobrief.pdf.

10
Conclusion

Sabrina Joseph

The work presented in this volume reaffirms certain findings articulated in the existing body of research on commodity frontiers. The authors, however, also broaden our understanding of commodity frontiers by exploring alternative frontiers hitherto little examined, deconstructing the political forces that propel capitalist expansion, shedding light on the active role of labour in shaping frontier development, and exploring local solutions to global problems generated by frontier expansion.

The various commodity frontiers explored in this book reaffirm Moore's view that capitalism's tendency is to 'accelerate environmental degradation, to intensify exploitation of labour and land (human and extra-human nature) and to globalize these exploitative and transformative production systems'.[1] Although the form and dynamics of socio-ecological degradation may vary across different frontier zones, it nonetheless characterizes capitalist expansion in agricultural frontiers from the Philippines to India and oil frontiers in the Western Amazon. Within a particular geographical area, furthermore, this degradation

S. Joseph (✉)
American University in Dubai, Dubai, United Arab Emirates
e-mail: sjoseph@aud.edu

S. Joseph (ed.), *Commodity Frontiers and Global Capitalist Expansion*,
Palgrave Studies in Economic History, https://doi.org/10.1007/978-3-030-15322-9_10

often intensifies and transforms as the shift is made from one commodity to another. Cottyn, for instance, demonstrate how frontier zones, far from being static, are often restructured—in the case of the Peruvian–Bolivian border region with the shift from silver to wool. Along the lines of Moore's research, her work demonstrates 'the relation between local ecological crises and the world economy's successive waves of restructuring and geographical expansion'.[2]

The work of Howarth et al. expands upon our understanding of commodity frontiers. By looking at the political ecology of protected areas and reserves, the authors provide us with insight on how the commodification of land involves not only direct exploitation through farming or mining, but 'exploitation' through appropriation, segregation and separation for the mutually related purposes of conservation and economic growth (via tourism). In certain respects, the delineation of land as a reserve or protected area provides a market-based solution to dealing with conservation issues, given that it involves the separation of humans from nature and tends to embrace an 'ecosystems services' view of nature's value to humans—which in practice usually results in monetary valuation and commodification.[3]

Political motivations of state and non-state institutions play a key role in shaping frontier dynamics and contributing to the expansion of frontier zones. Raymond Bryant and Sinead Bailey, in their book *Third World Political Ecology*, highlight how states have a history of being leading social and environmental actors, particularly given their focus on economic development. Their actions, moreover, are not only motivated by economic concerns, but also political and national concerns, be they internal or external.[4] Both Miller and Lockhart demonstrate how nationalist and development agendas often go hand in hand. Miller describes how state driven agricultural development of a frontier zone in the Philippines, motivated by a perception that economic modernization along these lines would prepare the country for a transition to independence, resulted in cultural and ecological transformation. As Lockhart argues, postcolonial states—in this case Chile—were not simply passive actors responding to global market forces, but active agents who pursued frontier expansion to consolidate state power, which in turn transformed political realities at the regional and international levels. Tandon's and Mello and Melkebeke's chapters highlight how developing states from India to South America and Africa perpetuated colonialist development agendas. In addition to states, Bryant and Bailey also indicate that multilateral institutions and businesses are dominant forces affecting the outcomes of environmental conflicts. For Miller, Declercq, Delgado and Howarth et al., however, the state and natural resource companies are not only leading actors in environmental conflicts or key agents of economic development, but the very forces that have instigated and defined capitalist expansion. As Declercq argues, technical experts and the mining companies they worked for played an instrumental role in establishing and expanding frontier spaces; they were adept at not only exploiting resources but organizing access to resources, often in harsh natural environments. In some cases, private companies and the state operated in similar ways. As outlined by Mello and Melkebeke, rubber collecting expeditions carried out by the state and by private companies in Congo had the same repercussions—plunder and destruction of villages and capturing/enslavement of people, resulting in the disruption of pre-existing economies and restructuring of social relations. Tandon's research, moreover, demonstrates how even more decentralized, participatory development agendas are not free from state involvement. As the research shows, although states have been at the forefront of capitalist development and keen to maintain their control over development discourses, they have also been slow in responding to the human and environmental ramifications of changes that ensue.

The research in this volume contributes to the existing scholarship on commodity frontiers by exploring the agency of labourers, peasants and local populations in actively shaping the dynamics of frontier expansion. Cottyn, Tandon, Delgado, and Mello and Melkebeke demonstrate how the resistance or active engagement of local populations and communities has impacted the management of natural resources, limited the extent of labour exploitation and land appropriation and shaped indigenous discourses on development. Looking at the rise of the working class in Chile, Lockhart explores how the labouring classes that emerged out of the mines in turn contributed to the internationalization of the Chilean labour movement. The advantage of taking a micro-approach rather than macro-approach to the study of commodity frontiers lies precisely in uncovering how local dynamics connect the frontier to the global economy. As highlighted by Stan B.-H. Tan, we must move away from perceiving peasants, labourers and communities as 'merely pawns in the "big game" of the corporate actors and doomed to subordination by capital and the State'.[5] The aforementioned chapters in this volume highlight that there is more work that needs to be done in understanding the locus of surplus production and capital accumulation at the local level. Indeed, there is a body of research that suggests that we need to consider the role of household units (including non-waged labour) rather than individual wage labour when analysing the role of workers within a frontier zone.[6] In his ethnographic research on China in the aftermath of the 2008 global financial crisis, Thomas Saetre Jakobsen argues that proletarianization is fading and new patterns of class formation have emerged whereby rural migrant workers, central to China's economy and dependent on the fluctuations of the global economy, are moving between the urban and agricultural workforces and not being dispossessed of their land; 'enterprises accumulate capital by not dispossessing the surplus population of their farmland, but by enlisting them in absorbing workforce reproduction'.[7]

While local populations have played a key role in contesting labour exploitation and land appropriation, Delgado's research also demonstrates how these same communities are often not completely opposed to frontier expansion, even when it is characterized by harmful health and environmental impacts. Ultimately, for these communities, the development of infrastructure and services that accompanies frontier expansion results in improvements that cannot simply be ignored. Thus, frontier zones are certainly not devoid of paradoxes. This is precisely what makes 'capitalism's unsustainability at the very largest and very smallest geographical scales'[8] so difficult to tackle and why starting with an understanding of local community dynamics is imperative. As summarized by W.M. Adams, 'development discourse does not hang in some kind of academic abstract, but is inextricably linked to sets of material relationships, to specific policies and to the exercise of power'.[9] While the role of communities in finding sustainable solutions to development is key, one cannot assume that 'community involvement' necessarily results in the implementation of ecologically friendly measures, a point also made by Tandon. We must be aware of the various social and economic factors at play within the community that influence access to and use of natural resources, particularly class and power relations. Interestingly, as Adams points out, modern-day sustainable development thinkers in the West have also tended to romanticize notions of community, overlooking the political, social and economic conflicts that shape community life.[10]

Finally, Tandon and Delgado draw attention to the fact that commodity frontier expansion, be it with agricultural production in India or oil extraction in the Amazon, has significantly transformed but also been shaped by the role of women. Their work builds on an existing body of literature that explores the relationship between gender and commodity production.[11] More comparative research is needed to understand the gendered dimensions of frontier expansion, but the research presented by Tandon and Delgado highlights that women's roles as mothers, labourers, activists, farmers and wives must be deconstructed in order to assess how frontiers have evolved in different regions of the world over time. Evidence provided by each of these authors indicates that the social, ecological and political transformations that accompany commodity frontier expansion have often had a gender-specific impact, requiring women to solve a particular set of challenges. Applying gender analysis to the study of commodity frontiers can shed light on the impact of socio-ecological degradation on women's roles as well as the roles of men and women in the production, extraction and consumption of commodities.

Notes

1. Moore, "'The Modern World System' as Environmental History? Ecology and the Rise of Capitalism," 347.
2. Ibid., 359.
3. Adrian Martin, "Global Environmental In/Justice, in Practice: Introduction," *The Geographical Journal* 179, no. 2 (2013): 101, 103.
4. Raymond L. Bryant and Sinead Bailey, *Third World Political Ecology* (London: New York: Routledge, 1997), 56, 61.
5. Stan B.-H. Tan, "Coffee Frontiers in the Central Highlands of Vietnam: Networks of Connectivity," *Asia Pacific Viewpoint* 41, no. 1 (2000): 56.

6. Richard E. Lee, "Critiques and Developments in World-Systems Analysis: An Introduction to the Special Collection[1]," *The Journal of Philosophical Economics* 4, no. 1 (2010): 10–12.
7. Thomas Saetre Jakobsen, "From the Workforce to the Household: Migrant Labor and Accumulation Without Dispossession," *Critical Asian Studies* 50, no. 2 (2018): 191.
8. Moore, "'The Modern World System' as Environmental History? Ecology and the Rise of Capitalism," 359.
9. W.M. Adams, *Green Development: Environment and Sustainability in a Developing World*, 3rd ed. (London and New York: Routledge, 2009), 8.
10. Ibid., 132–33.
11. Jemimah Njuki, Susan Kaaria, Angeline Chamunorwa, and Wanjiku Chiuri, "Linking Smallholder Farmers to Markets, Gender and Intra-Household Dynamics: Does the Choice of Commodity Matter?" *European Journal of Development Research* 23, no. 3 (July 2011): 426–43; Rachel K. Egharevba and Felicia A. Iweze, "Sustainable Agriculture and Rural Women: Crop Production and Accompanied Health Hazards in Women Farmers in Six Rural Communities in Edo State Nigeria," *Journal of Sustainable Agriculture* 24, no. 1 (2004): 39–51; and Anouk Patel-Campillo, "The Gendered Production-Consumption Relation: Accounting for Employment and Socioeconomic Hierarchies in the Colombian Cut Flower Global Commodity Chain," *Sociologia Ruralis* 52, no. 3 (July 2012): 272–93.

Bibliography

Adams, W.M. *Green Development: Environment and Sustainability in a Developing World*. 3rd ed. London and New York: Routledge, 2009.

Bryant, Raymond L., and Sinead Bailey. *Third World Political Ecology*. London: New York: Routledge, 1997.

Egharevba, Rachel K., and Felicia A. Iweze. "Sustainable Agriculture and Rural Women: Crop Production and Accompanied Health Hazards in Women Farmers in Six Rural Communities in Edo State Nigeria." *Journal of Sustainable Agriculture* 24, no. 1 (2004): 39–51.

Jakobsen, Thomas Saetre. "From the Workforce to the Household: Migrant Labor and Accumulation without Dispossession." *Critical Asian Studies* 50, no. 2 (2018): 176–95.

Lee, Richard E. "Critiques and Developments in World-Systems Analysis: An Introduction to the Special Collection[1]." *The Journal of Philosophical Economics* 4, no. 1 (2010): 5–18.

Martin, Adrian. "Global Environmental In/Justice, in Practice: Introduction." *The Geographical Journal* 179, no. 2 (2013): 98–104.

Moore, Jason. "'The Modern World System' as Environmental History? Ecology and the Rise of Capitalism." *Theory and Society* 32, no. 3 (June 2003): 307–77.

Njuki, Jemimah, Susan Kaaria, Angeline Chamunorwa, and Wanjiku Chiuri. "Linking Smallholder Farmers to Markets, Gender and Intra-Household Dynamics: Does the Choice of Commodity Matter?" *European Journal of Development Research* 23, no. 3 (July 2011): 426–43.

Patel-Campillo, Anouk. "The Gendered Production-Consumption Relation: Accounting for Employment and Socioeconomic Hierarchies in the Colombian Cut Flower Global Commodity Chain." *Sociologia Ruralis* 52, no. 3 (July 2012): 272–93.

Tan, Stan B.-H. "Coffee Frontiers in the Central Highlands of Vietnam: Networks of Connectivity." *Asia Pacific Viewpoint* 41, no. 1 (2000): 51–67.

Index

S. Joseph (ed.), *Commodity Frontiers and Global Capitalist Expansion*, Palgrave Studies in Economic History, https://doi.org/10.1007/978-3-030-15322-9

The manufacturer's authorised representative in the EU is Springer Nature Customer Service Centre GmbH, Europaplatz 3, 69115 Heidelberg, Germany. If you have any concerns regarding our products, please contact ProductSafety@springernature.com

Printed and bound by CPI Group (UK) Ltd, Croydon, CR0 4YY
25/09/2026
02222894-0003